MICROSOFT®
OFFICE 97
PROFESSIONAL
QUICK REFERENCE

D1263980

MICROSOFT®
OFFICE 97
PROFESSIONAL
QUICK REFERENCE

Robert Mullen with

David Day • Sheldon Dunn • David Field • Cheryl Kirk
Marilyn Kyd • Joyce Nielson • Sally Russell • Jan Snyder
Barrie Sosinsky

Microsoft Office 97 Professional Quick Reference

Library of Congress Catalog No.: 96-72201

ISBN: 0-7897-1061-7

99 98 97   6 5 4 '

Interpretation of the printing code: the rightmost double-digit
number is the year of the book's printing; the rightmost
single-digit number, the number of the book's printing. For
example, a printing code of 97-1 shows that the first printing
of the book occurred in 1997.

Screen reproductions in this book were created using Col-
lage Plus from Inner Media, Inc., Hollis, NH.

Credits

PRESIDENT
Roland Elgey

PUBLISHING DIRECTOR
David W. Solomon

EDITORIAL SERVICES DIRECTOR
Elizabeth Keaffaber

MANAGING EDITOR
Michael Cunningham

DIRECTOR OF MARKETING
Lynn E. Zingraf

ACQUISITIONS EDITOR
Angela Wethington

SENIOR PRODUCT DIRECTOR
Lisa D. Wagner

PRODUCT DIRECTOR
Dana S. Coe

SERIES DEVELOPMENT COORIDINATOR
Carolyn Kiefer

PRODUCTION EDITOR
Sarah Rudy

EDITORS
Patrick Kanouse
Patricia R. Kinyon
Christine Prakel
Brian Sweany

ASSISTANT PRODUCT MARKETING MANAGER
Christy M. Miller

TECHNICAL EDITOR
Midge Stocker

TECHNICAL SUPPORT SPECIALIST
Nadeem Muhammed

ACQUISITIONS COORDINATOR
Tracy M. Williams

SOFTWARE RELATIONS COORDINATOR
Patty Brooks

EDITORIAL ASSISTANT
Virginia Stoller

BOOK DESIGNER
Ruth Harvey

COVER DESIGNER
Nathan Clement

PRODUCTION TEAM
Marcia Brizendine
Jessica Ford
Trey Frank
Tim Neville
Lisa Stumpf

INDEXER
Nick Schroeder

Composed in *Century Old Style* and *Franklin Gothic* by Que Corporation.

About the Author

Robert Mullen is a Principal of The AskAmerica Group, directing a pool of computer publishing professionals that document existing and emerging technologies in a just-in-time publishing environment. Visit The AskAmerica Group at http://www.askamerica.com on the World Wide Web.

Robert is also an author, editor, and freelance writer who will find a way to believe in the Tooth Fairy as long as his young daughter Katherine continues to do so. Robert has authored or co-authored more than 25 computer books for people who are not satisfied with what they already know about computing.

Acknowledgments

Only expert authors provide the insight and background that clarify the best way to get a job done. That's why some of the best people in the business, real people getting real jobs done, were brought in to contribute to this book.

I'd like to thank the following people for their contributions to this book:

Barrie Sosinsksy   Barrie is a database developer and computer book author living in Eastern Massachusetts.

Sheldon Dunn   Sheldon has been in the software development profession for the past 15 years, working with companies such as Microsoft, Novell, Borland, Broderbund, and MicroPro. He is currently based in Sebastopol, CA and can be reached at sheldunn@sonic.net or 75720,2333 on CompuServe.

David Day   David is a computer book author and business consultant.

David Field   David Field is a professional trainer working with Microsoft Office products.

Jan Snyder   Jan Snyder is a software consultant in Virginia and has written and edited books for Que since 1993. More on Jan at this Web page: http://www.regent.edu/acad/schgov/asnyder/jan/.

Joyce Nielsen   Joyce J. Nielsen is an independent computer consultant, specializing in writing and developing books based on microcomputer software applications.

Marilyn Kyd   Marilyn Gratton Kyd has been writing short stories, articles, books, and computer-related materials for more than 25 years. Her business, WordMaster, which specializes in business and technical documentation, is located in Lynnwood, Washington.

Sally Russell   Sally is a technical writer and contributor to *The Beginner's Guide to Net Surfing*.

Cheryl Kirk   Cheryl is the author of *The Internet Phone Connection*, and a writer of a weekly column for a Pulitzer Prize-winning newspaper.

Each of these well-known writers has contributed their wit and aplomb in at least one topic of expertise, making this *Microsoft Office 97 Professional Quick Reference* one of the most valuable reference books on the subject of Microsoft Office 97!

Robert Mullen
Author

We'd Like to Hear from You!

As part of our continuing effort to produce books of the highest possible quality, Que would like to hear your comments. To stay competitive, we *really* want you, as a computer book reader and user, to let us know what you like or dislike most about this book or other Que products.

You can mail comments, ideas, or suggestions for improving future editions to the address below, or send us a fax at (317) 581-4663. For the online inclined, Macmillan Computer Publishing has a forum on CompuServe (type **GO QUEBOOKS** at any prompt) through which our staff and authors are available for questions and comments. The address of our Internet site is **http://www/quecorp/msoffice** (World Wide Web).

In addition to exploring our forum, please feel free to contact me personally to discuss your opinions of this book: I'm **73451,1220** on CompuServe, and I'm **dcoe@que.mcp.com** on the Internet.

Thanks in advance—your comments will help us to continue publishing the best books available on computer topics in today's market.

Dana Coe
Product Development Specialist
Que Corporation
201 W. 103rd Street
Indianapolis, Indiana 46290
USA

NOTE Although we cannot provide general technical support, we're happy to help you resolve problems you encounter related to our books, disks, or other products. If you need such assistance, please contact our Tech Support department at 800-545-5914 ext. 3833.

To order other Que or Macmillan Computer Publishing books or products, please call our Customer Service department at 800-835-3202 ext. 666. ▦

Table of Contents

Introduction

The *Microsoft Office 97 Professional Quick Reference* is the latest in a series of comprehensive, task-oriented references, which details how to use the features and functionality of the products that comprise Office 97. Compiled for the intermediate to advanced user who wants a concise, comprehensive reference, the *Microsoft Office 97 Professional Quick Reference* is loaded with detailed instructions outlining important tasks you need to complete.

The *Microsoft Office 97 Professional Quick Reference* presents the tasks most often sought by users of Access 97, Excel 97, Word 97, PowerPoint 97, Outlook, and Binder. The book also includes a comprehensive glossary with many terms and definitions that refer to the newest features in the latest Office product offering from Microsoft.

New Ways of Working

Que's Quick References help the reader cover the most ground with the least amount of hassle, and in a minimum amount of time! Tasks include steps that the reader can complete, and there are usually no more than five steps to any task.

The goal of the authors is to help you get your work done in the least amount of time, with a minimum of reading and learning. The authors know that your time is valuable to you, and that you may not need to use some of the included tasks very often. That's why each task in this book is written with economy in mind. The reader should be able to recognize a need, take this book off the shelf and complete a task within minutes; then put the book back on the shelf for future reference. It just doesn't get any faster or easier.

Expanded Coverage

Unlike previous versions, Que's *Microsoft Office 97 Professional Quick Reference* covers every major element of the Office 97 suite. More importantly, each product is covered separately, in its own dedicated section in this book. You no longer need a special book that covers your Standard or Professional version of Office 97. The *Microsoft Office 97 Professional Quick Reference* does it all!

Who Should Read This Book?

The *Office 97 Professional Quick Reference* is written for casual to advanced computer users who need a fast reference to Office 97 tasks and features. It is an ideal companion to Que's *Special Edition Using Microsoft Office 97 Professional*. The Quick Reference size makes it ideal for travel.

If you are upgrading from Office 4.x or Office 95 to Office 97, you will find this reference useful for finding new features and looking up new ways of getting a job done. If you are migrating from another suite, such as SmartSuite, this Quick Reference may be the right amount of instruction you need to transfer your know-how investment to new products.

If you are just starting to use Office software for the first time, or are a very casual user, you may want to consider Que's *User Friendly Using Microsoft Office 97* or *The Complete Idiot's Guide to Microsoft Office 97* as a book to get you up to speed. For a beginner or very casual task reference, check out Que's *Easy Microsoft Office 97*.

New Features of the Que Office 97 Quick Reference

If you take a moment to glance over the table of contents, you'll note that each Office 97 product has its own section in this book. Topics are organized into working groups under each Office product, with relative tasks sorted under each topic in alphabetical order. In some cases, tasks have been specially sorted by the authors when more than one task is best used when performed in conjunction with another task, or in the most intelligent order.

Content Tuned to Your Needs

You can't be expected to know everything, and yet, you don't have to be told everything either. That's why the Quick Reference authors have been given wide latitude in determining what extra information you might find valuable to complete a task. By tuning the presentation to your needs, you can spend less time sifting through background information, or cross-referencing related information just to be sure you're using a task appropriately. For example, authors often indicate which *conditions* must exist in order to complete a task. Authors explain why one task is best to use over another—all in very succinct text. Where it is obvious to you what conditions must exist or which task is best, you won't be slowed by text telling you what you already know.

Expert Advice

Expert authors know when a specific task is appropriate and when that task should be avoided. For example, there is no point in making a bulleted list if only one list item exists. This book tells you when a task is in order, and when you should avoid using a task when it's out of context or is not appropriate at a specific location in your document, database, or presentation. This expertise of the author transfers directly to your work through this expert author approach.

Navigation and Steps

Author expertise can also help keep tasks simple by including or eliminating steps that guide you to where you enter information or perform an action. Many of the tasks in this book detail how to get where you're going because the author believes that getting there is confusing for the reader.

In other cases, where your starting point is unknown or where you are likely to know where a menu or dialog is located, the authors keep it simple by not adding the navigational detail.

The same assumptions apply where individual actions can be compounded into a step. Beginners often need "baby steps" to avoid confusion. The need for such care soon passes for most, and the user is better able to work with a step that is a logical group of actions. The result is a more readable set of steps.

The authors have limited the length of commands and steps to just the words you need to read to complete each task in a minimum amount of time. Intermediate users of Windows-based applications rarely need to be told when to click the OK button!

Expert Mentoring

You also get background information, when appropriate, to the topic or task. Tasks are often introduced so that your understanding of the real purpose of the task is clarified. Although mentoring is best done through the full *Special Edition Using* series, there are times when a little mentoring before a task greatly enhances the understanding of that task or function. The authors keep this in mind while using their extensive user experience to determine when to provide that reinforcing conceptual information.

Conventions Used in This Book

This book uses certain conventions in order to guide you through the various tasks. Many tasks include tips, notes, warnings, and cautions. These are described in-depth in this section.

The authors have gone to great lengths to protect you from disaster, warning you of impending, often irreversible danger before you get in over your head. Warnings are just one way this Quick Reference will inform you when you need to know.

> **WARNING** AutoRecover does not save your documents—only certain recovery information! Be sure to save all documents you are working on at frequent intervals.

Notes often advise and direct you while you complete a task. Expect to find bobbles of great wisdom while you complete tasks.

NOTE Word 97 no longer has the AutoSave function that was in previous versions.

Tips offer expert input from those who really know the software. Tips often include time-saving solutions and ways to shortcut your way to success. If you're looking for a shortcut key, tips are where you'll find them!

TIP To see page borders in your document, you must be in Page Layout View.

The completion of some tasks may change several aspects of a document or the way your Microsoft Office products work in the future. Cautions inform the reader about unforeseen events that may not occur as expected. Cautions are not as severe as warnings, but you will want to read cautionary information.

CAUTION You must save entry and exit macros in the form file. If you save the macros elsewhere and then distribute the form, the entry and exit macros may not run because the macros aren't there.

A Comprehensive Glossary

With the Internet awareness of the Microsoft Office 97 product comes a lot of jargon that will be new to you. This book has a glossary of terms specific to who you are and what you're doing. These terms are contained in various sections of the book as italicized words. Look them up as you go along, or scan for any terms that you may not be familiar with. Ever wonder what a primary key is? You don't have to complete a task to find out. You can check out any term or definition in the glossary!

Task Reference

This Quick Reference is divided into sections, all dedicated to Office 97 software products. In each section, you will find an alphabetical listing of topics that are detailed with tasks.

To find all tasks that cover bulleted lists, for example, go to the Word section, find the task topic "Bulleted Lists," then turn to the tasks that cover activity in that topic area. Tasks follow one another, and are sorted in alphabetical order as well, unless there is special value in completing multiple tasks in order.

Related Books

No one book can cover all of the needs of every user. Que offers a complete line of Office 97-related titles. Look for Quick References on each of the Office 97 components as well as Windows 95. *Special Edition Using Microsoft Office 97 Professional* is the most complete tutorial and reference volume available for Office 97, and answers end-user questions with clear, concise, and comprehensive authority. Que's *Net Savvy Office 97* concentrates its content on getting the most of Office 97's extensive Internet and intranet features. Ask your bookseller for the availability of other Que titles.

Binder

Office Binder is an application that lets you group all your documents, workbooks, templates, and presentation files in one location. Binder enables you to add a single header or footer to all documents included in a *binder file*, print all files in a binder with a single command, or route the binder contents to other users over a network.

Binder Documents: Adding

You can add templates, documents, Web pages, and many other types of files to an Office 97 binder. Later, these documents can be collectively printed or viewed, or you can share Office binders on an intranet or on the Internet. Binder gives you the flexibility of easily adding new and existing documents.

Steps

1. Click the Show/Hide Left Pane icon (the double-headed arrow to the left of the File menu) on the menu bar to expand the Selection Pane.

2. Open the folder containing the document you want to add to the binder from either the Windows Explorer, My Computer, or from the desktop.

3. Drag the icon of the document to the *Left Pane* on the Binder window. An icon representing that document should be displayed in the Selection Pane; the document becomes a section in the binder and is shown open in the *Right Pane* of the Binder window.

   The menu bar and toolbar for the document's application are activated to allow you to work on the document from within the binder.

TIP You can add templates to your binder as well as documents you have created. Choose Section, Add, then click the tab for the type of document you want. Next, double-click the template tab type you want to add.

NOTE Not all file types can be placed in a binder. When you drag the icon over the open section pane and the cursor turns into a circle with a slash symbol, this means this document type cannot be read by Binder. ■

Binder Documents: Duplicating

There are times when you want to duplicate copies of a document to your Office Binder without having to find the original. Office Binder *sections* are separate documents (Word, Excel, PowerPoint, and so on.) grouped in a binder. These documents can be new, blank documents or existing documents.

Steps
1. Right-click the document icon in the Left Pane to select the document and display the shortcut menu.
2. Choose Duplicate from the shortcut menu and move the cursor in the Insert After field.
3. Double-click the existing section that you want the copied section to come after.
4. Click OK to add a copy of the selected section. A copy of the open section is inserted below the section you selected from the list.

Binder Documents: Hiding and Displaying

If you don't want a binder section to appear at the moment but you don't want to delete it, you can hide it and then display it again later.

To focus your attention on a particular section, oftentimes you might want to hide a section.

BINDER

Steps

1. Click the section you want to hide to select it. The Left Pane must be showing, if it isn't, click the Show/Hide Left Pane button.

2. Choose Section, Hide.

3. To unhide the section, choose Section, Unhide.

4. Double-click the section you want to unhide.

 TIP If you think you have forgotten to add a section, or you think you might have accidentally deleted a section, always check the Section menu's Unhide command to see if the section you thought you had deleted or forgotten to add is actually hidden.

Binder Documents: Viewing in Original Application

You can view a document or section in the application that originally created the document. The original application and the selected document will open. You can return to the binder when you're finished viewing the selected document.

Steps

1. In the Left Pane of the Binder window, click the section you want to view.

2. Choose Section, View Outside. The selected document will open along with the original application.

3. Choose File, Close and Return To when finished viewing.

Binder Sections: Deleting

Just as you would delete unneeded files to conserve disk space, you can delete unneeded sections to avoid clutter in your binders. If a section is no longer needed, or has been inadvertently added to your binder, you can delete it.

Steps

1. Click the section icon in the Left Pane to select the binder section you want to delete.

2. Choose Section, Delete.

TIP You can also delete a section by right-clicking that section and choosing Delete from the shortcut menu.

Binder Sections: Moving Within Binders

There may be times when you want to rearrange sections within your binder, perhaps into a more logical order or to group them into some other hierarchical order, such as introductory sections or supporting facts sections.

Rearranging your sections in this manner will make it easier for the reader to find and digest them. Binder makes it easy to move a section to another location within a binder.

Steps

1. Choose Section, Rearrange.

2. Click the section you want to move up or down in the Reorder Sections box.

3. Click the Move Up or Move Down button to position the section in the order you want.

Briefcase: Sharing Network Binders

For projects that involve working as a team or with other groups of people, using the Briefcase allows users to work more quickly, productively, and accurately to complete projects in a shorter amount of time. Using the *Briefcase* to share documents allows users to edit and revise documents as a group.

You can share your binders with other people by placing the binder file on the network. If more than one person will be working with the binder file, you can use the Briefcase option in Windows 95 to incorporate everyone's changes.

NOTE Briefcase is part of Windows 95, and is not available in Windows NT 3.51 Workstation. ■

Steps

1. Place your binder file on the network in a location where others can access it. You can use the File, Save As command and in the Save In box, select My Briefcase and give a file name, then click Save.

2. Tell the other users of the binder file to copy the binder file saved on the network to their local Briefcase.

3. Make sure when someone works on the binder file that they select Update All from the Briefcase menu. This ensures the changes will be made to the network binder file, and a copy of the binder will be placed in their Briefcase.

NOTE Binder headers and footers created by using the Binder Page Setup Header/Footer tab are not updated when using the Briefcase to update a shared copy of the binder. ■

Creating: New Binder Templates

If you've created a new binder that you'll want to use as a pattern for creating similar binders in the future, you can save the binder as a template. Before saving the binder as a template, be sure to delete any sections or information that you don't want to appear in every newly created binder that is based on your saved template.

You can create templates from Office binders you have already saved. These Binder templates can contain document templates and sections. Create *Binder templates* to speed up the creation of new binders. (See also "Templates: Using Built-In.")

Steps

1. Choose File, Open Binder and select the saved binder from which you want to base your template.

2. Add additional documents or sections as required.

3. Choose File, Save Binder As. The Save As dialog box appears.

4. Click Binder Templates in the Save As Type drop-down list.

5. Double-click the folder for the type of binder you are saving and type a name for the template in the File Name box. Click OK.

NOTE Make sure you save your Binder templates in the Templates folder where Microsoft Office was originally installed if you want that binder to appear in the Binder tab when you choose File, New Binder. ▓

Creating: New Binders

Office Binder enables you to take all documents, workbooks, templates, and presentations for a single project and create one location to store copies of these files. From there you can print preview an entire binder, or create a single footer or header for all files regardless of the type. Single binder files can also be viewed on a Web server and links can be created between Binder files and Office files. A new binder is used to combine and organize related files.

Steps

1. Choose File, New Binder.

2. Click the General tab.

3. Double-click the Blank Binder icon and a new Office Binder will open up.

 TIP When you start Office Binder, a blank binder is automatically created for you by default.

Deleting: Binders

When you delete a binder, although the sections will be deleted, the original documents used to create the sections will not be deleted because Binder uses pointers to the actual documents. Note that there is no delete option on Binder's File menu.

Steps

1. Open My Computer, Windows Explorer, or the folder where the binder you want to delete is saved.

2. Click to select the binder you want to delete.

3. Either drag the icon to the Recycle Bin, click the Delete button, or right-click and choose Delete from the shortcut menu.

NOTE The documents stored as sections in that binder are not deleted, only the binder itself. To delete the actual documents or templates the binder points to, locate those files with the Explorer, and delete them as you would any other file. ■

Opening: Existing Binders

To open an existing binder, all you need to know is that the binder does exist, and its location. This is useful if you don't want to start a new binder from scratch, if you want to review a binder created by someone else, or if you want to continue modifying a binder you've already created.

Steps

1. Choose File, Open Binder.

2. Click the drop-down list and the appropriate drive where the binder is stored in the Look In list box.

3. Locate and double-click the folder where the binder that you want to open is located.

4. Double-click the binder to select it.

TIP You can open binders stored on the World Wide Web or stored on an FTP server by supplying the full URL or FTP location where the binder is stored. For example, if the binder named mybinder.obd is stored on the Web server myserver.com, you would type **http://www.myserver.com/mybinder.obd** in the File Name field in the Open Binder dialog box.

Posting: To Microsoft Exchange Folder

If you have *Microsoft Exchange* installed on your system, you can post a binder file to a Microsoft Exchange folder so others can view it.

Steps

1. Open the binder file you want to post to the Exchange folder.

2. Choose File, Send To.

3. Click the Exchange folder.

4. Click the folder you want to post in the folder list dialog box.

NOTE   If you don't have Microsoft Exchange, you still can route binders by using any 32-bit e-mail program compatible with the Messaging Application Programming Interface (MAPI) or by using any 16-bit e-mail program that is compatible with Vendor Independent Messaging (VIM). ■

TIP   If you don't have access to e-mail, you can still share binders by putting the file in a network directory or saving it to a floppy disk.

Routing Slips: Creating

When you want to send a binder to several people at once via e-mail, you must first create a *routing slip*. By creating a routing slip, the binder file will be routed from one person to the next on the routing slip. Once the first person has reviewed it, it will be sent to the next person on the routing slip. Any time during the routing process you can track who has viewed the binder file. You can include individual names or choose a group alias to send the binder document to. After all the recipients have reviewed the binder, it will automatically be returned to you.

NOTE When you route a binder, it is sent as an e-mail attachment. Recipients must have Office Binder 97 installed on their systems to be able to read the routed file. ▪

Steps

1. Open the binder you want to route and choose File, Send To.

2. Click Routing Recipient and click the Address button to select the recipients that should receive the binder.

3. Type the recipients' names or select from the Address list box the names to be moved to the To box.

4. After adding all recipients in the To box, click OK.

5. Select any additional routing options you want to apply and click Route to send the binder to the recipients, or select Add Slip to add the routing slip.

NOTE You can change the order in which recipients will receive the binder by changing the order of the names in the list. Click the recipient's name to select it, then click the up or down arrow to move the name in the list. ▪

Routing Slips: Editing

Before proceeding with this section, see "Routing Slips: Creating." Rather than routing paper documents and later trying to compile changes, a more efficient way to allow other users to review or revise your documents is to route an electronic copy. This gives you more control over who receives the document, when they receive it, and the order in which they receive it. You can also specify that all recipients receive it at the same time.

If you are routing a document with an existing routing slip, you can edit it to add additional recipients.

Steps

1. Choose File, Open Binder to open the binder containing the routing slip you want to edit.

2. Choose File, Send To to display a drop-down list of three options: Mail Recipient, Routing Recipient, and Exchange Folder.

3. Choose Routing Recipient.

4. If you are the originator of the routed binder, change any of the routing slip options you want. If you are the recipient of the routed binder, change the order of the recipients by selecting the names, and clicking the up or down arrow to move their names within the list.

5. Click Route to route the binder, or click Add Slip to close the dialog box and keep working with the binder.

Sections: Moving to Other Binders

For organizational and file-sharing reasons, you may have a section in one binder that contains information that is actually needed in another binder. It's easy to move sections from one binder to another as you organize your projects based on your information needs.

Steps

1. Open both binder files.

2. Arrange the Binder windows so you can see both windows and section panes.

3. Click to select the section or sections you want to move in the first Binder window.

4. Drag the section or sections to the other Binder window and drop.

CAUTION   Make sure you click in the middle of the icon for the section you want, and not on the section title. Otherwise, Office will assume you are trying to rename the file.

Sections: Moving Outside Binders

For sections that have been created and modified within Binder, you may want to store them as an independent file to allow others to access the information contained in that particular section, but also prohibit access to other information or sections that may be confidential.

There are times when you want to transfer a section to another location of your computer such as a particular folder or a floppy disk drive. When you move a section to another location outside a binder, a copy of the actual section is placed at the intended location.

Steps

1. Arrange the Binder window so you can see the location where you will be placing the section.

2. Click to select the section or sections you want to move.

3. Drag the section to the location and drop, and Binder will make a copy of that section at the new location.

CAUTION   Make sure you have enough space at the intended location before you move a copy of the section. When you move a section outside of a binder, it is no longer being pointed to, but is an actual independent copy of the file.

Sections: Renaming

You should use a descriptive name to identify the contents of each section. This will save you time later by not having to search through many binder sections for information that you know is in your binder, but you're not sure where.

As you or other users create, add, and modify binder sections, you may want to rename the binder sections to reflect changes to the actual contents of a section.

Steps

1. Click to select the section you want to rename in the Left Pane.

2. Choose Section, Rename. The selected section's name is highlighted and activated for editing.

3. Type a new descriptive name for the section and press Enter. The section name is changed to reflect your update.

 TIP There are two other ways to rename a section. One is by clicking in the name of the section, then typing a new name. Another way is to right-click the section, then choose Rename from the shortcut menu.

Sections: Saving as Documents

As you build and modify your binder, sections that have been added and created within Binder can be saved as documents that are independent from Binder. This will not remove the section from the binder, the section will remain in the binder, and will also be an independent file for others to work on if needed.

For users that only need access to one section of a binder, you can save sections in your Binder as independent documents. This feature allows sharing of information on an as-needed basis. For example, another user may only need access to one section of a binder but not to the entire binder. This feature provides security for sensitive information, ability to selectively share information, and makes it easier for other users to access only the sections they need to see.

Steps

1. Click to select the section you want to save in the Left Pane.

2. Choose Section, Save As File.

3. Type the name of the file in the File Name box, and if necessary click to locate the directory or drive to save the file in the Save In box.

NOTE When you save the section as a separate file, the document is not removed from the binder. It will still be part of the binder. Use the Section menu's Remove command to remove a section from a pane. ■

Sending: Via E-Mail

You can share binder information with others by sending a copy of the binder through e-mail, or you can post a binder to a Microsoft Exchange public folder when you don't want to send it via e-mail. You can also post a binder to a Microsoft Outlook folder.

In order to send or route binders through e-mail, you need one of the following:

■ Microsoft Exchange (or other mail system compatible with the Messaging Application Programming Interface [MAPI])

■ Lotus cc:Mail (or other mail system compatible with Vendor Independent Messaging [VIM])

NOTE Not all e-mail gateways will be able to transfer binder files or will have very limited abilities in this area. Check with the administrator of the network to see if the binder file will work across the various gateways. ■

Steps

1. Make sure you are connected to the network and logged on to your e-mail account.

2. Open the binder file you want to mail.

3. Create a routing slip by choosing File, Send To.

4. Click Mail Recipient.

5. Address the mail message with the recipient's e-mail address.

TIP If the binder already has a routing slip attached, choose File, Send To, then click Next Routing Recipient and add the new recipient's e-mail address, then click OK.

Templates: Using Built-In

Binder templates save you time by keeping you from creating a new binder from scratch each time. The original template on which your new binder is based remains intact for use the next time you need to create another binder. Binder templates have been developed for a wide variety of different uses and already contain sections for some of the typical binders created for business needs.

Steps

1. Choose File, New Binder.
2. Click the Binders tab.
3. Double-click the Binder template you want to use.

NOTE Binder templates are saved in the Templates folder. If you want to add more templates, store them in the Microsoft Office\Templates folder so that the binder templates appear in the New Binder dialog box. ■

Unbinding: Into Separate Documents

You can unbind sections, then save those sections as separate documents. Binder sections are saved as separate documents in the same folder that contains that binder. When you unbind sections, the original binder still remains intact. Be sure all of the sections in the binder are closed before you try to unbind.

Steps

1. Locate the binder file you want to save as separate documents in your computer, using Windows Explorer.
2. Right-click the binder file.
3. Choose Unbind from the shortcut menu. The sections will then be divided into separate documents.

NOTE The Unbind command is not available in Windows NT Workstation 3.51, but you can still save each binder section as a separate document by using the section's Save File As menu option. ■

Outlook

Microsoft Outlook is your ultimate desktop management tool. With Outlook you can manage your e-mail messages, faxes, appointments, contacts, or your To-Do lists, as well as track all your activities. In addition, you can open and view documents, plus share information with others.

Address Book Entries: Creating

The *Address Book* contains addresses for fax recipients, Internet e-mail addresses, and addresses for recipients on other e-mail systems. These entries will appear when you click the Address Book button when sending a fax or e-mail.

Steps

1. Choose Tools, Address Book.
2. Choose File, New Entry from the Address Book's menu. A New Entry dialog box appears displaying a list of available types of address book entries.
3. Double-click to select the type of address this entry is from the list of available address book entry types.
4. Type the name, e-mail address, fax number, or business-related information based on the type of address you are adding. You MUST enter e-mail information to be able to get into any of the other tabs to enter information.
5. Click OK, then choose File, Close.

Calendar: Adding Appointments

The *Calendar* feature contains events, a date navigator to help you go directly to the date you want to view, a list of appointments, a taskpad that lets you outline your To-Do list, and a meeting planner. Appointments can have reminders attached to them that can be recurring if you choose. An appointment is an activity that you block time for, but that does not involve other people's resources. You can schedule appointments on other people's calendars if you have the permission to do so.

Steps

1. Choose File, New, and click Appointment. An untitled appointment dialog box appears.

2. Type a description for the appointment in the Subject field box.

3. Type a location where the appointment will be held in the Location field box.

4. Select the Start Times and End Times.

5. Change the options you want and click the Save and Close button on the toolbar.

 TIP You can schedule an appointment by going into Calendar, dragging across a block of time, right-clicking that block of time, and then choosing New Appointment from the shortcut menu.

Calendar: Scheduling Events

An *event* is an activity that lasts at least 24 hours or longer. An event is defined as lasting from midnight to midnight. You'll need to clear the All Day Event check box to enter specific times.

Steps

1. Click the Calendar icon from the Outlook bar.

2. Choose Calendar, New Event, and type the event description in the Subject field.

3. Type the location of the event in the Location field.

4. Choose the other options such as the Start Times and End Times, the Reminder time to remind you of the event, and the Categories associated with this event.

5. Click the Save and Close icon on the Standard toolbar.

Calendar: Scheduling Meetings

A meeting is an appointment, but instead of an appointment meant mainly for you, a meeting is an appointment to which you can invite other people and resources.

Steps

1. Click the Calendar icon in the Outlook bar.

2. Choose Calendar, New Meeting Request, and click the Meeting Planner tab.

3. Click the Invite Others button to invite the attendees and select their name from the list, or type the name of the person or resource to invite to the meeting.

4. For each name or resource select the Required, Optional, or Resources button. The required and optional attendees will appear in the Invite To field, and resources will appear in the Location field.

5. Click OK to scroll through the busy and free time listed for the prospective attendees.

 TIP To quickly schedule someone listed in your Contacts list, click the contact, then choose Contact, New Meeting with Contact.

Contacts: Creating

A *contact* is a detailed information sheet on a particular person or company. You can add all sorts of information about that contact including the phone number, Web page address, e-mail address, fax number, and business address.

Steps

1. Choose File, New.
2. Select Contact from the drop-down menu.
3. Type the full name of the contact in the Full Name field.
4. Add the additional information such as phone number, business address, e-mail address, or Web page.
5. Click the Save and Close button on the Standard toolbar.

E-mail: Sending Messages

Cutting-edge electronic mail enhancements include AutoName Check to help ensure your e-mail message is sent to the intended recipients quickly. Outlook automatically checks the validity of e-mail names while you compose your message.

AutoPreview displays the first few lines of the body of your message so it isn't necessary to open every message. This feature can significantly reduce the time you spend reading e-mail.

E-mail can quickly be sent within a network or throughout the Internet with the click of a button.

Steps

1. Click the Mail button in the Outlook bar and choose File, New.
2. Click Mail Message from the drop-down menu and enter the e-mail address of the recipient(s).
3. Type the subject in the Subject field.
4. Enter the message in the Message field.
5. Click the Send button on the Standard toolbar.

TIP   If your e-mail is operating slowly, eliminate any sounds or notifications in the Options dialog box. Also, make sure you have at least 16M of RAM memory if you are using Word as your e-mail editor.

E-mail: Setting Up

In order to use e-mail with Outlook, you must first configure Outlook. You can receive e-mail from the Internet, within an intranet, through Microsoft Mail, through cc:Mail on a LAN, or from an Exchange Server.

Steps

1. Choose Tools, Services.

2. Click the Services tab, then click the Add button.

3. Select Microsoft Exchange in the Available Information Services box and click OK.

4. Click the General tab, then type the name of the Microsoft Exchange Server in the Exchange Server field.

5. Type the name of the mailbox you use and select the options you want, then click OK twice. Make sure you exit and restart Outlook to ensure the changes take effect.

NOTE   If you do not know the name of the Exchange Server or mailbox, check with your network administrator. ▪

Folders: Creating

Folders can contain all elements of Outlook in addition to any type of document stored on your computer. Folders allow you to organize your appointments, faxes, e-mail messages, and documents into easily accessible items.

Steps

1. Choose File, New; then click Folder (or press Ctrl+Shift+E).

2. Enter the name of the folder in the Name field.

3. Select the items to be stored in this folder from the Folder Contains drop-down list.

4. Enter the description of this folder in the Description field.

TIP When you make changes to entries in a folder, they may not show up immediately. To force Outlook to refresh folder views, choose View, Refresh, or press F5.

Information: Archiving

As your Outlook mailbox grows, messages will fill up in your box. You may not immediately need old messages, but may still want to save them. In this case, you would *archive* them to another file.

You can manually or automatically archive Outlook information, or you can have AutoArchive delete old items.

Steps

1. Choose File, Archive. The Archive dialog box is displayed.

2. Select whether to AutoArchive all folders, or just an individual folder by choosing the appropriate radio button.

3. Select the date to start the archiving in the Archive Items Older Than drop-down list box.

4. Type the name of the archived file in the Archive File list box and click OK.

CAUTION Outlook can archive only those items stored in a mail folder. This includes Word, Excel, or PowerPoint documents. A file not stored in a mail folder cannot be archived.

Information: Copying

By integrating your desktop, Outlook allows you to move and share information easily between Office files and items in Outlook. This feature helps save you time by eliminating the need to retype data. You can copy information from one folder to another.

Steps

1. Click to select the items you want to copy.

2. Choose Edit, Copy to Folder.

3. Click to select the folder you want to copy the items into.

 TIP To select more than one item to copy, hold down the Ctrl key and click the items. To select a group of items, click the first item in the list. Hold down the Shift key and select the last item of the group.

Information: Deleting

Information that is outdated or no longer needed can easily be deleted from any folder within Outlook.

Steps

1. Click to select the items you want to delete.

2. Choose Edit, Delete.

3. The items will be placed in the Deleted Items folder. You can retrieve them later if you have not deleted them from the Deleted Items folder.

 TIP You can also press the Delete key to delete selected items. To quickly empty the Deleted Items folder, choose Tools, Empty Deleted Items.

Information: Finding

You can copy, move, find, and delete just about any type of information in Outlook. You specify what you want to look for by entering keywords and telling Outlook where to look for your information.

Steps

1. Choose Tools, Find Items.

2. Select where to look for the information, such as in e-mail messages, files, tasks, and so on. The kinds of

options you'll have to chose from vary depending on
what kind of information you choose in the Look For
box.

3. Enter the keywords to search for in the Search For
Word(s) box, or select the type of file you want to look
for in the In box to search for items in the subject field,
message body, and frequently used text fields. Again,
your choices will vary depending on what you want to
search for.

4. Specify other options such as the sender of the message,
the date the file was created or modified, or Journal
entry type.

5. Click the Find Now button.

Information: Moving

Unlike copying, where the original stays in the same location,
moving will actually move the item you select.

> **CAUTION**   Make sure you remember where you move information.
> If you forget where you have moved information, use the Tools, Find
> Items command.

Steps

1. Click to select the items you want to move.

2. Choose Edit, Move to Folder.

3. Click to select the folder you want to move the items into.

Journal Entries: Creating

The *Journal* is a new component to help you keep track of any
information that goes through your personal computer. Outlook Journal can be used to find Office files or Outlook items
based on when the file was last modified instead of what it was
named or where it was saved. Journals look much like project

charts. Activities can automatically be recorded in your journal, including e-mail messages, meeting requests, and task requests.

Steps

1. Choose File, New and click to select New Journal Entry from the drop-down menu (Crtl+Shift+J).

2. Type the subject of the journal entry in the Subject field, and choose the Entry type from the drop-down list.

3. Specify the Start date and Duration.

4. Enter the text for the Journal entry.

5. Click the Save and Close button on the Standard toolbar.

TIP Double-click the subject of the journal entry in the Journal window to expand that journal entry.

Notes: Creating

Notes in Outlook are much like Post-It notes. You can add a note at any time and refer back to that note by clicking the Notes icon in the Outlook toolbar.

Steps

1. Choose File, New, and then click to select Note from the drop-down menu (Ctrl+Shift+N).

2. Type your note.

3. Click the Close button to close and save the note.

NOTE To read the notes you have written, click the Notes icon in the Outlook toolbar. The notes you have created will be listed, with a portion of the note displayed in the Outlook window. ■

TIP You can sort the way notes are displayed by choosing View, Sort.

Outlook: Customizing

You can add individual components in Outlook, or you can delete those components you may not use. Outlook can be set to automatically start each time you start your computer. You can also control what options show when you first open Outlook.

Steps

1. Close all programs you have opened.
2. Choose Start, Settings, Control Panel.
3. Double-click the Add/Remove Programs icon.
4. Click Microsoft Office on the Install/Uninstall tab.
5. Click Add/Remove and follow the removal instructions.

TIP   Refer to Microsoft Outlook's Help file for information on all the additional features installed when Outlook is initially installed.

NOTE   Make sure you are still using the same CD-ROM drive designator you used when you originally installed Outlook. If the drive designator has changed, re-run the setup from the Outlook CD-ROM. ■

Profiles: Copying

Outlook builds upon and extends the Windows Messaging System by providing standard interfaces for connecting e-mail clients and applications. These interfaces allow you to copy a profile from one service profile to another. (See also "Profiles: Creating.")

Steps

1. Select Tools, Services.
2. Click the Services tab.
3. Select the Information Service you want to copy in the list box.

4. Click the Copy button.

5. Select the profile to copy the service to, then click OK twice.

Profiles: Creating

A *profile* is a stored setting that defines how Outlook is set up for a particular user. That setting may contain pointers to a particular address book and settings for mailbox options.

You create multiple profiles when you use different information services, such as having connections to a commercial service and an Internet service provider, or when there are multiple users for one machine.

Outlook can start with the same profile every time, or you can be prompted to select a profile each time you start.

Steps
1. Choose Start, Settings, Control Panel.

2. Double-click the Mail and Fax icon.

3. Click the Services tab, then click Show Profiles.

4. Select the desired profile on the General tab.

5. Click Add and follow the Inbox Setup Wizard.

Profiles: Deleting

You can easily delete service profiles that are no longer needed. (See also "Profiles: Creating" and "Profiles: Copying.")

Steps
1. Select Start, Settings, Control Panel.

2. Double-click the Mail and Fax icon.

3. Click the Services tab, then click Show Profiles.

4. Click the General tab, then click the profile you want to delete.

5. Click the Remove button.

> **CAUTION** Make sure you know which profile you are deleting. When you delete a profile you will delete information to connect to that service.

Remote Mail Access: Setting Up

Remote mail allows you to retrieve your mail from another location outside your current network. You can send and receive messages at home or on the road. Download message headers to preview the sender and subject before downloading or deleting entire messages.

Steps

1. Install Outlook on the remote computer you will be communicating with.

2. Create a personal folder on your hard drive.

3. If necessary, download the Address Book to your computer's hard drive.

4. Set the options for mail delivery in the mail delivery service.

5. Select the messages to be delivered to your personal file folder, exit, and restart Outlook.

Tasks: Creating

Tasks are items you add to your Task list. Tasks can be assigned start dates and end dates, percentage complete, and priority. Tasks also have the ability to set a reminder alarm when the task is due.

Steps

1. Choose File, New, and select Task from the drop-down list (Ctrl+Shift+K).

2. Enter the title of the task in the Subject field and specify the due date if applicable.

3. Specify the Status from the drop-down list and specify the Priority and Percentage Complete if necessary.

4. Click the Reminder check box to create a reminder alarm if necessary.

5. Specify the Categories as required, and click the Save and Close button on the Standard toolbar. If you don't have the task maximized, you can't see the Categories option.

 TIP To modify a task, double-click the task subject or due date. To check off the task, click the check box to the left of the task in the Task window.

OUTLOOK

Word

Word 97 is Microsoft's latest entry into the race of the word processing software products. Word 97 is an upgrade from Word 7 for Windows 95 and is designed to connect every word processor software user to other computer users on their local network and the Internet.

In this section, most of the commonly requested functions and features of Word 97 are outlined in a task-oriented style that's easy to use. The information helps you access tasks that enable you to step your way through many of the latest features in Word 97.

Alignment: Center

Headlines for a title page or lyric stanzas are often centered on a page, ragged on both left and right margins.

Steps

1. Position the cursor anywhere within the text of the paragraph you want centered (or select a group of paragraphs).
2. Click the Center button on the Formatting toolbar.

All the text within the paragraph (or paragraphs) you selected becomes centered. Any unselected text following a carriage release remains unaffected. Right and left margins are both ragged.

Alignment: Justify

To give text a more formal appearance, you can justify it to make it fill the line fully to both margins. Word fills out each line by adding space between words (except for the last line in a paragraph, which is flush left).

Steps

1. Position the cursor in the paragraph.
2. Click the Justify button on the Formatting toolbar.

Alignment: Left

You can align text both horizontally and vertically on a page. Default text alignment is ragged-right, flush with the left page margin.

Steps

1. Position the cursor anywhere within the text of the paragraph you want to left align (or select a group of paragraphs).
2. Click the Align Left button on the Formatting toolbar.

All the text within the paragraph (or paragraphs) you selected becomes aligned with the left margin. Any unselected text following a carriage return remains unaffected. The right margin remains ragged.

Alignment: Right

You can also make text flush with the right margin, with the left side ragged.

Steps

1. Position the cursor anywhere within the text of the paragraph you want to right align (or select a group of paragraphs).
2. Click the Align Right button on the Formatting toolbar.

All the text within the paragraph (or paragraphs) you selected becomes aligned with the right margin. Any unselected text following a carriage return remains unaffected. The left margin remains ragged.

Alignment: Vertical

Word can automatically align text in the vertical page space. The default vertical alignment is "top," where lines begin at the top of the page and are spaced according to the current line space settings. You can also center text, making the space between top and bottom equal. Or, justify text vertically to automatically add line spacing to evenly fill the entire page. If there aren't enough lines remaining to fill the page, justified text has the same effect as "top" alignment.

Steps

1. Choose File, Page Setup.
2. Click the Layout tab (if it isn't already displayed).
3. Choose Top, Center, or Justified from the Vertical Alignment drop-down list box.
4. Click OK to close the dialog box and apply the change.

AutoComplete: Starting

AutoComplete is part of Word's extensive automatic text feature that also includes AutoFormat and AutoCorrect. After you type the first few characters of a word, such as a day of the week or month, AutoComplete can automatically insert the item in your document.

AutoComplete can insert the following elements:

- Today's date
- A day of the week
- A month
- Your (default author's) name
- Previously stored AutoText entries (called *glossary entries* in previous versions of Word)

Steps

1. Choose Tools, AutoCorrect.
2. Click the AutoText tab.

3. Select the check box marked Show AutoComplete Tip for AutoText and Dates. Clear the check box to turn the feature off.

4. Click the OK button to close the dialog box and apply the changes.

AutoComplete: Using

The AutoComplete feature also can fill out words that identify a text or graphics selection saved earlier. Because AutoComplete can insert any length of text, this feature can save you an enormous amount of typing.

Steps

1. Begin typing the word, for example, **Janu** for January.

2. Word displays a suggestion box. You can take one of several steps:

   ■ Press Enter or the F3 key to accept and complete the word after the completed word.

   ■ If you type a space after the completed word rather than Enter, Word also proposes the current date, for example, January 1, 1997.

   ■ If you simply continue typing, Word cancels AutoComplete and restores your text as entered.

NOTE See also "AutoText: Using AutoComplete" to learn how to create entries that AutoComplete can automatically insert. ■

AutoComplete: Using AutoCorrect

Word 97's *AutoCorrect* feature corrects many common typing errors as you type them. Word fixes these errors:

■ Double capitals at the beginning of a word

■ Lowercase letter beginning a sentence (immediately after a period)

- Lowercase letter beginning a day of the week
- Capitalization from a Caps Lock key left on (reverses the capitalization and automatically turns off Caps Lock)
- Commonly misspelled words (including some grammatical errors)

AutoCorrect also lets you insert special symbols. Word 97 even provides automatic correction for some short word strings.

You can control which AutoCorrect features you want to use and also create a list of grammatical exceptions to exclude from automatic correction.

Steps

1. Choose Tools, AutoCorrect. Click the AutoCorrect tab to bring the AutoCorrect sheet to the front.

2. Select or clear check boxes for four different kinds of capitalization correction and for the option to Replace Text As You Type.

3. Click the Exceptions button to open the AutoCorrect Exceptions dialog box. Make any desired changes to prevent certain abbreviations that are formed with a period from automatically capitalizing the next word. Word 97 gives you a list of such abbreviations (such as etc. and misc.), and you can add your own.

4. Click OK to close the AutoCorrect Exceptions dialog box. In the AutoCorrect dialog box, click OK to close the dialog box and apply the changes.

AutoFit: Applying to Table Entries

If you apply AutoFit to a table with multiple lines, Word widens the column to fit the text, returning the row to single-line spacing.

Steps

1. Select at least one cell in the column of table entries you want to be automatically fitted. (See the following caution.)

2. Choose Table, Cell Height and Width. The Cell Height and Width dialog box is displayed.

3. Click the Column tab and then click the AutoFit button. Clicking the AutoFit button closes the dialog box and Word automatically adjusts the column to a width as narrow as possible to fit the widest text in each selected column.

CAUTION To use AutoFit on more than one column at a time, be sure to select each column of cells in its entirety. Otherwise, Word adjusts the space in only the selected cells, making their column width different from other rows in the table. (Of course, this may be the effect you want.)

AutoFit: Making Equal Width Cells

For symmetry, you may want to make columns in a table equal width. It's easiest to let Word 97 do this for you.

Steps

1. Select cells in at least two columns to be balanced.

2. Choose Table, and either Distribute Rows Evenly or Distribute Columns Evenly. Word automatically makes all the selected rows as wide as the widest one.

 TIP To select multiple rows or columns in a table, click one row or column, then hold down the Shift key while you click others (without losing the selection for the first one).

AutoFormat: Changing AutoFormat Options

AutoFormat is a series of format adjustments Word makes to your document, either as you type or when you apply a format. You can choose which of many format controls you want to apply. Word includes AutoFormat as a part of the AutoCorrect feature.

Word applies AutoFormat effects automatically when your text contains certain characters. You can apply these effects to selected text or to an entire document. The other option, AutoFormat As You Type, applies most of the same formats as you enter text. You can separately select which formatting features you want to apply for AutoFormat or AutoFormat As You Type.

Here are a few of Word's AutoFormat features:

- Creates a numbered list when you begin a line with a number followed by a period, hyphen, closing parentheses, or > character, and then enter a space or tab followed by some text.

- Creates a bulleted list when you begin a line with an asterisk, one or two hyphens, the > character, or an arrow composed of -> or =>, and then enter a space or tab followed by some text.

- Substitutes a typographical fraction for one entered using the / (front slash) key, such as 1/2.

You can find a complete list in the Word Help list under AutoFormat.

Steps

1. Choose Tools, AutoCorrect. The AutoCorrect dialog box appears.
2. Click the AutoFormat or AutoFormat As You Type tab.
3. Select the check boxes for the features you want.

AutoRecover: Enabling

AutoRecover is a new Word feature that saves certain information on any documents you have open to your disk at timed intervals. If a document you are working on becomes corrupted due to a power failure or malfunction, Word may be able to recover its contents using this information.

When you restart Word after a failure, it senses possible document problems. Word then opens the special file saved by the AutoRecover function and attempts to automatically restore documents.

Steps

1. Choose Tools, Options.
2. Click the Save tab to bring the Save sheet to the front.
3. Select the check box marked Save AutoRecover Info Every.
4. Enter the time duration in the Minutes spin box (from 1 to 120) for AutoRecover's automatic save of recovery information.

WARNING AutoRecover does not save your documents—only certain recovery information! Be sure to save all documents you are working on at frequent intervals.

NOTE Word 97 no longer has the AutoSave function that was in previous versions. ■

AutoSummarize: Using

Microsoft has included a new feature in Word 97 called *AutoSummarize*, which automatically generates an abstract or summary of a document. At the same time, AutoSummarize compiles a list of the most heavily used words and phrases and creates a keyword list that becomes one of the document properties.

You can have Word highlight key points directly in the text of your document, insert a separate summary at the beginning, or create an entirely separate summary document.

Steps

1. Choose Tools, AutoSummarize. The AutoSummarize dialog box is displayed.

2. Select the level of detail you want the summary to contain.

3. Double-click where you want the summary created (highlighted, at the top of the document, or as a separate document).

AutoText: Inserting

To save tedious re-typing, you can quickly insert text phrases into your document that you saved earlier as AutoText entries.

Steps

1. Click to select the entry point in your document.

2. Choose Insert, AutoText.

3. Select the AutoText item you want from the submenu of pre-defined greetings and salutations (each of which has a second submenu).

or

Click AutoText from the submenu to open the AutoText dialog box and select from the complete list of AutoText entries. (The AutoText tab should be automatically selected.)

AutoText: Saving AutoText Entries

Some generally useful AutoText entries are included with Word 97, and you can add more items to the list.

Steps

1. Select the text or graphic element you want to store.

2. Choose Insert, AutoText, New (or press Alt+F3).

3. Word suggests an identifying name for the new entry; you can accept the name or enter your own. The entry is stored in the current document template.

NOTE If you want the AutoText entry to be inserted as a paragraph, be sure to also include in your selection the paragraph mark (¶) at the end of the text block. You can make paragraph marks visible by clicking the paragraph mark symbol in the Standard toolbar. Or triple-click the paragraph to select the text and paragraph mark.

If you save an AutoText text item without a paragraph mark (or if you save a graphic), no paragraph formatting is saved with it. ■

TIP Ordinarily, AutoText items are saved in the Normal template, making them available to all documents. You can choose to save them in individual templates, making the items available only to the documents linked to those templates. You also can copy AutoText entries between templates, so you can include your AutoText elements with documents used on other PCs.

AutoText: Using AutoComplete

If you know the beginning text of your AutoText entry, simply begin typing it in your document where you want it to appear. As soon as Word recognizes the matching entry, it opens a box showing the first few words of that entry. To confirm (and place the entire entry in your document), press Enter or F3.

Steps

1. Choose Insert, AutoText, AutoText. The AutoCorrect dialog box opens with the AutoText sheet on top.

2. Select the Show AutoComplete Tip for AutoText and Dates check box to enable or remove the check mark to disable this feature.

3. Click OK to close the dialog box and enable or disable the feature.

Backup: Accessing a Backup Document

You'll need to access the backup copy of your document if you want to cancel an editing session you've already saved, or if your current document file is missing or becomes corrupt.

Steps

1. Click the Open button to display the Open dialog box.

2. In the Files of Type list box, select All Files.

3. In the file window, open the folder that contains the original document file.

4. Select the file named BACKUP OF [ORIGINAL DOCUMENT NAME]. If you have file Details turned on, the document Type column shows this file as a Microsoft Word Backup Document.

5. Click the Open button to close the dialog box and open the backup copy of the file.

TIP To cancel edits on a document that has been saved, simply close the file without saving it. To cancel edits and begin a new editing session, re-open the document. Word confirms your desire to revert to the saved file. If you do, the most recently saved document replaces what is on-screen.

Backup: Enabling Automatic Backups

In most cases, you should have a backup copy of the document you're working on. If the current document is somehow lost or corrupted, or if you decide to cancel an editing session, you'll need that backup.

Steps

1. Choose Tools, Options.

2. Click the Save tab to bring the Save sheet to the front. Place a check mark in the Always Create Backup Copy check box to enable this feature.

3. Click OK to close the dialog box and apply the change.

Now, when you save an existing document, it's saved with the original name you've given it, and the previously saved file is renamed BACKUP OF [ORIGINAL DOCUMENT NAME].

CAUTION   When you create a new document and then save it, only one file exists. Word creates a backup copy only on the second and following times you save the document. Therefore, you cannot cancel edits on a new document until you have saved it twice.

NOTE   If you select Always Create Backup Copy, Word clears the check box for Allow Fast Saves, because a fast save does not save a full copy of the document. You cannot have both check boxes selected. ■

Bookmarks: Deleting

You may want to delete a bookmark that's no longer useful from your document.

Steps

1. Choose Insert, Bookmark.
2. Select the name of the bookmark to be deleted from the Bookmark Name list box.
3. Click the Delete button. The selected bookmark name is removed from the list box and the document.
4. Click the Close button to close the dialog box and return to the document.

NOTE   If you delete all the selected text or other element marked by a bookmark, the bookmark itself is also deleted. ■

Bookmarks: Jumping to a Bookmark

You can go directly to any bookmark you've placed in a document.

Steps

1. Choose Insert, Bookmark. The Bookmark dialog box is displayed.

2. Select the name of the bookmark marking the place you want.

3. Click the Go To button. The dialog box is closed and the cursor moves to the location of the bookmark. If the bookmark marks a range or a graphic, the entire range is selected in the document.

Bookmarks: Placing

A bookmark is a named marker for a block of text, a cell, range of cells, an entire table or a graphic, or simply a position in a document. First you enter a bookmark where you want it, then you can jump to it or cite it as a reference in a field or formula. Word can also use bookmarks for cross-references or to create index entries.

Steps

1. Click in your document where you want the bookmark to be—a location, a block of text, or an object.

2. Choose Insert, Bookmark. The Bookmark dialog box is displayed.

3. Enter your new bookmark name in the Bookmark Name text box. You also can select an existing name from the list, and Word moves the bookmark from its existing location to the place you have selected.

4. Click the Add button to add the bookmark to the bookmark list and close the dialog box.

Borders and Shading: Adding a Border

You can add borders around selected text, paragraphs, individual pages, or every page in your document. You can also add borders to entire tables or selected cells within it, and also to graphic objects. Borders can be complete boxes or lines around any of the four sides of the selected element.

Steps

1. Select the text or graphic to which you want to add a border.

2. Choose Format, Borders and Shading. The Borders and Shading dialog box is displayed. Click either the Borders tab for text or paragraph borders, or the Page Border tab for page borders.

3. Select the setting for the style border you want and select Style for the line style, color, and width.

4. Select the border position by clicking the edges of the Preview window or clicking the buttons surrounding it. Choose Paragraph, Cell, or Table from the Apply To drop-down list box to apply the border to selected text or to the entire paragraph.

5. Click OK to close the dialog box and apply the border effect.

TIP To see page borders in your document, you must be in Page Layout View.

Borders and Shading: Adding Shading

You can fill a table, paragraph, or selected text with background shading effects. You can choose from an overall fill in various percentages of black (shades of gray), or from a group of provided fine line patterns. You can also select an available system color to use for the fill instead of black.

Steps

1. Select the text that you want to be shaded.

2. Choose Format, Borders and Shading. The Borders and Shading dialog box is displayed. Click the Shading tab to bring the Shading sheet to the front.

3. Choose the fill pattern and color you want.

4. Choose what element you want to apply shading to—text or paragraph.

5. Click OK to close the dialog box and apply the shading.

TIP If you apply borders or shading to a paragraph, you don't need to select the entire paragraph; just click anywhere within it. To apply borders to a page, click anywhere within the page and select the Page Border tab in the Borders and Shading dialog box.

Callouts: Deleting

You may want to remove a callout you previously placed in your text.

Steps

1. Click the callout to select it, displaying its border.

2. Press the Delete key to remove the callout and its text.

Callouts: Editing a Callout Box

A callout is a special type of drawing object used to display text with a border. A common use for callouts is the text shown in comic strips. You can move or size a callout box.

Steps

1. Click anywhere on the callout with your mouse to display the callout handles.

2. Click the border where the cursor changes to a four-headed arrow. With the four-headed cursor, move the callout box to the new location in your document.

3. To change the callout's size, drag one of the hollow box handles on the edge of the outline.

4. Click the mouse anywhere outside the callout box to complete the operation.

Callouts: Entering

Word 97 gives you a set of pre-defined callouts of various shapes that you can place anywhere on the page. You can also enter and edit the callout's text, change its size, and adjust the leader line.

Steps

1. Choose Insert, Picture, AutoShapes. The AutoShapes toolbar appears. (You also can get AutoShapes by clicking AutoShapes on the Drawing toolbar.)

2. Click Callouts (the last button) on the AutoShapes toolbar and select the callout outline shape you want from the 20 pre-defined callout shapes.

3. Place the resulting plus sign (+) cursor in the document and hold down the left mouse button to drag the callout to the size you want.

4. If the cursor is not displayed in the center of the callout, click in the callout. Then, enter or edit the text you want.

Captions: Adding

Captions are short text phrases placed on a table, figure, equation, or other document item. You can use captions to identify or explain the item or to add a text tag for any purpose.

Add captions to items already in your document or have Word automatically include a caption whenever you add an item.

Steps

1. Select the item for which you want a caption.

2. Choose Insert, Caption. The Caption dialog box is displayed.

3. In the dialog box, enter the caption text in the Caption text box.

NOTE   You can even insert a caption in advance of the item you want to associate with it. But remember, the caption is numbered in sequence, so it increases the numbers of all following captions. ■

Captions: Automating

You can choose to have Word automatically supply a caption for your choice of items—figure, table, or equation—as well as any Windows object. You can add your own label category for items as well. Word also can automatically number the captions in sequence as you enter them, in your choice of formats.

Steps

1. Choose Insert, Caption. The Caption dialog box is displayed.
2. In the Caption dialog box, click the AutoCaption button. The AutoCaption dialog box is displayed.
3. Place check marks in the check boxes in the Add Caption When Inserting list box for the items you want captions for.
4. Click the OK button to close the dialog box and apply the changes.

Now, whenever you insert an item of the types you checked, Word enters a caption and numbers it. At the same time, Word updates all other captions. For example, if you insert a table between Table 1 and Table 2, the new table becomes Table 2, and Table 2's caption automatically changes to Table 3.

Captions: Modifying Automatically

Word updates field codes automatically in a document, but only if you select that option. See also "Captions: Modifying Manually."

Steps

1. Choose Tools, Options. The Options dialog box is displayed. Click the Print tab to bring the Print sheet to the front.
2. Place a check mark in the Update Links check box in the Print Options group to enable this feature.
3. Click OK to close the dialog box and apply the change.

TIP Captions are special Word fields. If your document displays a character string enclosed in {} brackets where the caption should appear, this is the field code. To display the actual caption text, select the entire field code, right-click it, and select Toggle Field Codes from the shortcut menu.

CAUTION If you delete the automatically supplied number from a caption, it becomes a simple character string and is no longer a caption. In this case, the caption is not included in the numbering sequence for that category of item.

Captions: Modifying Manually

Captions are inserted in your document as special Word fields. You can edit captions in-place as if they were ordinary text, except for the automatically supplied caption numbers.

You can even change or delete the label without affecting the label category. (For example, you can edit the word Table, and Word still considers this entry to be a caption for a table.)

To delete a caption, select the entire caption and press Delete. When you delete a caption, Word does not automatically update fields for other captions in the same item category.

Steps

1. Select any displayed field and right-click it.
2. Select Toggle Field Codes from the shortcut menu.

Chapters: Creating in a Document

Chapters divide a document into sections by content. Each section has its own title, and often, its own internal page numbering. Word provides for these functions in several ways.

You can lay out your document with chapters as you create it, or you can use a separate master document that coordinates a number of subdocuments, each of which might be a chapter. See also the "Master Documents" tasks to learn how to use that feature.

A document consists of a single section with a single style unless you choose to break it into separate sections.

Steps

1. Place chapter headings in the document using the built-in Heading 1 format.

2. Choose Format, Bullets and Numbering. The Bullets and Numbering dialog box appears. Click the Outline Numbered tab to bring the Outline Numbered sheet to the front.

3. Click the format that shows the chapter numbering that you want to use.

4. Click OK to close the dialog box and apply the numbering format.

Chapters: Using Chapter Numbers

Once you've set up chapter divisions, you can have Word 97 automatically number pages within each chapter.

Steps

1. Choose Insert, Page Numbers. The Page Numbers dialog box is displayed.

2. In the dialog box, select the position and alignment of numbers on the page from the Position and Alignment drop-down list boxes, respectively.

3. Click the Format button to open the Page Number Format dialog box and select the check box marked Include Chapter Number.

4. Click OK to close the Page Number Format dialog box and accept the changes. Click OK to close the Page Numbers dialog box and return to your document.

Charts: Creating from a Datasheet

Word 97 lets you insert various types of charts into your document. These charts are created using numbers and labels from either a datasheet you fill out, or from an existing table in your document. A datasheet appears as a small spreadsheet, with pre-formatted row and column titles and sample numbers in its cells.

Steps

1. Choose Insert, Object. The Object dialog box is displayed. Click the Create New tab to bring the Create New sheet to the front.

2. In the Object Type list box, double-click Microsoft Graph 97. A bar graph with an associated datasheet appears in your document.

3. Edit the datasheet by changing numbers and row and column titles to conform to the data you want displayed.

4. Click off the datasheet when you're ready to update the chart; the datasheet disappears.

Whenever you want to edit the chart, double-click it to display the datasheet.

 TIP While the datasheet is displayed, Word dynamically modifies the Standard toolbar to show a chart button. Click that button to display and select from a graphic list of available chart types.

Clip Art: Editing

You can edit the size and proportions of any *clip art* you've previously inserted in your document.

Steps

1. Click the clip art to display its box.

2. Drag the handles to change the size or proportions. To keep the original proportions (*aspect ratio*), hold down the Shift key while you drag one of the corner boxes.

3. Click anywhere in the document to complete the operation.

Clip Art: Inserting

You can choose to install clip art and access an extended clip art gallery on CD, as part of the OfficeTools selection. You can select from this collection of useful drawings to insert anywhere in a document.

Photographic art from the Pictures gallery can be inserted the same way. You can use commercial photo collections or scan in your own (using other applications and equipment).

Steps
1. Click where you want the art to appear.
2. Choose Insert, Picture, From File.
3. Using the Look In drop-down list box, navigate to, and select your clip art file. Click insert. The picture is inserted into your document.

Clipboard: Copying

You can copy text, graphics, or other objects into the Windows Clipboard, which serves as a temporary storage area. From there, you can later paste these elements into one or more other places in your document. The Clipboard stores only the most recent set of elements.

The Clipboard enables you to copy and paste almost any Windows object. For example, you can use the Clipboard for sound and music files, for animations, and even for movie clips. See also "Clipboard: Pasting."

Steps
1. Select the text or object.
2. Choose Edit, Copy.

Clipboard: Cutting

You can cut text, graphics, or other objects from your document for later use elsewhere. When you cut, the Windows Clipboard serves as a temporary storage area from which you can later paste the element.

The Clipboard enables you to cut and paste almost any Windows object. For example, you can use the Clipboard for sound and music files, for animations, and even for movie clips.

Steps

1. Select the text or object.

2. Choose Edit, Cut.

Clipboard: Pasting

You can paste previously cut elements from the Clipboard into your document. The Clipboard applies the most compatible format it has. For example, if you copy Microsoft Excel worksheet data into a Word document, you get a formatted table.

You can paste almost any Windows object from the Clipboard into your document. For example, you can use the Clipboard for sound and music files, for animations, and even for movie clips.

Steps

1. Position the cursor to where you want the text or object.

2. Choose Edit, Paste.

 TIP You can control the type of element the Clipboard pastes in your document. Instead of simply pasting, choose Edit, Paste Special, then select the format you want.

Color: Adding to Drawing Objects

You can color both the lines and fill of drawing objects. You can choose from all available system colors for either line or fill. You can also fill clip art boxes using these same colors.

Steps

1. Select the object you want to color.

2. Click and select AutoShape from the Drawing toolbar.

3. For either line or fill, click the mouse on the Line Color or More Fill Color's down-arrow button on the Drawing toolbar to display the color chooser.

4. Choose a color from the standard palette or click More Colors to display the entire available color wheel.

TIP   Instead of using a color from the More Colors color wheel, you can click the Custom tab and select any mix you want from the red-green-blue primary colors. (Remember, these custom colors may appear dithered—having internal patterns—when displayed or printed.)

You can click Fill Effects to select gradient or pattern fills—or even use a photo to fill the drawing object!

Color: Adding to Text

You can apply color to selected text in your document. You have 16 choices available: 12 solid colors, black, white, and two shades of gray. These colors should render well on almost any display, or on any color printer. Text defaults to black, but you can change it easily.

Steps

1. Select all characters you want to modify.

2. Select the Font down arrow button from the Formatting toolbar.

3. Choose the color you want from the Color list box.

Columns: Creating to Format Text

You can use columns to format your text on a page. The standard Word layout is "newspaper style," with all columns the same width, and where text flows from the bottom of one column to the top of the next. You can set the width for each column separately if you want.

Steps

1. Switch to Page Layout View (click the Page Layout View button at bottom left of the document window).

2. Select the text (or to format the entire document with columns, select the document).

3. On the Standard toolbar, click the Columns button.

4. Drag the pointer to select the number of columns you need.

 TIP   If you want columns in text frames, comment boxes, or headers and footers, you must use a table. Newspaper columns aren't available.

Columns: Creating in Tables

When you insert a new table, you can click and drag to specify the number of columns, or (using a pen tool) draw the table in place. (See also "Tables: Adding or Deleting Cells.")

Steps

1. Select one or more table columns immediately to the right of where you want your new column(s). (The number of new columns to be inserted will equal the number of existing columns you select.)

2. Right-click and point to the Insert Columns entry on the shortcut menu. New columns will be inserted to the left of the selected columns.

Columns: Removing Newspaper-Style Columns

You can remove newspaper-style (text) columns you previously inserted.

Steps

1. Switch to Page Layout view (click the Page Layout button at bottom left of the document window).

2. Select the text (or to format the entire document with columns, select the document).

3. On the Standard toolbar, click the Columns button.

4. Drag the pointer to reduce or eliminate columns.

Columns: Removing Table Columns

You can easily remove one or more columns from tables in your document.

Steps

1. Select one or more table columns you want to remove.

2. Right-click and point to the Delete Columns entry on the shortcut menu.

Comments: Inserting

You can add a comment to text or other item as you review a document to provide a note to other readers. This text appears in a yellow box, and is not printed with the document unless you want it to be.

Steps

1. Select the text or item you want to attach a comment to.

2. On the Reviewing toolbar, click the Insert Comment button.

   or

   Choose Insert, Comment.

3. Type your comment in the separate pane that appears at the bottom of your screen.

Your comment appears on the text line, with your initials, followed by a sequential comment number.

TIP If you have a sound card and microphone, you can add voice comments to your document. If you have pen features, you can write your comment.

NOTE If you want your comments to appear in the printed text, you can check the Comments check box in the Options dialog box, in the Include with Document group on the Print sheet. ■

Cross-References: Inserting

You can insert a cross-reference in your text to refer to a numbered or sequential element, such as a table or chapter heading. Word makes sure the reference is adjusted for changes in numbering or page position as the document is changed.

Before you use a cross-reference, of course, the referenced item must already be in your text.

Steps

1. Enter text up to the point where you want the reference.
2. Choose Insert, Cross-Reference. The Cross-reference dialog box is displayed.
3. Select Numbered Item, Heading, Bookmark, Footnote, Endnote, Equation, Figure, or Table from the Reference Type list box.
4. Click the Insert button to insert the reference in your text and close the dialog box.

Date and Time: Inserting

Word can access the date and time from your computer system's internal clock. You can easily insert an entry in your document showing the date and/or time, in several formats. You can have Word update the entry automatically if you want.

Steps

1. Select the position you want for the entry.

2. Choose Insert, Date and Time. The Date and Time dialog box is displayed.

3. Choose the date or time text format that you want to insert from the Available Formats list box. Place a check mark in the Update Automatically check box to enable automatic updating of the date and/or time whenever the document is opened or printed.

4. Click OK to close the dialog box and apply the change.

NOTE The date or time shown is a text string indicating the moment you entered it—unless you click the Update Automatically check box in the Date and Time dialog box from Step 3 in the preceding steps. If you do, Word places a field in your document that it automatically updates to the current time when you print it. ■

Dictionary: Adding Entries to a Custom Dictionary

Once you've created a custom dictionary, you can add words to it. If you have several custom dictionaries, you'll need to select the one designated for the particular word category. The easiest way to add entries to your custom dictionary is when you do a spell check.

Steps

1. Click in your document where you want the spell check to begin.

2. Click the Spelling and Grammar button on the Standard toolbar to open the Spelling and Grammar dialog box and begin the spell check.

3. When Word finds and highlights a word that fails spell check but you want it accepted (and ignored in future checks), click the Add button. The word is added to your custom dictionary.

Dictionary: Creating Custom Dictionary

Word provides a large, built-in word dictionary for use in spelling checks. Word also has a custom dictionary, and you can create more custom dictionaries to store spellings of words not in the basic dictionary. You may want to maintain separate custom dictionaries for various categories of words, such as legal or technical.

Steps

1. Choose Tools, Options, and click the Spelling & Grammar tab in the Options dialog box.

2. Click the Dictionaries button and then the New button. The Create Custom Dictionary dialog box is displayed.

3. Type the name of your new dictionary in the File Name text box.

4. Click the Save button to create the new custom dictionary and return to the Custom Dictionary dialog box. Click OK to close the Custom Dictionary dialog box and OK again to close the Options dialog box.

Dictionary: Enabling Custom Dictionary

If you want Word to use your custom dictionaries, they must be enabled. You need to enable each dictionary and also the use of custom dictionaries.

Steps

1. Choose Tools, Options. The Options dialog box is displayed. Click the Spelling & Grammar tab to bring the Spelling & Grammar sheet to the front.

2. Be sure the check box marked Suggest From Main Dictionary Only is not checked; this allows the custom dictionaries to be employed.

3. Click the Dictionaries button. The Custom Dictionaries dialog box is displayed.

4. Place a check mark in each of the check boxes for any dictionaries in the Custom Dictionaries list box that you want to be used in spell checks.

5. Click OK to close the Custom Dictionaries dialog box and OK to close the Options dialog box.

Documents: Adding Envelopes

Word gives you an easy and automated method to create and format envelope text. Although you can print an envelope by itself, it's usually easier to add one to the top of your letter document. That way, you can print the envelope with the document.

After you have created a letter, Word can automatically extract the recipient address from your salutation and format an envelope.

Steps

1. Choose Tools, Envelopes and Labels. The Envelopes and Labels dialog box is displayed.

2. Click the Envelopes tab to bring the Envelopes sheet to the front.

3. Click the Options button to open the Envelope Options dialog box where you select envelope type, text size, and font.

4. Click OK to close the Envelope Options dialog box. Enter the delivery (recipient) and return address text in the Delivery Address and Return Address text boxes.

5. Click the Add to Document button to close the dialog box and create an envelope, adding the envelope to the top of your document.

NOTE   While you're in the Options list box from Step 3 in preceding section, you can click the check box for the delivery point bar code (which encodes the recipient's ZIP code above the address) and also the FIM-A Courtesy reply mail (which puts alignment bars to the left of the stamp area). These bar codes may speed up handling of your letter. The FIM-A option is not available until the bar code option is activated. ▪

Documents: Closing

When you're done viewing or editing a document, you can close it. Closing documents not in use can speed up response time as well. Because you're so often closing documents, the easiest method is to use the keyboard.

Steps

1. Make sure the document you want to close is the active document (if you have more than one open).

2. Type Alt+F, then C.

TIP If you want to close the document but save it with a new name or in a new folder, type Alt+F, then A (for File, Save As). This creates a new document but leaves the old one intact. Next, close the document by pressing Alt+F, then C, as before.

If you want to close Word entirely, simply type Alt+F, then X.

Documents: Comparing Two Versions

If you are editing or reviewing a document, you may want to see the differences between two versions (or editing levels). Word lets you easily compare two different copies of a document.

Steps

1. Open one of the two documents you want to compare.

2. Choose Tools, Track Changes, Compare Documents. The Select File to Compare With Current Document dialog box is displayed.

3. In the dialog box, double-click the other document to compare (or type the name and click Open).

4. Review the document's changes, which appear in a different color.

Documents: Creating

You can create a new blank document based on a template or wizard, or you can get just a plain blank page.

Steps

1. Choose File, New.

2. Select the General tab and double-click the Blank Document button.

Documents: Using Templates

An even easier way to open a new blank document is to simply click the New button on the left side of the toolbar. You can create a new blank document based on a template.

Steps

1. Choose File, New.

2. Select the tab that is relevant to the type of document you want to create.

3. Double-click the icon for whichever template you want to use.

Endnotes: Inserting

An endnote is exactly like a footnote—an explanatory or identifying note referenced in your text—but it's placed in a list at the end of your document rather than at the bottom of a page. You can choose to use either footnote or endnote style in your Word document.

Steps

1. Click in your text where you want to place the endnote reference.

2. Choose Insert, Footnote. The Footnote and Endnote dialog box is displayed.

3. Select the Endnote option button in the Insert group at the top of the dialog box and click OK to return to the document.

4. Enter the note in the open pane at the bottom of your text.

Equations: Inserting

Word provides an elaborate set of equations, which calculate or determine various values that are displayed in fields in your text.

You can build your own equations by entering a field and then selecting the operators and arguments you want, but it's much easier to use the Microsoft Equation Editor—an optional *applet*. With the Equation Editor, you can build your equation elements from lists of operators, variables, and symbols.

Steps

1. Click in the document where you want to insert the equation.

2. Choose Insert, Object. The Object dialog box is displayed. Click the Create New tab to bring the Create New sheet to the front.

3. From the Object Type list box, double-click Microsoft Equation 2.0 to launch the editor.

4. Build your equation using the Equation Editor.

5. To insert the equation and return to Word, click in your document.

TIP For detailed information on the Equation Editor, see the separate help topic about it on Word's Help menu.

Field Codes: Displaying

Word provides you with the ability to embed Field Codes for a variety of information and functions. Field Codes include the author's name, original document creation date, HTML functions, database functions, and many more fields. When a Field Code is inserted in a document, the text is displayed, rather than the Field Code, regardless of the view mode.

Steps

1. Position the Insertion tool at the point of the field text.

2. Choose Tools, Options. The Options dialog box appears.

3. Click the View tab in the Options dialog box.

4. Click the Field Codes check box in the right column of the Show group to turn the display of Field Codes on or off.

5. Click OK to close the Options dialog box and return to your document. When Field Codes is turned on (checked), the Field Codes are displayed rather than the field text.

 TIP To switch between viewing the field code and its result, right-click in any field, then select Toggle Field Codes from the shortcut menu. This command toggles all field codes in your document simultaneously.

Fields: Deleting

Word uses fields to include derived or calculated information in your document. For example, a field can show the date, the results of an equation, or stored strings, such as author name. A field also can display the page number or count, a numbered caption, or a link or reference to a bookmark or other document element, or to a file.

Steps

1. Select the entire field you want to delete.

2. Press the Delete key.

Fields: Formatting Form Fields

By creating a form using form fields, you can provide features to allow a user to enter text, select items from *list boxes*, and click *check boxes*. These automation tools make forms easier to use and enable you to restrict user entries to a set of pre-defined choices.

Word provides three categories of form fields: the text field to fill in text, the check box field to select choices or options, and the drop-down field to access a drop-down list box structure.

Steps

1. Choose View, Toolbars, Forms to display the Forms toolbar on-screen.

2. Click the Text Form Field button, Check Box Form Field button, or Drop-Down Form Field button for the field type you want.

Fields: Inserting

Some fields are inserted automatically or interactively, such as those for mail merge, indexes, and tables. You can create other fields by typing the proper format or using the Equation Editor.

Word saves the field definition as a field code. You can choose to display this special code (or equation) or the result of the field. If you know how to format the proper field code and structure, you can directly enter a field in your document.

Steps

1. Click in your document to position the field.

2. Choose Insert, Field. The Field dialog box is displayed.

3. From the Categories list box, choose the type of field you want, and choose the field keyword you want from the Field Name list box.

4. If the Options button is not dimmed, click it to select options for that field type. After making these selections in the Field Options dialog box, click OK to return to the Field dialog box.

5. Click OK to insert the field and close the dialog box.

Files: Deleting

Sometimes you will need to delete objects, such as text or graphics in a document or a file, from your computer system. In earlier versions of software, you might have needed to close a program and use a different program or even DOS to delete a file. Word includes the commands to delete the contents of an open document from your system with a few keystrokes.

Steps

1. Choose File, Open. The Open dialog box appears.

2. Using the Look In box and the File Name text box, select the file you want to delete.

3. Right-click the selected file name.

4. Click Delete on the shortcut menu that appears.

5. Click Yes in the Confirm File Delete dialog box to send the selected file to the Recycle Bin, or No to cancel the deletion.

Files: Opening from Windows Explorer

When browsing in Windows Explorer, you can open any .doc file and simultaneously start Word 97.

Steps

1. Open Windows Explorer and find the file you want to open.

2. Double-click the file name. Word 97 will start and simultaneously open the selected file so you can immediately begin working on it.

Files: Opening from Within Word 97

You can open a file from within Word 97 whether your file is on your hard disk, a floppy disk, or a network server.

Steps

1. Choose File, Open (or press Ctrl+O).

2. Find the file you want to open.

3. Either double-click the file or highlight it, then click Open.

Files: Opening While Starting Word 97

You can set the properties of Word 97 so that each time it starts, it automatically opens a specific document as a template.

Steps

1. In Windows 95 right-click the Word 97 shortcut icon, choose Properties, and select the Shortcut tab.

2. At the end of the startup path, type a space followed by /t in the Target text box.

3. Type the full file name, including path, of the file you want Word 97 to automatically open each time the program starts.

Files: Saving with a New Name

Files can be created once, have minor changes, and then be saved with a new name by using the Save As dialog box. The Save As dialog box can also be used to save files in a different format.

Steps

1. Choose File, Save As. The Save As dialog box is displayed.

2. Enter the new file name in the File Name text box.

3. Navigate through the folder structure in the Save In drop-down list box to save the file in a folder other than the original.

Find and Replace: Formatting and Styles

The Find and Replace (sometimes called search and replace) features of Word 97 enable you to search for and optionally replace text that has specific formatting or styles and substitute another format if you want.

Steps

1. Choose Edit, Replace (or press Ctrl+H) to open the Find and Replace dialog box.

2. Click the Find tab to bring the Find sheet to the front, and then click the More button to open additional search and format options.

3. From the Format list, select the formatting you're looking for.

4. Click the Replace tab to bring the Replace sheet to the front, move to the Replace With drop-down list box, and select the formatting to replace the original material.

5. Click the Replace button (to replace the next format occurrence) or Replace All (to replace all occurrences). When finished, click the Close or Cancel button to close the Find and Replace dialog box.

Find and Replace: Special Characters

You can search for and optionally replace special document characters including paragraph marks, tabs, column breaks, page breaks, and the like.

Steps

1. Choose Edit, Replace to open the Find and Replace dialog box.

2. Click the Replace tab, move to the Find What drop-down list box, and then the Special button (if the Special button isn't visible, click the More button).

3. From the Special list, select the special character or document markup you're looking for.

4. Move to the Replace With drop-down box and select the special character to replace what's found.

5. Click the Replace button (to replace the next character occurrence) or Replace All (to replace all occurrences).

Forms: Protecting

You can create forms for data entry and then protect them from unintended changes by other users by setting the Protect Document parameters. The Protect Document dialog box is used to either protect the entire form currently selected or to protect sections of the form.

Steps

1. Choose Tools, Protect Document. The Protect Document dialog box is displayed.

2. Click the Forms option button to specify that the document is a form.

3. Click the Sections button if you want to protect only selected parts of the form. The Section Protection dialog box is displayed.

4. Click the check box to the left of any sections that you want to protect from user changes.

TIP   Protection can be removed for the current form by choosing Tools, Unprotect Document.

NOTE   The form can be protected and unprotected by clicking the Protect Form button on the Forms toolbar (if the Forms toolbar is displayed). ■

CAUTION   If you use a password to protect the form and lose the password, it will not be possible to reopen the document or to remove the protection.

Hyphenation: Automatic

Automatic hyphenation occurs as you are typing. You control the amount of space between the end of the hyphenated word and the right margin (called the hyphenation zone), and you can specify how many consecutive lines can contain hyphenated words.

Steps

1. Choose Tools, Language, Hyphenation.

2. Choose Automatically Hyphenate Document.

3. In the Hyphenation Zone text box, enter the distance (in inches) you want and leave between the end of the last word in the line and the right margin (the default is 1/4 inch).

4. In the Limit Consecutive Hyphens To text box, enter or choose the number of consecutive lines that can be hyphenated (the default is no limit).

TIP If you make the hyphenation zone wider, you reduce the number of hyphenated words but probably create a very ragged right margin. To reduce the raggedness, make the zone smaller.

Hyphenation: Disabling Automatic

There may be occasions when you prefer to control when and where hyphenation occurs in a document. You may even prefer no hyphenation. When you want to be totally in charge of hyphenation, you must disable or turn off the default automatic hyphenation feature.

Steps

1. Select the text you want exempted from automatic hyphenation.

2. Choose Format, Paragraph.

3. Click the Line and Page Breaks tab.

4. Click Don't Hyphenate.

NOTE If you previously marked the selected text for No Proofing, Word does not apply hyphenation. ■

Hyphenation: Installing the Hyphenation Tool

Hyphenating words in your work can help create a cleaner and more professional appearance in the finished document, especially when you have justified text or narrow columns. You can hyphenate in two ways: automatically or manually.

Steps

1. Make sure all programs are closed.
2. Click the Windows Start button, choose Settings, Control Panel.
3. Double-click the Add/Remove Programs button.
4. On the Install/Uninstall tab, click Microsoft Office (if you installed Word 97 via the Office Setup program) or Word 97 (if you installed Word 97 individually) and then click the Add/Remove button.

NOTE If Word 97 was installed from a CD-ROM, and if you have changed the letter of your CD-ROM drive since that installation, you must run Setup again from the CD-ROM. If you are running any files from the CD-ROM, you must uninstall Word 97 and reinstall it from the CD-ROM. ■

NOTE If you are running Word 97 on Windows NT Workstation 3.51, you need to take the following step to add or remove components of Word. You must start Word 97 Setup or Office Setup the same way you did when you first installed Word 97 and follow the screen directions. ■

Hyphenation: Manual

When you want to exercise complete control over where and when to use hyphenation, use the manual hyphenation feature.

This allows you to govern the physical appearance of your document.

Steps
1. Select the text you want to subject to hyphenation.
2. Choose Tools, Language, Hyphenation.
3. Word 97 scans your document, and if it finds a word that is a candidate for hyphenation, it displays that word with the hyphenation in place. Click Yes if you approve of the suggested hyphenation, or move the cursor to the position you prefer and then click Yes.

Hyphenation: Non-Breaking

When you have a compound word or phrase that you do not want hyphenation to break between lines, you can insert a non-breaking hyphen. For example, you would use non-breaking hyphens to keep the word hand-me-down all on one line.

Steps
1. Position the cursor where you want to insert the hyphen and click.
2. Press Ctrl+Shift+−.

Hyphenation: Optional

When you want to hyphenate a word not included in the hyphenation dictionary, you can assign an optional hyphen. This step allows Word to hyphenate the word at the end of a line, but if later editing moves the word to the beginning or middle of a line, the hyphen disappears.

Steps
1. Position the cursor where you want to insert the hyphen and click.
2. Press Ctrl+−.

Importing: Databases from a File

Importing files from other word processors into Word is usually an automatic process. Just open the file, and if Word recognizes the file or document format, Word converts the file to its
native format and displays it.

A few simple converters are built in to Word. You also can
choose to install over 30 import converters, including ones for
most major word processors. In Word 97, you can now import
HTML files, used on the World Wide Web.

If it cannot positively identify the file format, Word may prompt
you to confirm which type it is before converting. If this
doesn't work, you may need to open the file in the application
that created it and save it again in one of the formats Word
recognizes.

You can select data from Access or another database and insert it into your Word document. You can use Word to sort and
filter the data you want, or you can use Microsoft Query, an
applet in the Office suite.

Steps

1. Choose View, Toolbars, Database to display the Database toolbar. Click the Insert Database button on the
   toolbar. The Database dialog box is displayed.

2. Click the Get Data button to open the Open Data Source
   dialog box, then select your data source file.

3. Click Open to open the file.

4. Click the Query Options button and select your sort and
   filter options in the Query Options dialog box. Click OK
   to close the dialog box and return to the Database dialog
   box.

5. Click the Insert Data button, indicate the data range
   in the Insert Data dialog box, and click OK to close the
   dialog box and place the data into a table in your
   document.

TIP If you want to dynamically update the data in your table if the source changes, be sure to select the query check box marked Insert Data as Field in the Insert Data dialog box.

Indents: Permanent Hanging

Usually when you create bibliographic entries, glossaries, bulleted lists, numbered items, or even résumés, you use hanging indents.

Steps

1. Choose Format, Paragraph and select the Indents And Spacing tab.

2. Under the Indentation heading, click Special and choose Hanging.

3. In the By text box either choose the desired indentation spacing or type in your own (in inches). Click OK and all text will be indented as specified until you change the settings.

Indents: Temporary

Sometimes you just want a bit of text to be indented in a hanging indent format; for example, when quoting a section of text or creating a list.

Steps

1. Choose Tools, Options, and select the Edit tab. Verify that the Tabs and Backspace Set Left Indent box is selected. If it is not, choose it now.

2. Type the text that goes on the left side of the page.

3. Press Tab and type the text you want indented. Keep typing until text wraps to the next line. It will wrap so that it is flush left.

4. Position the cursor at the front of the second line and press Tab until the second line of text is aligned where

you want it. All subsequent word wrapping will be automatically indented to this position.

NOTE You can drag the indent markers on the ruler to change the indent, or you can change settings using the Format, Paragraph command. ■

Indexes: Creating Concordance Files

A concordance file is a two-column table that lists text you want included in the index on the left. On the right are the subjects the text relates to in the index. For example, if your subject listing is political parties, you might want to include democrats, republicans, independents, reform party, libertarians, and so on. In this example, the named parties would be listed on the left, and the subject listing would be repeated each time on the right.

Steps

1. Choose File, New (or just click the New button on the Standard toolbar).

2. Click the Insert Table button on the Standard toolbar and create a two-column table.

3. In the left column, type the text you want Word 97 to search for and mark as an index entry (XE). Remember that you must type this text exactly as it appears in the document. (Using our example, you would type **democrat**, **republican**, and so on).

4. Press Tab. In the right column, type the corresponding subject word or phrase (in the example, this would be **political parties**). If you want subentries, just end the main entry with a colon and then type the subentry.

5. Repeat Steps 3 and 4 until you have finished identifying all the items for the index. Then save the file.

TIP Enter all forms of the words you want included in the index to be sure your index is comprehensive. Using the earlier example, for **republicans** you would also include **GOP**, **republican**, and any other form of reference you can think of.

You can make this job easier by opening both the original document and the concordance file and arranging them side-by-side. Then you can scroll through the document to find items for inclusion in the index and copy text from one file to the other.

Indexes: Cross-Referencing

Cross-references can direct readers to other areas in the index that may provide them with related information.

Steps

1. Select the text you want to mark for entry into the index.
2. Press Alt+Shift+X. The Mark Index Entry dialog box is displayed.
3. Click the Cross Reference option button in the Options group.
4. In the Cross Reference text box (which already includes the word *see*), type the cross-reference information.
5. Click Mark and then Close.

Indexes: Inserting a Custom Index

Sometimes it is necessary to select the index entries or format the index yourself. This is called a custom index.

Steps

1. Make sure all entries for inclusion in the index are properly marked.
2. Position the cursor where you want the index to begin and click one time.

3. Choose Insert, Index and Tables, then select the Index tab.

4. Choose From Template in the Formats box and click Modify. The Style dialog box comes up. Click Modify here too, to bring up the Modify Style dialog box.

5. Choose Format and select the format you want to change. Click OK to close the dialog box and return to the Style dialog box. Then click OK or Apply to close the dialog box and OK to close the Index and Tables dialog box.

Indexes: Inserting a Standard Index

The usual location for an index is to start on a new page at the end of the document.

Steps

1. Make sure all entries for inclusion in the index are properly marked.

2. Position the cursor where you want the index to begin and click once.

3. Choose Insert, Index and Tables, then select the Index tab.

4. Choose either the Indented or Run-in option button in the Type group. Then select From Template, Classic, Fancy, Modern, Bulleted, Formal, or Simple in the Formats scroll box, and click OK.

Indexes: Marking Entries

You can create an index that contains words, phrases, and symbols by marking those items for entry. Then you choose an index design and build the index. Word 97 does all the hard work by reading the entire document and collecting the entries, sorting them alphabetically, referencing their page numbers, finding and removing duplicates, and then displaying all the information in the format you chose for the document.

Before Word 97 can build the index, you must first mark all the words, phrases, and symbols for inclusion.

Steps

1. Either select the text or symbol you want marked for entry into the index, or at the point where you want to insert an index entry, type your own text.

2. Press Alt+Shift+X.

3. To create a main index entry, edit the text that you see in the Main Entry text box or type in your own text. If your text is a symbol, type ;# (semicolon and pound sign) after the symbol.

4. To create a subentry, type the appropriate text in the Subentry text box. If a third-level entry is necessary, type ;# (semicolon and pound sign) after the second-level text and then type the third-level text.

5. Click Mark to include this entry in the index or click Mark All to include all occurrences of this entry in the index. Then click Close.

You can enter more entries by just selecting text (or clicking after the desired text), clicking in the Main Entry text box to replace the old entry with a new one, or by typing over the old entry in the Main Entry text box with whatever new text you want included. Be sure to click Mark or Mark All. Then just repeat Steps 3 and 4 from the preceding list of steps.

NOTE If you select Mark All, Word 97 marks (in hidden text format) the first occurrence of each entry that exactly matches the original entry as an XE field (XE=Index Entry).

If you don't see the XE field and want to see it, click the Show/ Hide button on the toolbar. ■

Indexes: Marking Entries with Concordance Files

When you mark entries using a concordance file, Word 97 searches through the open document looking for the exact occurrence of the text in the left column of the concordance file. Word uses the text in the right column as the subject name. Only the first occurrence of an entry in a paragraph is used.

Steps

1. Choose Insert, Index and Tables. Select the Index tab.

2. Choose AutoMark, and type the name of the concordance file you want to use in the File Name text box.

3. Choose Open.

TIP You can automatically mark all occurrences of words, phrases, and symbols by clicking Mark All in the Mark Index Entry dialog box, but using the concordance file automatically marks multiple words, phrases, and symbols.

Indexes: Marking Entries over Entire Pages

Sometimes you want your index entries to cover a range of pages to ensure that nothing is accidentally left out. This can be done by specifying the range of pages.

Steps

1. Select the text range you want marked as an index entry, then choose Insert, Bookmark.

2. Assign a name to this text in the Bookmark Name text box and click the Add button.

3. Go back to the document. At the end of the text you marked with the bookmark, press Alt+Shift+X to open the Mark Index Entry dialog box.

4. In the Main Entry text box, type the word or phrase you want to appear in the index for the marked text.

5. Click Page Range in the Options section. In the Bookmark text box, type the name you assigned to this text
(in Step 2). Click Mark and then Close.

Letter Wizard: Modifying a Letter

The *Letter Wizard* can not only guide you through the steps
necessary to create a letter, it can help you modify letters as
well.

Steps

1. Open the document you want to change or finish.

2. Choose Tools, Letter Wizard.

Letter Wizard: Starting Using Office Assistant

The Letter Wizard guides you through four elements in creating a letter: Letter Format, Recipient Info, Other Elements, and
Sender Info.

In Letter Format, the Wizard guides you through selecting
such things as how to position the date line and what it should
contain; what page design and layout you want to use; and
whether you are using pre-printed letterhead (and if so, how
much of the paper the letterhead takes up).

The Recipient Info enables you to choose an address from the
address book or type it in on the spot. This element offers four
salutation types (Informal, Formal, Business, and Other).

Other elements include whether you want a Reference Line,
Mailing Instructions, Attention vs. Attn, a Subject Line, and
Courtesy Copies.

The Sender Info enables you to choose an address from the
address book, type it in on the spot, or even omit a return
address. This element offers closing options and enables you
to include or exclude your job title, company name, writer/
typist initials, and enclosures.

WORD

Steps

1. Start your letter with a salutation that begins with **Dear** or **To** (for example, Dear John or To Whom It May Concern). Follow this word with a comma or colon and press Enter. The Office Assistant automatically opens.

2. Click Get Help with Writing the Letter and follow the Wizard's advice and instructions.

Letter Wizard: Starting Without Office Assistant

If you have turned off the Office Assistant feature, you can still use the Letter Wizard. In fact, you can start the Letter Wizard any time you need help with a letter.

Steps

1. Choose File, New. Select the Letters and Faxes tab, then double-click the Letter Wizard button.

2. Fill in the letter according to the Wizard's advice.

3. If you want to send just the one letter, click Send One Letter in the Wizard and follow the instructions for the four areas where help is offered. If you want to send letters to a list of addresses, click Send Letters to a Mailing List, and the Wizard directs you to the Mail Merge feature.

Line Numbers: Inserting

Line numbers can be useful in documents that are carefully tracked for content, such as legal or technical works where explicit text references are needed. You can add line numbers to any part or all of your document.

Steps

1. In Page Layout View, select the text you want to be numbered.

2. Choose File, Page Setup to open the Page Setup dialog box, then click the Layout tab.

3. In the Apply To list box, choose where you want to apply numbering—the selected text or the whole document.

4. Click the Line Numbers button to open the Line Numbers dialog box, click the check box marked Add Line Numbering, and select other options.

5. Click OK to apply numbering and OK again to return to the document.

CAUTION Word displays line numbers in the left margin (or to the left of each column). If the page has too little margin, Word can neither display nor print line numbers. Increase the margins to remedy this problem.

Links: Automatically Updating Linked Objects

If you have turned off the default automatic linking feature, you can easily restore it.

Steps

1. Choose Edit, Links.

2. Select the linked object(s) you want to update.

3. Choose Automatic.

Links: Breaking Connections

You can leave an object in your destination file but break its connection to the source file. However, if you want to reconnect the link, you must insert the linked object again.

Steps

1. Choose Edit, Links.

2. Select the linked object(s) you want to break away from the source file.

3. Click Break Link.

Links: Manually Updating Linked Objects

Word 97 automatically updates linked objects, but you can
disable that feature and manually update links. When you
manually update linked objects, you prevent them from being
automatically updated each time you open or print the destination file or change the source file while the destination is open.

Steps

1. Choose Edit, Links.

2. Select the linked object(s) you want to update. You can
   select multiple objects by holding down the Ctrl key and
   clicking each linked object you want to include in the
   update.

3. Choose Manual.

NOTE If you do not have any linked objects in your file, the
Links command is not available. ■

Links: Preventing a Linked Object from Being Updated

You may have a circumstance when you want to update some
links but not all of them. For example, if the location of your
file has changed, you would want to update that specific link
but leave the other links intact.

Steps

1. Choose Edit, Links.

2. Select the linked object(s) you want to exclude from the
   update.

3. Click Locked.

4. Click the Update Now or OK button to return to the
   document.

Links: Reconnecting Linked Objects

If you broke the connection between a linked object and its destination file, you can re-establish that link.

Steps

1. Choose Edit, Links.
2. Select the linked object(s) you want to reconnect.
3. Click Change Source and in the File Name box, type the name of the file you want to reconnect to.

NOTE If you direct the object to a different file, that file must have been created in the same program as the original source file. ■

Links: Updating Linked Objects When You Print

Regardless of whether you have set link updates to manual or automatic, you can always update linked objects when you print the document.

Steps

1. Choose Tools, Options.
2. Select the Print tab and click Update Links in the Printing Options box.

Links: Updating Links Manually

Regardless of the link update setting, you can update whenever you want to.

Steps

1. Choose Edit, Links.
2. Select the linked object(s) you want to update.
3. Choose Update Now.

TIP An even quicker way to update links on demand is to select the linked object and then press <F9>.

Lists: Changing Indent Levels for Bulleted or Numbered Lists

You can easily change the indent level for bulleted or numbered lists as you type. Each indent level has its own format for bullet or number style, which Word automatically applies.

Steps

1. To change the level, press the Tab key immediately after pressing Enter to begin a new line.

2. To outdent an item, press Shift+Tab.

3. To change the level for lines you've already entered, select the lines and press Tab or Shift+Tab as just described.

Lists: Choosing a Bullet or Number Style

You can easily create bulleted or numbered lists in Word 97, or apply numbers or bullets to already existing lists. You can choose from a number of built-in bullet styles or use any character in any Windows font as a bullet (including special symbol fonts such as Wingdings).

Steps

1. Right-click the left margin where you want to begin your list.

2. Choose Bullets and Numbering from the shortcut menu.

3. Click the Bulleted or Numbered tab.

4. Double-click the box showing the style you want.

5. Begin typing without moving the selection point.

NOTE   You also can start a bulleted or numbered list by clicking the marked buttons on the Formatting toolbar. ■

Lists: Creating Bulleted Lists

You can easily create bulleted lists in Word 97, or apply bullets to already existing lists. You can choose from a number of built-in bullet styles or use any character in any Windows font as a bullet (including special symbol fonts such as Wingdings).

Steps

1. Start a line with *, -, or > followed by a space. Word automatically creates the bulleted list when you press Enter. (Word then substitutes bullet styles for these ordinary text characters.)

2. To end the list, press Enter twice. Word automatically removes the last (unused) bullet and the extra line.

Lists: Creating Numbered Lists

For numbered lists, Word has built-in number, letter, and Roman numeral styles. Word also has a series of outline numbering styles that automatically format indented lists. For any of these styles, you can customize the font, relative position, indent, and starting number or letter.

You don't need to select any special formatting to create an ordinary numbered list. If you remove any line in a numbered list, Word automatically renumbers the remaining lines.

Steps

1. Start a line with a number followed by a period,), or >. Word automatically creates the numbered list when you press Enter.

2. To end the list, press Enter twice. Word automatically removes the last (unused) number and the extra line.

Lists: Customizing Bulleted or Numbered Lists

You can easily customize a Word list you have already entered. You can change number or bullet styles for an entire list at any time. You also can convert between numbered, outline-formatted, and bulleted lists.

Steps

1. Select all lines of the bulleted or numbered list you want to customize.

2. Right-click the selection and choose Bullets and <u>N</u>umbering on the shortcut menu. The Bullets and Numbering dialog box is displayed.

3. Select the <u>B</u>ulleted or <u>N</u>umbered tab.

4. Double-click the box showing the style you want.

Lists: Entering and Modifying an Outline

Word has a series of outline numbering styles that automatically format indented lists. For any of these styles, you can customize the font, relative position, indent, and starting number or letter.

Steps

1. Right-click your selection and choose Bullets and <u>N</u>umbering on the shortcut menu.

2. Click the O<u>u</u>tline Numbered tab and double-click the outline format you want.

 TIP If you select an outline style that contains the text Heading 1, you get text formatted in very large font sizes. These styles create headline text best used for screen presentations and title sheets.

Lists: Inserting a Custom Bullet Character

You can choose a custom bullet character from a built-in list or choose any character from a Windows font. You also can change font size or indent for the bullet.

Steps

1. Select all lines of the list you want to customize.

2. Right-click the selection and choose Bullets and <u>N</u>umbering on the shortcut menu.

3. Click the <u>B</u>ulleted tab and double-click to select one of the custom bullets shown.

4. If you want a new custom bullet, click the Customize button and then the <u>F</u>ont and <u>B</u>ullet buttons in the Customize Bulleted List dialog box.

5. Click OK to apply the style and exit the dialog boxes.

TIP   You can even add animation to your bullets! While you're in the Font selection box described in Step 4, click the Animation tab to add one of several motion effects in the Animations list box to the bullet. (These effects will appear on-screen only when the document is opened in Word 97.)

Lists: Removing Bullets or Numbering

You can easily remove bullets or numbering you previously added to a section.

Steps

1. Right-click your selection and choose Bullets and <u>N</u>umbering on the shortcut menu.

2. Double-click the None box to remove all bullet and number formatting and exit the menu.

Macros: Adding to Forms

A macro is a collection of instructions and commands that execute a single task for you automatically. Any time you have a time-consuming or repetitive task, you can create a macro to perform it for you. In addition to streamlining your work, macros reduce errors because they reduce your keystrokes.

Steps

1. Open the template file for the form to which you want to add macros.

2. On the Forms toolbar, turn off protection by clicking the Protect Form button. You can tell when Protection is on by checking the toolbar. If Protection is on, then all buttons will be disabled (except Form Field Shading and Protect Form).

3. Create the macros you want to use (or copy them from another form), then double-click the form field to which you want to assign them.

4. If you want to run the macro when the insertion point enters the form field, click Entry. If you want the macro to run when the insertion point leaves the form field, click Exit.

CAUTION You must save entry and exit macros in the form file. If you save the macros elsewhere and then distribute the form, the entry and exit macros may not run because the macros aren't there.

Mail Merge: Adding to Main Documents

While still in the Mail Merge Helper, you can create the data to be used in the finished document.

Steps

1. With the Mail Merge Helper open and the document type already defined, choose Get Data under the second topic, Data Source.

2. Choose Create Data Source.

3. Add or remove field names until you have defined the data fields, then click OK.

4. Name and save your data file. A pop-up window will appear inviting you to key in your data.

5. Choose Edit Data Source and key in your merge data. When you're done, click OK.

Mail Merge: Creating Databases Manually

When you use Mail Merge Helper to create the data source, your data cannot contain more than 31 fields of information. If you require more than 31 data fields, you must create your data elsewhere.

Steps

1. Open a new file and start entering data.

2. Separate each field with a tab or a comma in both the header record and the data itself. Because some of the data may include commas, tabs are the best choice.

3. When a data field is empty, insert two separators (unless it's the last field).

4. Enclose the data for a field in quotation marks ("") if any of the following characters are in it: tab or comma (whichever one is used as the separator); line break or paragraph mark; the list separator specified on the Number tab of the Regional Settings Properties; or quotation marks (yes, this means you will have two sets of quotation marks).

Mail Merge: Creating Main Documents

The Mail Merge feature enables you to create form letters, mailing labels, envelopes, catalogs, or lists. To do this, you create a main document and merge it with a data source.

When you're creating a new data source, be sure to give some consideration to its form and content before you start entering data. Keep these points in mind:

- Include enough data fields so your records are as inclusive and comprehensive as you need them to be.

- Make sure that any data you may want to sort by is in a field all by itself (in other words, if you want to sort by city, don't include city and state in the same data field).

- Include enough information to make the list versatile. For example, if your source is an address list, don't include just the name and address; include a salutation as well, or make the person's title (Mr., Mrs., Dr.) separate from the name so you can use the list to create the salutation separate from the address.

NOTE The easiest way to merge data is to use the Mail Merge Helper. This process involves three steps. First, you create the document you'll be merging data into; next you create the data; and finally, you merge them together. ■

Steps

1. Open a new file (or a previously created file with which you now want to merge data).

2. Choose Tools, Mail Merge, and click Create under the first topic, Main Document.

3. Choose the type of document you want to create.

4. If you want to create a new document and have already opened a blank new file, or if you already opened an existing file and want to merge with it, click Active Window. If you want to create an entirely new file, click New Main Document.

Mail Merge: Creating Merged Documents

After you create your Main Document, including the positioning of all your data fields, and after you create the data file, you are ready to merge them to produce your finished, merged document or documents.

TIP Before you merge the data with the document, it's a good idea (especially if the data file is large) to check for errors. Choose Check Errors and choose an error-checking process.

Steps

1. With the Mail Merge Helper open, choose Merge.

2. Select a destination for the newly created, merged file.

3. Choose whether to print a blank line when a data field is empty.

4. Choose Merge.

Mail Merge: Defining Data Fields

After you create the Main Document and define the data to be merged into it, you must create or edit the document so it includes the appropriate data fields.

Steps

1. Create or type your Main Document.

2. Position the cursor where you want to insert a data field and click Insert Merge Field (on the Mail Merge toolbar).

3. Click the data field you want inserted.

4. Repeat Steps 1-3 until you have completed your Main Document.

5. Name and save your Main Document.

Mail Merge: Printing Selected Records

Sometimes you don't want to print the entire database but only specific records.

Steps

1. With the Mail Merge Helper open, choose Query Options under the third topic, Merge.

2. Choose the Filter Records tab.

3. Choose which field you want to use as your selector.

4. In the Comparison field, choose the appropriate instruction (for example: like, not like, greater than, less than).

5. In the Compare To field, type the data you want to include in the merge. If you want other records, indicate whether they must conform to the same criteria (by choosing AND), or if they can conform to other criteria (OR). Repeat this process until you have selected all the records for merging.

Mail Merge: Using External Data Sources

The easiest way to merge data with a document is to use the Mail Merge Helper. However, other data sources are available. For example, you can use data files from Microsoft Access; Microsoft Excel; a personal address book created with Microsoft Exchange server, Outlook, or Schedule+ 7.0; or other lists created using MAPI-compatible messaging systems.

Steps

1. With the Mail Merge Helper open, choose Get Data under the second topic, Data Source.

2. Choose Open Data Source or Use Address Book.

3. Find and click the appropriate file.

4. If the data requires editing, choose Edit.

Mailing Labels: Changing Label Size or Creating a Custom Label

It's easy to switch from one label to another. You can do this by either switching to a different specific pre-defined label or by modifying the label measurements to conform to your unique needs.

Steps

1. Choose Tools, Envelopes and Labels, and select the Labels tab.

2. Choose Options and select your printer type (Dot Matrix or Laser and Ink Jet).

3. From the Label Products box, select the label brand you're using. From the Product Number box, select the specific label you're using.

4. Choose Details to change any measurements or choose New Label to establish your own set of measurements.

Mailing Labels: Creating Multiple

Most of the time, you'll want to print a whole sheet of mailing labels.

Steps

1. Follow Steps 1-3 in preceding section.

2. In the Print box, choose Full Page of Same Label.

3. Make sure the label sheet(s) are inserted in your printer and choose Print.

Mailing Labels: Creating Single

You can create a single mailing label for one address, you can print the same address on multiple labels, or you can merge a list of addresses and print them on a sheet of labels. You also can change the size of a mailing label or even create a custom label.

Most of the time you'll want to create a whole sheet of labels, but once in a while you just need one.

Steps

1. Choose Tools, Envelopes and Labels, and select the Labels tab.

2. If the default label is not the one you want, choose Options and select the right one.

3. If the address you want is not automatically displayed in the Address text box, type the right one.

4. In the Print box, choose Single label and specify the location of the label on the label sheet.

5. Make sure the label sheet is inserted in your printer and choose Print.

Mailing Labels: Merging Data

You may also have a frequent need to create mailing labels using a database of addresses. It is easy to merge that data with the labels.

Steps

1. Choose Tools, Mail Merge. Then choose Create and select Mailing Labels.

2. If the underlying document is the one you want to be your main document, choose Active Window; if you prefer to create a new document, choose New Main Document.

3. Under Data Source, choose Get Data and either Create a new data source or Open a data source. You can create a new data file or use data already entered in your personal address book, Outlook Address Book, or Schedule+ Address Book.

4. After you identify or establish your data, click Set Up Main Document and choose the labels you want to use, inserting the appropriate merge fields in the Sample Label text box. At this point you also can include Postal Bar Codes.

5. Choose Merge and then select a destination (new document, printer, electronic mail, or electronic fax). Choose Print.

Master Documents: Creating

A Master Document is like a book containing many chapters or subdocuments. Rather than try to create a huge, hard-to-manage file, you can create chapter files and link them to-gether under the umbrella created by the Master Document. This method also enables you to create a table of contents, index, or other cross-referencing tools that cover all relevant files.

You have the full range of normal formatting available to you when you create a Master Document and the subdocuments within it. Although the Master Document serves as the orga-nizer or umbrella, you can treat each subdocument as a stand-alone entity.

Steps

1. In a new document, choose View, Master Document.

2. Using standard outlining techniques, outline your document by typing the heading for the main document first and then the subordinate subdocuments.

3. Type whatever text (if any) you want for each subdocument.

4. Select the subheadings and all associated text. Click the Create Subdocument button on the Master Document toolbar.

5. Save the Master Document using the File, Save As command.

NOTE Word 97 saves the Master Document and each subdocument, automatically assigning names based on the subdocuments' headings. You can edit the individual files or you can go into the Master Document and expand it to include all the files, then edit there.

If the Create Subdocument button is not present on the Master Document toolbar, click the Expand Subdocuments button on the Master Document toolbar. ■

Master Documents: Printing

You can print the Master Document in two ways. You can print the document so it appears as an outline, showing the names of the files and their positions within the Master Document, but not including any text from those files. Or you can print the entire document including all the text from all the subdocuments.

Steps

1. Open the Master Document in Master Document View.

2. Click the Expand Subdocuments button on the Master Document toolbar.

3. Show as much or as little of the document as you want by clicking the Expand or Collapse buttons on the Master Document toolbar. You can show the first line only of a body of text; show headings only; show text and headings; or show headings and text in just about any combination you desire.

4. Choose File, Print.

5. Choose the printing options you want and print.

Master Documents: Using Existing Word Documents

You can format a Master Document using existing Word 97 document files.

Steps

1. Create a Master Document and make sure it is displayed in Master Document View.

2. Expand all the subdocuments by clicking the Expand Subdocuments button on the Master Document toolbar.

3. Position the cursor where you want to insert the existing file (make sure one blank line comes before and after this position).

4. Click the Insert Subdocument button on the Master Document toolbar and type the name of the file you want to insert.

5. Click Open.

Object Alignment: In Relation to Each Other

When you place several objects on a page, you may want to align them relative to each other to maintain equal spacing or to make their centers, or top or bottom edges line up.

Steps

1. Select all drawing objects you want to align to each other.

2. On the Drawing toolbar, click the Draw button.

3. From the drop-down menu, select Align or Distribute to open the Align or Distribute submenu.

4. Click the alignment you want for the collection of selected objects from Align Left, Align Center, Align Right, Align Top, Align Middle, Align Bottom, Distribute Horizontally, Distribute Vertically, or Relative to Page.

 TIP From the same menu, you can also distribute the selected objects evenly across the page using Distribute Horizontally or Distribute Vertically.

Office Assistant: Closing

The *Office Assistant* is present to guide you through your work. By default it is on, but you can turn it off.

Steps

1. Click the Office Assistant button in the toolbar to open it.

2. Click Options, and in the Assistant Capabilities box make sure the Help With Wizards option is not checked. If it is checked, click once to deselect it.

Office Assistant: Customizing

You can change the appearance of the Office Assistant as well as the type of information it displays, and when it displays that information.

Steps

1. Make sure the Office Assistant is open. If it is not open, click the Office Assistant button in the toolbar.

2. Click Options, and select the Gallery tab.

3. Click Next or Back to view the choices and select the one you like best.

NOTE The Microsoft Office CD-ROM must be installed in order to access the different Office Assistants.

continues

continued

The Mother Nature and Genius Office Assistants are not available
unless you install from CD-ROM, and if you choose them, your
video monitor and adapter must support at least 256 colors. ■

Office Assistant: Getting Help

The Office Assistant is your instantly accessible guide whenever you have questions.

Steps

1. Make sure the Office Assistant is open. If it is not open,
   click the Office Assistant button in the toolbar.
2. Click Options, and select the Options tab.
3. Click the tip options you want to be active to put a check
   mark in the box (or click a box to de-select an option).
4. Click Reset My Tips when you're done to make sure all
   the changes are recorded.

Office Assistant: Opening

If you have previously closed (i.e., turned off) the Office Assistant and want to restart it, you may do so.

Steps

1. Click the Office Assistant button in the toolbar to open it.
2. Click Options, and in the Assistant Capabilities box make
   sure the Help With Wizards option is checked. If it is not
   checked, click once to select it.

Outlines: Creating in Outline View

When you use the *Outline View* to create an outline, you can
expand or collapse headings to minimize or maximize the
amount of text visible at any time.

Steps

1. Open a new file, and choose View, Outline.
2. Type in your first heading. The Outline View will automatically format it for the Heading 1 style.
3. Type in all other headings using the drag-and-drop feature to indent them as necessary to achieve the desired subordination.
4. When you're ready to add text to the headings, just choose View, Normal or View, Page Layout. The body text will be formatted using the "Normal" style.

Outlines: Creating Traditional

You can type headings and subheadings in a simple, numbered style. This option does not impose heading styles on the various level headings but keeps everything in the same style. This style of outline is limited to nine levels.

Steps

1. Open a new file, and choose Format, Bullets and Numbering.
2. Click the Outline Numbered tab, and choose a format that does not include "Heading 1." Click OK.
3. Type your list, being careful to press Enter after each entry.
4. Move numbered items to their designated level by selecting that text and then clicking the Increase Indent button or the Decrease Indent button.

Outlines: Formatting Paragraphs

You can create an outline by assigning outline levels to paragraphs.

Steps

1. Select a paragraph in the file you want to convert to outline form.

2. Choose Format, Paragraph and select the Indents and Spacing tab.

3. Select a level from the Outline Level box.

4. Switch to Outline View from the View menu and the format will automatically be adjusted.

Page Breaks: Inserting Manual

When you insert manual page breaks, you can choose whether to simultaneously create new sections (by breaking before the page end), or to break at all odd or even pages.

Steps

1. Position the cursor where you want the page to break and click.

2. Choose Insert, Break.

3. Choose Page Break. Click OK.

Page Numbers: Inserting in Documents

You can give the pages of your documents page numbers and you can position and format those page numbers as you want.

Steps

1. Choose Insert, Page Numbers.

2. Select the position and alignment for your page numbers.

3. If you want page one to show a page number, be sure there is a check mark in the Show Number on First Page box.

NOTE You can start the document using any page number you want. So, if you are tracking a document through several separate files, you can still maintain uninterrupted pagination. If you are working with a Master Document, just add page numbers to the header or footer and pagination will occur smoothly. ■

Page Numbers: Inserting in Headers/Footers

You can insert page numbers into your headers and footers.

Steps

1. Choose View, Header/Footer.

2. Position the cursor within the header or footer where you want the page number to appear. You can precede the page number with some text, like the word Page followed by a space.

3. Click the page number button in the Header/Footer toolbar.

4. If you have changed header/footer text to a font other than the default, remember to change the format of the page number field code as well.

5. Close the header/footer.

Page Setup: Changing Default Page Layout

This final bit of page formatting enables you to choose whether your headers and footers are the same throughout the document, or change from odd page to even page. You can elect to print the header/footer on all pages except the first page; and you can specify how you want text positioned on the page. The defaults start all sections on a new page and align all text with the top of the page.

Steps

1. In the Page Setup dialog box, select the Layout tab.

2. Select where you want new sections to start.

3. When you're working with headers and footers, indicate whether you want different headers and footers for odd and even pages. Also indicate if you want the first page to carry a different header or footer than subsequent pages (this gives you a chance to apply the header/footer to all pages except the first one).

4. Select the vertical alignment you prefer to position text on the page. The "justified" option works only when the page is filled with text.

5. In the Apply To box, indicate to what portion of the document you want these changes to apply. If you want them to apply to all future use of this template, click Default, then click Yes.

Page Setup: Changing Margins

The default margin settings are one inch top, bottom, right, and left. The default gutter margin is zero and the header/footer default is one half inch. You can change these defaults on a document-by-document basis, or you can permanently change the default.

Steps

1. In a new file, choose File, Page Setup. Select the Margins tab.

2. Either select or type in the margins you prefer for all sides, including the header/footer.

3. If you will be binding the document and want the inside margin to remain constant, click Mirror Margins to toggle that feature on and off.

4. In the Apply To box, indicate to what portion of the document you want these changes to apply.

5. If you want these changes to apply to all future use of this template, click Default, then click Yes.

Page Setup: Changing Paper Size

With Word 97 you can work with many different sizes of paper and you can print in either portrait (vertical) or landscape (horizontal) orientation. The default is standard 8.5 × 11-inch paper in a portrait orientation.

Steps

1. In the Page Setup box, select the Paper Size tab.

2. Select the paper size that matches your needs from the Paper Size box.

3. If your paper measurements are not included in the Paper Size box, type in the appropriate measurements in the Width and Height text boxes (you can scroll through and select what's there, or you can overtype with your unique requirements).

4. Choose the orientation you prefer.

5. In the Apply To box, indicate to what portion of the document you want these changes to apply. If you want them to apply to all future use of this template, click Default and then Yes.

Page Setup: Changing Paper Source

The Paper Source tab tells your printer where to go to get the first page of a document, and then where to go to get all subsequent pages. The default is Default tray (Auto Select) for all pages.

Steps

1. In the Page Setup dialog box, select the Paper Source tab.

2. Select the location or source of the first page of each document for your printer.

3. Select the location or source of all subsequent pages for your printer.

4. In the Apply To box, indicate to what portion of the document you want these changes to apply.

5. If you want these changes to apply to all future use of this template, click Default, then click Yes.

Paragraphs: Displaying Marks

There are a number of editorial marks that are included in your text, but most of the time, those marks are invisible. You can elect to turn them on, however, and see exactly what is going on within each paragraph.

Steps

1. Choose Tools, Options, and select the View tab.

2. In the Non-printing Characters section, click the characters you want to see displayed on-screen.

NOTE No matter which characters you choose to display, they will remain non-printing characters and will never appear in your printed text. ■

Paragraphs: Formatting Line and Page Breaks

Formatting paragraphs to control where lines and pages break gives you control over the overall appearance of your document.

Steps

1. Position the cursor anywhere within the paragraph you want to format, and choose Format, Paragraph.

2. Select the Line and Page Breaks tab.

3. Click to toggle on and off the various options. Click OK when you are finished.

Paragraphs: Formatting with Menu Commands

The Format/Paragraphs menu allows you to control indents and spacing, line and page breaks, and tabs.

Steps

1. Position the cursor anywhere within the paragraph you want to format, and choose Format, Paragraph.

2. Select the Indents and Spacing tab and specify the format you want to apply to this (and all selected) text.

3. You can open the Tabs formatting dialog box from this tab if you want. Click OK when finished.

Paragraphs: Tabs

When you set tabs, you gain control over how indented or tabular material is presented in your document, giving it a more professional and clean appearance.

Steps

1. Position the cursor anywhere within the paragraph where you want to define tabs.

2. From the bottom of either the Indents and Spacing tab or the Line and Page Breaks tab, click Tabs.

3. In the Tab Stop Position text box, type in the desired tab measurement or click one from the list and redefine it.

4. If you want the default tab stops to be different from one-half inch, then type the desired default in the Default Tab Stops text box.

5. Define whether or not you want a leader between tabs and if so, which one. Click OK when finished.

NOTE Because Word 97 displays text in a what-you-see-is-what-you-get manner, you must click What's This in the Help menu, or press Shift+F1 to see what formatting instructions apply to any given text. ■

Pictures & Graphics: Converting Floating Pictures to Inline Pictures

While inline pictures stay where you put them, floating pictures can "float" with the text.

Steps

1. Click the floating picture to select it.

2. Choose Format, Picture.

3. Select the Position tab and click Float Over Text to uncheck the box. This changes the picture to an object.

Pictures & Graphics: Hiding

When pictures, clip art, and other graphics are displayed in your document, they can slow down scrolling speed. You can speed up scrolling by hiding the graphics.

Steps

1. Make sure you are using Page Layout View (from the View menu).

2. Choose Tools, Options, and select the View tab.

3. If your picture was inserted as an inline picture, click Picture Placeholders to put a check in the box; if your picture was inserted as a floating picture, click Drawings to turn off that check.

NOTE When you hide inline pictures, you will see a box marking the spot where the picture goes. When you hide floating pictures, you will see nothing in their place. ■

Pictures & Graphics: Inserting

Word 97 comes with its own collection of clip art and pictures which are stored in the *Clip Gallery*. You can choose an image from the Clip Gallery, or you can insert a picture from another source. All imported pictures (in other words, those that come from a source other than the Word 97 Clip Gallery) are imported as floating pictures. You can drag floating pictures to any position on the page. You can also convert them to inline pictures, which will anchor them to the position where they were inserted.

Steps

1. Position the cursor where you want the picture to be inserted.

2. Choose Insert, Picture, and select Clip Art.

3. Choose the Clip Art tab, click the category that you want, and browse till you find a suitable piece of clip art.

4. When you find the clip art you want, double-click it and it will automatically be inserted in your document.

5. When you have the 4-way crosshair arrow cursor, you can move the clip art to any position on the page.

Pictures & Graphics: Wrapping Text

When you include a graphic in a text document, you can choose how you want the text to wrap around the graphic from among several options.

Steps

1. Select the graphic around which you want to wrap text.

2. Choose Format, Picture, and select the Wrapping tab.

3. Select the wrapping style you prefer and adjust the spacing (distance from text) if necessary.

Printing: In Draft Mode

You can print any file created in Word 97. An advantage offered by Word 97 is the ability to print in Draft Mode. This speeds the process and reduces the burden placed on the printer when the document is heavy with graphics.

Printing in Draft Mode eliminates formatting and most graphics, thus speeding up the print job. Some printers do not support this feature.

Steps

1. Choose Tools, Options, and select the Print tab.

2. In the Printing Options section, click the Draft Output check box to turn it on. Click OK when you finish making your choices in this section.

WORD

Printing: In Print Preview

Often it is a good idea to preview a print job before actually sending it to the printer. If everything looks fine, you can send the job to the printer without exiting the print preview screen.

Steps

1. Choose File, Print Preview, or click the Print Preview button in the toolbar.

2. If you feel the text is good enough to print, choose File, Print, or click the Print button in the Print Preview toolbar.

Printing: To a File

You can print a document to a file for later printing to a printer, even one other than your own.

Steps

1. Choose File, Print, and in the Printer Name box select the printer on which you will print the document. This tells Word 97 in which printer language to save the file.

2. Click Print to File to put a check in the box.

3. Click OK, then assign a name to the file in the File Name text box.

Proofing: In Another Language

In order for Word 97 to spell check in another language, you must first load the appropriate dictionary. Many foreign language dictionaries are available from third-party sources.

Steps

1. Make sure the appropriate foreign language dictionary has been loaded and activated.

2. Choose the foreign language text that you want to proof.

3. Choose Tools, Language, Set Language, and set the desired language.

4. Mark the text as the appropriate language.

5. Check the spelling by turning on the AutoCorrect feature, or choose Tools, Spelling and Grammar.

NOTE   If you need to check the spelling of a document that contains a foreign language but you have not installed the foreign language dictionary, then click No Proofing in the Mark Selected Text As box. ■

Properties: Entering Document Properties

When you define properties for documents, Word saves these settings with all documents. The properties settings include a Title, Subject, Author's name, Company, and other information. The document properties can be included in the printout or viewed by choosing File, Properties.

Steps

1. Choose File, Properties. The Document Properties dialog box is displayed.

2. Click the Summary tab to bring the Summary sheet to the front and enter the information. The Author and Company information defaults to the names that Word was registered to during the setup.

NOTE   The author's name can also be changed by choosing Tools, Options, and then clicking the User Information tab to bring the User Information sheet to the front. Change the author's default name in the Name text box. ■

TIP   If you want to have the author's name set for the current file only, click the Summary tab in the Properties dialog box and enter the author's name there. Entering the author's name in the Properties dialog box overrides the name entered in the Options dialog box.

Readability Testing: Documents

Word provides a tool within the *Spelling and Grammar tool* to check the readability of your document. The Readability Statistics tool provides the means to quickly check your text for ease of reading or complexity of thought processes. The readability statistics are shown as a school grade level to indicate the level of comprehension needed to understand the document. The Show Readability Statistics check box is set to off by default.

Steps

1. Choose Tools, Options. The Options dialog box is displayed.

2. Click the Spelling & Grammar tab to bring the Spelling & Grammar sheet to the front.

3. Click the Show Readability Statistics check box to enable or disable the display of statistics. Close the Options dialog box by clicking OK.

4. Choose Tools, Spelling and Grammar. The readability statistics are displayed after the Spelling and Grammar operation is completed.

NOTE You can also set the option to check readability statistics when you run the Spelling and Grammar tool by clicking the Options button in the Spelling and Grammar dialog box. Then click the Show Readability Statistics check box, and click OK to close the dialog box and continue the Spelling and Grammar operation. ■

CAUTION If you have already run the Spelling and Grammar tool with Show Readability Statistics set to off, it is necessary to choose Tools, Options to set Show Readability Statistics on and then rerun the Spelling and Grammar tool.

Repaginating: In the Background

Word can automatically repaginate your document while you are entering new text and making changes. While you make changes to your document, Word can reorder and renumber the pages according to the insertions, deletions, and text changes. The Background Repagination option is set to on by default.

Steps

1. Click the View menu to determine if your document is in the Normal view mode. If not, click Normal to change the View mode.

2. Choose Tools, Options. The Options dialog box is displayed.

3. Click the General tab to bring the General sheet to the front.

4. Click the Background Repagination check box to enable or disable the automatic repagination of your document. Close the Options dialog box by clicking OK.

NOTE Online Help in Word for background repagination is found under the topic of "Page Numbers, Automatic Repagination." ■

Revision Marks: Customizing

You can use revision marks to automatically indicate sections of text that have been changed. As you insert, delete, or change text, the original text is displayed and printed with special marks.

Steps

1. Choose Tools, Options. The Options dialog box is displayed.

2. Click the Track Changes tab to bring the Track Changes sheet to the front.

3. Make the desired changes in the Inserted Text, Deleted Text, Changed Formatting, or Changed Lines groups. The changes can be seen in the Preview boxes to the right of each of these groups. Close the Options dialog box by clicking OK.

4. To display the revision marks, choose Tools, Track Changes, Highlight Changes. The Highlight Changes dialog box is displayed.

5. Click the Track Changes while Editing check box in the Highlight Changes dialog box to enable and disable the display of revision marks. Continue editing your document.

NOTE   If you have the Tools toolbar displayed, you can customize the revision marks by clicking the Highlight Changes button. To enable and disable the display of revision marks, click the Track Changes button on the Tools toolbar. ■

CAUTION   Changes made whenever Track Changes while Editing is set to off will not be displayed or printed with revision marks even when Track Changes while Editing is set to on.

 TIP   Revision marks can also be customized in the Highlight Changes dialog box by clicking the Options button and making the changes in the Track Changes dialog box that is then displayed.

Scanning: Pictures

Office 97 provides the means to scan pictures and insert the images into your document. If you have a scanner attached to your PC, you can use Word to call the Microsoft Photo Editor and then insert the captured picture into your document.

Steps

1. Choose Insert, Picture. Click From Scanner in the Picture submenu. Microsoft Photo Editor is opened and your scanner is intialized.

2. Choose File, Select Scanner Source to set up your scanner. Highlight your scanner and click Select to close the Select Source dialog box.

3. Choose File, Scan Image, and capture the image. Make any desired changes to the image in Microsoft Photo Editor.

4. Choose File, Exit and Return to return to Word and insert the image at the insertion point in your document.

NOTE It is necessary to be in Page Layout View to see the image. When you insert the scanned image, Word automatically switches to Page Layout View. If you switch back to Normal View, the image is not displayed. ■

Section Breaks: Removing

Section breaks are used not only to break a document into a series of sections, many times labeled as chapters, but section breaks can also be used to reset counters in input footnotes, figure captions, and so on.

If you have placed section breaks such as a Next Page break in your document, at some time you may want to remove a break.

Steps

1. Choose View, Page Layout.

2. If the section break mark is not visible, click the Show/ Hide button in the Standard toolbar. (If the Standard toolbar is not displayed, choose View, Toolbars, and click Standard.)

3. Move the insertion tool to the front of the section break that you want to remove.

4. Choose Edit, Clear, or press the Delete key on your keyboard.

Shading: Paragraphs

Word lets you emphasize the text in your document by adding shading and color behind your text. You can create an eye-catching effect for text in the main body of the document or in separate text boxes, such as with sidebars.

To add background shading to your document, just move to the paragraph you want to format. Or, select as much contiguous text as you want.

Steps

1. Place the insertion tool anywhere within the paragraph to be emphasized.

2. Choose Format, Borders and Shading. The Borders and Shading dialog box is displayed.

3. Click the Shading tab to bring the Shading sheet forward.

4. Click the shading or color you want to use in the Fill group.

or

To create a combination of shading and color, select from the Style and Color drop-down boxes in the Patterns group at the bottom of the Shading sheet.

5. The effect of your choices is shown in the preview to the right of the Shading sheet. Click OK.

NOTE To set the color of the text, choose Format, Font. Click the Font tab and pick the desired color from the Color drop-down box. ■

> **CAUTION** Selected Shading may not be displayed as it will be printed. It is necessary to experiment with the percentage of shading that your printer will best support.

Shapes: Adding Shadows and 3-D Effects

You can add shadows and 3-D effects to shapes and drawing objects that you have inserted in your document. This is most effective when your document is going to be used on the Web.

Steps

1. If the Drawing toolbar is not displayed, choose View, Toolbars, Drawing.

2. From the Drawing toolbar, click the Autoshapes button and select a shape to place in your document from one of the six groups of shapes: Lines, Basic Shapes, Block Arrows, Flowchart, Stars and Banners, or Callouts, provided with Word.

3. Click and drag the basic shape of the object. Then, click the Select Objects button in the Drawing toolbar and click the placed object.

4. Click the Shadow or 3-D button on the far right of the Drawing toolbar and select the desired effect.

5. To further enhance the placed object, click the Fill Color down arrow button on the Drawing toolbar and select a color from the palette.

NOTE Shadow and 3-D effects cannot be combined to enhance a drawing object or shape. If an effect is already set, selecting a different effect will replace the original with the new. ■

TIP If a shape is not visible after being placed in the document, double-click the object and select a line or fill in the Format AutoShape dialog box that is displayed.

NOTE Shadow and 3-D effects are turned off by clicking the Shadow or 3-D button in the Drawing toolbar and selecting No Shadow or No 3-D, respectively. ■

Shapes: Deleting

Sometimes, you may place a drawing object in a document that you later decide is not needed. Deleting the shape is as simple as deleting text.

Steps

1. Select the object to be deleted by clicking it.

2. Choose Edit, Clear; or press the Delete key on your keyboard.

Sorting: Tables

Word provides the ability to create tables of information of different types that can be used in many ways. An important table function is the ability to sort the data.

Steps

1. Create a table by choosing Table, Insert Table. The Insert Table dialog box is displayed.

2. Specify the number of Columns and Rows in the Insert Table dialog box, and click OK to close the dialog box. A table is inserted at the insertion point in the document.

3. Enter data in the columns and rows of the table. Select the columns and rows to be sorted using the mouse or the keyboard.

4. Choose Table, Sort. The Sort dialog box is displayed.

5. Select the column to use as the primary sort key in the Sort By field. Then select the Type of data and the order—Ascending or Descending. Click OK to close the dialog box and complete the sort.

NOTE International users can set the Sort options to their specific language by clicking Options in the Sort dialog box and selecting the desired language from 56 variations in the Sorting Language field. These include nine versions of English and 15 versions of Spanish. ■

Sorting: Text

While Word provides the means to sort information set up in tables, it is not necessary to use a table to sort text. Place the text in column form in the document to be sorted.

Steps

1. Create several rows of text in a document. Select the text to be sorted using the mouse or the keyboard.

2. Choose Table, Sort. The Sort dialog box is displayed.

3. Select Paragraph or Field as the primary sort key in the Sort By field. Then select the Type of data and the order—Ascending or Descending. Click OK to close the dialog box and complete the sort.

4. If you have more than one column of text to be sorted, you can sort using up to three columns by entering the the first sort column in the first Then By field, the second in the second field, and so on.

NOTE Multiple columns of text that are to be sorted must be separated with tabs. The same number of tabs must be placed in each row even if there is no data for every column of every row. ■

NOTE Online Help in Word for sorting text is found under the topic of "Lists, Sorting." ■

> **CAUTION** If you try to perform a multi-column sort and some of the selected rows do not have the same number of tab-separated columns, the two Then By sort fields are disabled. All columns must have the same number of tabs to enable the secondary sort fields.

WORD

Spacing: Changing Paragraph Spacing

You can customize your paragraph spacing in Word for the spacing between paragraphs and the spacing between the lines in specified paragraphs.

Steps

1. Place the insertion tool in the paragraph to be modified, or highlight all of the contiguous paragraphs to be changed.

2. Choose Format, Paragraph. The Paragraph dialog box is displayed.

3. Click the Indents and Spacing tab to bring the Indents and Spacing sheet to the front.

4. To change the spacing before or after the specified paragraphs, change the value(s) in the Before and After fields of the Spacing group in the middle of the Paragraph dialog box.

5. To customize the spacing between the lines of the specified paragraphs, select from one of the options in the Line Spacing field. If you set Line Spacing to At Least, Exactly, or Multiple, you set the spacing in the At field to the right of the Line Spacing field.

TIP If you are unhappy with the changes you have made, use Ctrl+Z to undo paragraph formatting quickly. The paragraph will be returned to the format it was set to before the change.

Special Characters: Inserting

The standard keyboard used on a computer cannot include all of the characters that you might need. Whether you need to print a character from a different language, or have to include a special symbol like the trademark symbol, you can use the Symbol tool to include thousands of special characters.

Word provides you with the ability to place characters and symbols in your document that are not on the standard keyboard.

Steps

1. Place the insertion tool at the point in the paragraph that you want to place a symbol or special character.

2. Choose Insert, Symbol. The Symbol dialog box is displayed. Click the Symbols tab to select a symbol.

3. Select the font set that contains the symbol you want to insert in your document in the Font drop-down list box. For example, select Wingdings.

4. To view a symbol in the displayed table, click the symbol. The symbol is then displayed in an enlarged and high-lighted view. To insert the symbol, click the Insert button.

5. Click the Close button to close the dialog box and return to your document.

Spelling: Finding Double Words

You search for and delete repeated words (such as and and) not with Find and Replace but with the spell check feature. Simply begin spell checking, and when Word reaches double words, it gives you the option of removing one.

Steps

1. Position the insertion point in your document where you want spell checking to begin.

2. On the Standard toolbar, click the Spelling button.

3. Word displays the Spelling and Grammar dialog box and scans through your document. When Word finds a repeated word, you can click the Delete key to remove it.

Spelling: Changing Spelling Options

The Spelling tool in Word checks your spelling on command—as you work, after you are finished, or whenever else you need to use it. In addition to the extensive dictionary in Word, you can also create your own custom dictionary to expand the Spelling tool's comprehension.

Steps

1. Choose Tools, Options. The Options dialog box is displayed. Click the Spelling & Grammar tab to bring the Spelling & Grammar sheet to the front.

2. Select the spelling options you want in the Spelling group of the Spelling & Grammar sheet.

3. To select custom dictionaries or to change the language you want to use, click the Dictionaries button in the Spelling group.

4. In the Custom Dictionaries dialog box, you can create or select your own dictionaries, or load additional Microsoft or third-party dictionaries.

5. To select from 56 different languages to use, click the Language drop-down list box, and select the language.

Spelling: Checking Your Document

Word offers you the ability to run the Spelling tool manually or to check spelling as you type. By default, Word will try to correct misspelled words as you type them.

Steps

1. Start typing your text. Word will automatically correct words it recognizes.

2. After typing your document, choose Tools, Spelling and Grammar, or click the Spelling and Grammar button on the Standard toolbar. The Spelling and Grammar dialog box will be displayed and will indicate the language dictionary being used in the title bar.

3. As words that are not in the standard dictionary or your selected custom dictionary are found, they will be displayed in the Not in Dictionary frame of the dialog box in a different color.

4. Click the Ignore button to ignore a selected word in the specified occurrence, or click the Ignore All button to ignore all occurrences of the word in the entire document.

5. If the word is correctly spelled but not found in the dictionary, you can add the word to your custom dictionary by clicking the Add button.

NOTE You can revert changes back to their original spelling by clicking the Undo button on the bottom row of the Spelling and Grammar dialog box, rather than closing the dialog box and using Ctrl+Z. ■

Startup: Starting Word

Word can be customized to start with a specific document open on-screen, or to run a pre-defined macro. You can create complex routines that will guide a reader throughout a document using Word as a tool in the background.

Adding a switch in the path definition, Word can be started while launching or not launching add-ins or macros; or by opening documents. Customizing Word with a special startup is accomplished from the desktop of Windows.

Steps

1. If Word is already running, close it and return to the desktop. From your Windows desktop, right-click the Word button.

2. Select Properties from the shortcut menu. The Microsoft Word Properties dialog box is displayed.

3. Click the Shortcut tab.

4. Include any of these switches separated from the path name in the Target field for the specified action: /a disables the launching of add-ins; /l *addinpath* launches a specified add-in; /m disables macros on Startup; /m*macroname* launches a specified macro; /t *filename* opens a document in Word as a template.

5. Entering a path name in the Start In field specifies the folder to use as the default destination and source for your files. Click OK to close the dialog box and return to the desktop. Then run Word by double-clicking the button.

WORD

NOTE You can also assign a shortcut key combination to start Word from the Windows desktop rather than using the mouse. ■

NOTE You can change the Word button to one of the buttons supplied with Windows or from third-party libraries. ■

Styles: Applying

Style sheets make creating documents with different text characteristics an easy task. Create style sheets once and use their automatic formatting capabilities to quickly create your documents.

An easy method to ensure that sections of your document have the same formatting as other related sections is to define and apply styles.

Steps

1. Place the insertion tool in the paragraph to have a style applied, or highlight all of the contiguous paragraphs to be formatted.

2. Choose Format, Style. The Style dialog box is displayed.

3. Click the style that you want to apply to the selected paragraph from the Styles list box. You can see the effect of the style in the paragraph preview to the right.

4. Click the Apply button to close the dialog box and apply the style to the paragraph.

NOTE If you have previously defined styles for different documents and do not see the style you want to apply for the current document in the Styles list box, click the List drop-down list box below the Style list box, and select All Styles. All styles defined for any document will then be available in the Style list box. ■

Styles: Deleting

Word provides you with the ability to both define and delete style definitions from the current document.

Steps

1. Choose Format, Style. The Style dialog box is displayed.

2. Click the style that you want to delete from the Styles list box.

3. Click the Delete button in the Style dialog box.

4. A confirmation dialog box is displayed asking if you want to delete the style. Click the Yes button to delete the style from the current document.

NOTE If a style has been applied to paragraphs in the document, deleting the style does not remove the formatting from the paragraphs. ■

Styles: Gallery

Word comes with 15 pre-defined templates in its Style Gallery. The templates have text and paragraph formatting already defined for visual clarity and impact. These templates can be applied when you create new documents or to a pre-existing document.

Steps

1. Open the document you want to apply a template to from the Style Gallery.

2. Choose Format, Style Gallery. The Style Gallery dialog box is displayed.

3. Click the template that you want to apply in the Template list box. A preview of the template style is displayed in the Preview Of frame to the right.

4. Click OK to close the dialog box and apply the template style to the open document.

NOTE   All styles from the template can be viewed in the Style dialog box when Styles in Use is selected in the List field when the template has been applied to a document. ■

Symbols: Creating Shortcut Keys

Word provides you with the ability to place characters and symbols in your document that are not on the standard keyboard. Special characters and symbols can be inserted in your document without opening the Symbol dialog box by pressing the key combination you have assigned as the shortcut key.

Steps

1. Choose Insert, Symbol. The Symbol dialog box is displayed.

2. Click either the Symbols or Special Characters tab and select the desired symbol or special character.

3. Click the Shortcut Key button to open the Customize Keyboard dialog box.

4. With the cursor in the Press New Shortcut Key field, press the key combination you want to assign the symbol or character.

5. Click the Assign button to assign the shortcut key to the selected character. Click Close to return to the Symbol dialog box, and click Close to return to your document.

NOTE   Symbols and special characters may have more than one shortcut key assigned. As you go through the previous steps, if you assign more key combinations, you will see each one added to the Current Keys list to the right of the Press New Shortcut Key field. ■

CAUTION   If the key combination is already assigned to a different symbol or character, a message to this effect is displayed below the Press New Shortcut Key field. If you then click the Assign button and close the dialog box, the previous assignment will be removed and the new shortcut key assignment will take effect. Going back into the Customize Keyboard dialog box and removing the shortcut key assignment will restore the original assignment.

Symbols: Removing Shortcut Keys

Special characters and symbols can have shortcut keys assigned to speed character insertion. If you have mis-assigned shortcut keys or otherwise want to remove an assignment, you can make the change in the Customize Keyboard dialog box.

Steps

1. Choose Insert, Symbol. The Symbol dialog box is displayed.

2. Click either the Symbols or Special Characters tab and select the desired symbol or special character.

3. Click the Shortcut Key button to open the Customize Keyboard dialog box. Select the shortcut key to be removed in the Current Keys list box.

4. Click the Remove button to delete the shortcut key from the list.

5. Click the Close button to return to the Symbol dialog box, and click Close to return to your document.

NOTE If the key combination was previously assigned to a different symbol or character, removing the shortcut key assignment will restore the original assignment. ■

Table of Contents: Creating

When creating a large document, such as a book, a table of contents (TOC) is an important component. Word provides the means to create simple or complex tables of contents, as well as other types of tables and indexes using heading styles placed in the text of your document.

Word provides a valuable tool by giving you the ability to create tables of contents based on embedded headings and other styles.

Steps

1. In your document, apply headings from the built-in styles to the appropriate paragraph headings.

2. Choose Insert, Index and Tables. The Index and Tables dialog box is displayed.

3. Click the Table of Contents tab to bring the Table of Contents sheet to the front. Select a table format from the Formats list box. The table format can be seen in the Preview frame to the right.

4. By default, page numbers are created in tables of contents. To turn page numbers off or on, click the Show Page Numbers check box.

5. Click the Right Align Page Numbers check box to turn alignment on or off. When the box is checked, page numbers are displayed and printed against the right margin. Otherwise, the headings are followed by one space and the page number. Click OK to close the Index and Tables dialog box and create the table of contents.

Tables: Adding or Deleting Cells

When you want to present information in a table format, maybe one including grids or framing to delineate the data, the Table tools provide a speedy way to organize the data. Information can be quickly transferred into a table layout and returned to a simple text layout.

When you create a table, you are asked to specify the number of rows and columns. At some time in the future, you may decide to add or delete cells from the table.

Steps

1. In the table you want to change, highlight a cell that you want to insert additional cells in relation to.

2. Choose Table, Insert Cells. The Insert Cells dialog box will be displayed. If you did not highlight a cell or series of cells, the Insert Cells option will not be seen on the Table menu.

3. In the Insert Cells dialog box, select whether to insert the new column or row of cells to the right or above by clicking the Shift Cells Right or Shift Cells Down option buttons, respectively.

4. Selecting the Insert Entire Row or Insert Entire Column radio buttons places a new row above or a new column to the left of the current cell, respectively.

5. In all cases, click OK to close the Insert Cells dialog box and insert the cells into the table.

NOTE If you select an entire row or series of contiguous rows, or if you place the cursor in a cell rather than highlighting the cell, Insert Rows will be shown in the Table menu. When you select an entire column or series of contiguous columns in a table, Insert Columns will be shown in the Table menu. ■

Tables: Changing to Text

The information in a table can be easily converted to text in your document. The text can be converted and placed in the document as separate paragraphs, or as delimited columns of text.

Steps

1. Create a table in your document and enter text in some or all of the cells.

2. Highlight the row(s) or the entire table that you want to convert to text.

3. Choose Table, Convert Table to Text. The Convert Table to Text dialog box is displayed. If the option is not displayed in the Table menu, make sure that you have selected the entire row(s).

4. Select how you want the text to be converted and placed in the document by clicking the Paragraph Marks, Tabs, Commas, or Other option buttons.

5. Click OK to close the dialog box and to convert the table to text.

Tables: Changing Text to a Table

You can create tables from existing text simply by using the Convert Text to Table option. The existing text can be either contiguous paragraphs, or text delimited with tabs, commas, or user-defined delimiters.

Steps

1. Enter several rows of text, separating the text into columns with tabs, for example. Highlight the rows of text that you want to convert to a table.

2. Choose Table, Convert Text to Table. The Convert Text to Table dialog box is displayed.

3. Select the number of columns you want to have in the table in the Number of Columns field. If you enter more columns than you have in the delimited text, empty cells will be created in the extra columns. Specifying fewer columns than you have will create extra rows between your rows and place the text from your extra columns in the extra rows.

4. Word will try to determine the delimiters you have used in your text. If you want to set the delimiters manually, select from the options in the Separate Text At frame at the bottom of the dialog box.

5. Click OK to close the dialog box and convert your text to a table.

Tables: Creating with Table Wizard

The Standard toolbar includes the Insert Table button for creating quick tables with the Table Wizard.

Steps

1. Choose View, Toolbars. Check the Standard check box to display the Standard toolbar if it is not visible on the desktop.

2. Place the insertion point in your document where you want the table to be inserted.

3. Click the Insert Table button on the Standard toolbar to open the Table Wizard, a four row by five column grid.

4. As you move the mouse pointer across the grid, highlighting the initial number of rows and columns, you will see the table definition displayed immediately below the grid.

5. Click the bottom-right corner of the grid to define the size, close the Wizard, and insert the table in the document.

NOTE The Table Wizard allows a maximum of four rows and five columns. If you need more rows or columns, place the insertion point in the table and click the Insert Rows or Insert Columns button on the Standard toolbar. ■

Tabs: Changing Default Tabs

Tabs are important when placing text in documents. Tabs can align text on its left edge, right edge, centered on a defined point, or you can align numeric data on its decimal for best visual clarity.

When Word is installed, the Ruler has a set of default tab stops every .5 inch (if you have set your copy to use inches). You can change the tab stops to any setting you want in addition to, or instead of, the default tab stops.

Steps

1. Choose Format, Tabs. The Tabs dialog box is displayed. If you want to clear all of the default tab stops, click the Clear All button.

2. To change the default tab stops to a different, but consistent setting, click in the Default Tab Stops field and enter the new value, for example enter .25 inches. Tab stops will be set every quarter inch based on these settings.

3. To replace the default tab stops with specific non-consistent tab stops, first click the Clear All button. Then enter each specific tab stop location in the tab stop position field, clicking the Set button to enter each location in the Tab Stop Position list.

4. To add specific tab stops in addition to the default tab stops, just enter the locations in the tab stop position field and click the Set button after each entry. After clicking the Set button for each position, the location appears in the Tab Stop Position list.

5. Click OK to close the dialog box and apply the new tab stops settings to the Ruler.

Tabs: Using the Ruler to Set

Tab stops can be added to the Ruler by simply clicking the Ruler at the appropriate position.

Steps

1. If the ruler is not displayed, choose View, Ruler to display the Ruler in the Editing window.

2. Move the mouse pointer over the Tab button to the left of the Ruler to see the type of tab currently set.

3. To change the type of tab, click the Tab button. The Tab button will cycle between Left Tab, Center Tab, Right Tab, and Decimal Tab. Set the button to the type of tab you want to set on the Ruler.

4. With the type of tab set, move the mouse pointer to the exact location that you want the tab to be set, and click the Ruler.

5. Tabs can be moved on the Ruler by using the mouse to click and drag the tab to the desired location. To remove an existing tab from the Ruler, use the mouse to click and drag the tab off of the Ruler.

Templates: Changing

Templates are designed to make the creation of documents easy. If you want to create a new template based on an existing template, the easiest way is to open the template, make the changes, and save it with a new file name.

Steps

1. Choose File, Open. The Open dialog box is displayed.

2. Select Document Templates in the Files of Type drop-down list box to display all templates. If necessary, change the folder, using the Look In drop-down list box to move to the appropriate folder.

3. When you have located the desired template, double-click the file name to open it in the Editing window.

4. A Warning dialog box may be displayed if there are macros in the template. Click Enable Macros to open the template.

5. Make the desired changes to the template. If you want to save the template with the same name, press Ctrl+S. To save the template as a new template, choose File, Save As, enter the new file name in the File Name field, and click the Save button.

CAUTION   Word does not include the necessary software to scan for or remove a virus. It is important to have current virus protection software if you intend to download files from online services or to swap disks with sources you are not sure are virus-free.

WORD

Templates: Saving and Naming

After creating or changing an existing template, you can save it to a new file name or use the existing file name.

Steps

1. To open an existing template, see also "Templates: Changing" and follow the steps.

2. To create a new template, choose File, New. The New dialog box is displayed.

3. Click the tab of the folder containing the type of document template you want to create. Then select the document type and click the Template option button in the Create New frame in the bottom-right corner of the dialog box.

4. Click the OK button to close the dialog box, and make the desired changes to the template.

5. If you have opened an existing template and want to save it with the same name, press Ctrl+S.

Text: Adding Drop Caps

You can easily add a drop capital to a paragraph. Begin by entering your paragraph of text in the usual way, including the initial letter.

Steps

1. Click anywhere in the paragraph.

2. Choose Format, Drop Cap. The Drop Cap dialog box is displayed.

3. Select None, Dropped, or In Margin from the Position group.

4. Select the formatting to apply from the Lines To Drop and Distance From Text spin boxes. Click OK to close the dialog box and apply the effect.

Text: Adding and Removing Lines

You can enhance the appearance of the text in your documents by using lines on-screen, in printouts, on the Web, and so on. You can also change the color of the lines to enhance your document.

Steps

1. Select the text to be enhanced with the use of lines and color.

2. Choose Format, Font. The Font dialog box is displayed.

3. Click the Font tab to bring the Font sheet to the front.

4. Select the underline you want by selecting from the nine styles in the Underline drop-down list box. You can select a color to display and print the text in by selecting from the eight different colors in the Color drop-down list box. The effect of the change can be seen in the Preview frame at the bottom of the dialog box.

5. Click the OK button to close the dialog box and apply the change to the text.

Text: Changing Case

You can easily change the case of an entire block of selected text. For example, you may want to capitalize a head or convert running text to have initial caps. This is especially useful when you're inserting unformatted text.

Steps

1. Select the text whose case you want to change.

2. Choose Format, Change Case. The Change Case dialog box is displayed.

3. Choose from the Sentence Case, Lowercase, Uppercase, Title Case, or Toggle Case option buttons to indicate the case format you want to apply to the selected text.

4. Click OK to close the dialog box and apply the format change.

TIP If you have AutoCorrect turned on, Word automatically capitalizes the first letter of a sentence and days of the week. Word also repairs double-capitals and even reverses the effects of an accidental Shift Lock.

Text: Changing Character Colors

You can enhance the appearance of your documents with the judicious use of color on-screen, in printouts, on the Web, and so on.

Steps

1. Select the text to be enhanced with the addition of color.
2. Choose Format, Font. The Font dialog box is displayed.
3. Click the Font tab to bring the Font sheet to the front.
4. Set the color you want to enhance the selected text with by selecting a color from the Color field. The effect of the color can be seen in the Preview frame at the bottom of the dialog box.
5. Click OK to close the dialog box and apply the color to the text.

NOTE To set the background color of the text, choose Format, Borders and Shading. Click the Shading tab to bring the Shading sheet to the front. Select the desired background color and shading to apply to the selected text. ■

Text: Changing Font Sizes

You can enhance the appearance of your documents with the judicious use of fonts in different sizes on-screen, in printouts, when used on the Web, and in other uses.

Steps

1. Select the text to be enhanced with the use of a different font size.
2. Choose Format, Font. The Font dialog box is displayed.

3. Click the Fo_n_t tab to bring the Font sheet to the front.

4. Set the font size you want by selecting a size from the predefined _S_ize list box, or by manually entering a size in the _S_ize text box. The effect of the size change can be seen in the Preview frame at the bottom of the dialog box.

5. Click the OK button to close the dialog box and apply the font size change to the text.

Text: Changing Font Type

You can enhance the appearance of your documents with the judicious use of different font types on-screen, in printouts, on the Web, and so on.

Steps

1. Select the text to be enhanced with the use of a different font type.

2. Choose F_o_rmat, _F_ont. The Font dialog box is displayed.

3. Click the Fo_n_t tab to bring the Font sheet to the front.

4. Set the font type you want by selecting a font from the predefined _F_ont list box. The effect of the font type change can be seen in the Preview frame at the bottom of the dialog box.

5. Click OK to close the dialog box and apply the font type change to the text.

NOTE You can also enhance your document by selecting a different font style from the Font Style list box. For example, when creating a bibliography for a paper, use the Italic font style for the title of a book rather than enclosing the title in quotes. ■

Text: Deleting

You can quickly delete any text or other element in your document.

Steps

1. Select the text or other elements to delete.

2. Press the Delete key.

CAUTION Any item you delete is lost and is not placed on the Clipboard. The item cannot be pasted elsewhere. But, you can click the Undo button to reverse your most recent delete action.

Text: Hiding

Word enables you to enter text in your documents that you can hide from view and from printing.

Steps

1. Select the text you want to hide.

2. Choose Format, Font. The Font dialog box is displayed.

3. Click the Font tab to bring the Font sheet to the front.

4. Click the Hidden check box in the Effects group to hide the selected text in the document.

5. Click the OK button to close the dialog box and hide the text.

NOTE To view hidden text, choose Tools, Options and click the View tab. Click the Hidden Text check box and close the dialog box. All hidden text can then be viewed. To remove the hidden characteristic, select the now visible text and repeat the previous steps, unchecking the Hidden check box in the Font dialog box. ■

NOTE To print hidden text, click the Options button in the Print dialog box. In the next dialog box, click the Hidden Text check box and close the dialog box. Then finish the Print steps. ■

Text: Using Superscript and Subscript

Text can be displayed and printed as superscript or subscript text through the Font dialog box.

Steps

1. Select the text to be set to superscript or subscript.
2. Choose Format, Font. The Font dialog box is displayed.
3. Click the Font tab to bring the Font sheet to the front.
4. Click the Superscript or Subscript check box in the Effects group to set the desired effect.
5. Click the OK button to close the dialog box and apply the change to the text.

Text: Using Word Count

With the Word Count tool, you can determine your word count and more. It makes it easy to show, for example, that you have met the size requirements for a college paper. Wherever you need an informative word count, Word provides the means to count how many pages are in your document, as well as how many words, characters (with and without spaces), paragraphs, and lines.

Steps

1. Open a document in Word.
2. Choose Tools, Word Count. The Word Count dialog box is displayed with all the document statistics.
3. By default the Word Count tool only checks the main document. If you want to include any footnotes and endnotes in the count statistics, click the Include Footnotes and Endnotes check box to turn the option on or off.
4. Click the Close button to close the dialog box and return to the Editing window.

NOTE To print the word count statistics, choose File, Print. In the Print dialog box, click in the Print What drop-down list box in the bottom-left corner and select Document Properties from the list. Click OK to close the dialog box and print the document properties, including the word count statistics. ▦

Text: Using Zoom Tool

At times, it may not be as easy as you would like to read a document on-screen because of attributes such as font size, screen size, screen resolution, and so on. The Zoom tool allows you to increase or decrease the image size on-screen without affecting the final output.

You can set the zoom magnification to the numbers listed in the zoom box, or enter your own percentage. You can also display the entire width of the document. When you are viewing the document you can set the view to Whole Page or Many Pages.

Steps

1. Open a document in Word.

2. From the menu bar, choose View, Normal.

3. Now choose View, Zoom. The Zoom menu is displayed.

4. Click one of the Zoom To magnification factors. You can see the effect of the change in the Preview frame to the right.

5. Click the OK button to close the dialog box and change the view mode.

NOTE To view the document at a magnification factor other than one of the pre-defined choices, enter the factor in the Percent field in the bottom-right corner of the Zoom dialog box. ▦

Text Boxes: Inserting Floating

Text boxes can be used to always keep text in a specific location relative to other objects such as graphics or related paragraphs. Using the other tools, such as the Borders and Shading tool, you can create visual emphasis for all of your documents.

The text boxes can also include their own visual enhancement with sidebars that are set apart from the main text of a news article. Floating text boxes can be linked to specific text, graphics, Web links, or other points in documents.

Steps

1. Choose Insert, Text Box. A cross-hair cursor appears.

2. Click and drag the cross-hair cursor to indicate the location and size of the text box.

3. After releasing the mouse button, the text box is displayed with the insertion tool inside the box. Enter your text, insert a graphic, or place any desired object or material in the text box.

4. Click outside the text box to return to the Editing window. To return to the text box, click in the box and start editing again.

NOTE If you insert a graphic in the text box, the box will automatically change its size and shape to contour to the graphic. If you then add a caption to the graphic in the box, the box does not automatically resize itself to accommodate the caption. You will need to manually click and drag the box frame to display and print the caption. ■

Text Boxes: Removing

Removing a text box is as simple as removing text from your document.

Steps

1. Click the text box to be removed.

2. To remove the text box completely, press the Delete key on your keyboard, or choose Edit, Clear.

3. If you want to move the text box or copy it to another location, choose Edit, and either Cut or Copy respectively. Then point the insertion tool to the desired location and press Ctrl+V or choose Edit, Paste.

NOTE All objects such as links, text or graphics, fills, and other formatting follow the text box if you move or copy it to another position in your document. ■

Text Boxes: Rotating

Word provides the ability to change the orientation of text in a text box while the main text in your document remains in a traditional horizontal layout. Using the Text Box toolbar and the Format Text Box dialog box, you can rotate a text box and text into a vertical, left- or right-facing direction.

Steps

1. Choose Insert, Text Box. A cross-hair cursor appears. Click and drag the cross-hair cursor to indicate the location and size of the text box. After releasing the mouse button, the text box is displayed with the insertion tool inside the box.

2. Enter your text, insert a graphic, or place any desired object or material in the text box. Click outside the text box to return to the Editing window.

3. Click the text box.

4. Choose View, Toolbars, Text Box. The Text Box toolbar will be displayed.

5. Clicking the Change Text Direction in the Text Box toolbar will rotate the text in the text box first to a left-facing vertical orientation, then to right-facing vertical,

and finally back to horizontal. After selecting the desired text direction, click and drag the text box frame to resize the box to accommodate the new text direction.

Thesaurus: Using

You use the Thesaurus in the same way you use a Spell Checker. Essentially, select the text that you want to replace, then invoke the Thesaurus.

Steps

1. Select the word that you want to look up in the document or text box.

2. Choose Tools, Language, Thesaurus.

3. The Thesaurus dialog box will be displayed with the selected word in the Looked Up field and major synonyms displayed in the Meanings list box immediately below. A list of minor synonyms for the highlighted synonym in the Meanings list box are shown in the Replace with Synonym list box to the right.

4. Click the Replace button to close the Thesaurus and replace the selected word with the word indicated in the Replace with Synonym field.

NOTE The use of a particular synonym, such as a verb or noun, is shown to the right of the possible synonyms in the Meanings list box. This helps to ensure that the original word is replaced with a grammatically correct equivalent. ■

Toolbars: Adding Buttons

Toolbars are made up of icons and buttons to speed access to commands and functions. Word is installed with 14 pre-defined toolbars covering the most commonly used commands. You can also add to the existing toolbars and create your own custom toolbars.

WORD

Steps

1. If the toolbar you want to add a button to is not open, choose View, Toolbars. Then click the desired toolbar in the submenu.

2. Choose View, Toolbars, Customize. Or, using your mouse, right-click the toolbar and select Customize from the menu.

3. In the Customize dialog box, click the Commands tab.

4. Select from the function categories shown in the Categories list box to the left to display the different pre-defined Word commands in the Commands list box to the right. When you have found the command you want to add to the toolbar, click and drag the command to the desired location on the toolbar.

5. To further customize the button, with the Customize dialog box open, click the button in the toolbar and then click the Modify Selection button in the dialog box. Make the desired changes and press Enter on your keyboard. Click the Close button in the Customize dialog box to close the box and return to the Editing window.

NOTE If a command that you want to add to a toolbar has no button, a shortcut key is shown as a character with an underline. Pressing Alt+ that key will run the command. If there is already a matching shortcut key on the Word menu, the menu will take precedence. To change the button shortcut key, select Modify Selection in the Customize dialog box, click Name and move the & to a position before a different letter in the command string. ■

Toolbars: Creating

Word comes with 14 pre-defined toolbars, but to save space on-screen it may be easier to create your own toolbar. Then, with only your personal toolbar displayed, you have instant access to the tools and commands that you use the most.

Steps

1. Choose View, Toolbars, Customize. The Customize dialog box is displayed.

2. Click the Toolbars tab to bring the Toolbars sheet to the front. Then, click the New button. The New Toolbar dialog box is displayed.

3. Enter the name you want to give to your new toolbar in the Toolbar Name text box. Then, select whether to make the toolbar available to all documents by selecting Normal, or pick a specific document name in the Make Toolbar Available To drop-down list box. Click OK to close the New Toolbar dialog box.

4. Now, with the new toolbar displayed in front of the Customize dialog box, click the Commands tab of the Customize dialog box.

5. Select from the function categories shown in the Categories list box to the left to display the different pre-defined Word commands in the Commands list box to the right. Click the Close button in the Customize dialog box. The new toolbar is displayed as a floating toolbar.

TIP   To place the floating toolbar on any of the four borders, click and drag it to the desired edge and release the mouse button. The toolbar is now displayed as a toolbar on the selected border.

Toolbars: Displaying or Hiding

When Word is installed, only the Standard and Formatting toolbars are displayed in the Editing window. To display or hide pre-defined or customized toolbars, choose View, Toolbars, or use the Customize dialog box.

Steps

1. Choose View, Toolbars.

2. If the toolbar you want to display is not visible in the Editing window, there will be no check mark to the left of the toolbar name in the Toolbar submenu. Click the toolbar name in the submenu to display the toolbar in the last location it was shown in the Editing window.

3. To hide a toolbar, repeat Step 2, clicking the desired toolbar name to remove the check mark and removing the toolbar from view.

TIP Toolbars can also be hidden from view simply by right-clicking the toolbar and then clicking the toolbar name to remove the check mark.

NOTE   If the toolbar to be hidden is a floating toolbar, click the Close button in the upper-right corner of the toolbar. ▮

Toolbars: Moving

Toolbars can be displayed on the borders of the Editing window or as floating toolbars in front of the Editing window. Floating toolbars can be sized, shaped, and moved anywhere on the screen.

Steps

1. If the toolbar you want to move is not open, choose View, Toolbars. Then, click the desired toolbar in the submenu.

2. Click and drag the toolbar to a different border. As you move, the toolbar changes its functions to match the border. When you are where you want to be, release the mouse button.

3. If you want to change a toolbar to a floating toolbar, click and drag the toolbar to the Editing window. Floating toolbars can be dragged anywhere in front of the Editing window, or returned to a position on a border of the window.

4. The order in which the toolbars are displayed on the borders can be changed by dragging the toolbars above or below one another (if the desired toolbars are on a horizontal border).

NOTE   To remove a toolbar from view, right-click any toolbar and click the desired toolbar's name to remove the check mark next to the name. ■

NOTE   Toolbars can also be placed on other toolbars. Click and drag the toolbar to the toolbar you want to make it a part of. Combining toolbars is not recommended because the combined buttons are not all visible or accessible. ■

Toolbars: Resizing and Reshaping

See "Toolbars: Moving" before reading this section. Floating toolbars can be resized or reshaped however you want. The form of the floating toolbars will always be the minimum size necessary to show all buttons and options.

Steps

1. If the toolbar you want to resize or reshape is not open, choose View, Toolbars. Then, click the desired toolbar in the submenu.

2. Move the mouse pointer over one of the edges of the toolbar until the pointer changes into a double-headed pointer and click and drag the edge as desired. The form will reshape it as you resize it.

Tracking: Changes

Different professions use revision marks to track changes in documents. In places where more than one person contributes to a document, each person can be assigned their own colors to indicate who made which changes. After all contributions have been made, the Track Changes tool provides the means

WORD

to review all suggestions and to accept or reject the individual changes.

Tracking changes involves marking changes and then reviewing the suggested changes. It is necessary to use revision marks for the Track Changes tool to later review the changes. See also "Revision Marks: Customizing" to see how to mark changes.

Steps

1. Choose Tools, Track Changes, Highlight Changes in the submenu. The Highlight Changes dialog box is displayed.

2. Click the Track Changes while Editing check box to turn tracking on or off. All changes made with the box checked can be accepted or rejected later using the Track Changes tool.

3. Make the desired changes to your document.

4. When finished editing, choose Tools, Track Changes. Then, click Accept or Reject Changes in the submenu. The Accept or Reject Changes dialog box is displayed.

5. Click the Find button to start the review of your document. As the marked changes are encountered, you will be prompted to accept or reject each change. Click the Accept or Reject buttons to indicate your action.

Undo: Undoing Edits

One of the most valuable commands of word processing software is the capability to undo editing or other changes made to a document. Changes may be recovered using Undo between document saves.

Whether you want to recover text that was intentionally or accidentally changed, change formatting, or remove a placed figure, the Undo command is as simple as pressing a shortcut key.

Steps

1. Open an existing document and edit some text. Now, change the formatting of part of the text. Possibly, add a figure to your document.

2. Press Ctrl+Z, or choose Edit, Undo to revert an edit to what it was before the specific change.

3. Changes can be made back for at least 10 changes using the Undo command.

NOTE To change back to what the text was before the Undo command was used, press Ctrl+Y or choose Edit, Redo. ■

Views: Using Page Layout View

The Page Layout View provides you with the means to see the overall visual effect of your page or pages. All text, objects, or other elements specified to be viewable are displayed in a page layout.

Steps

1. Open a document in Word.

2. Choose View, Page Layout. The page (or pages if you have specified a multiple page view) will be displayed in a compressed view.

3. To return to an editing view, choose View, Normal.

NOTE All editing functions can be accomplished while in the Page Layout View, but, because of the compressed view text editing can be difficult. However, moving non-text elements can be accomplished easily and with good results. ■

Views: Using Print Preview

You might at times want to see how your document will look before you print it out. Print Preview displays your document in a full page mode and has a Zoom tool to take a closer look at the document.

Steps

1. Open a document in Word.

2. Choose File, Print Preview. The document is shown as large as is possible. If the viewed document is more than one page in length, click the vertical scroll bar to view subsequent pages.

3. To get a closer view of a section of the document, move the mouse pointer to the section you want to view. The mouse pointer changes to a magnifying glass with a + symbol in the center. Click the area that you want to see.

4. To return to the full page view, position the mouse pointer, now a magnifying glass with a - symbol in the center, and click.

5. To return to the Editing window, choose View, Normal.

NOTE You can also open a Print Preview by clicking the Print Preview button in the Standard toolbar. ■

Views: Viewing One or Two Pages

Word comes with different ways to look at your document while you are working on it. You can view an outline of your text while you are expanding upon it, or view how it will all look as a printout.

If you want to see the overall visual look of your document, it is possible to see it in a full page (though not readable) view, as one page, as two pages, or up to six pages at once. The view reflects how the document will appear, according to the output device you have previously selected.

Steps

1. Open a document that is several pages in length.

2. Choose View, Page Layout. By default, Word displays documents in the one page view, displaying the document so that one page fills the screen from the top to the bottom of the available window.

3. If the viewed document is more than one page in length, click the vertical scrollbar to view subsequent pages.

4. Now choose View, Zoom. The Zoom dialog box is displayed.

5. Click the Many Pages option button in the Zoom To group. Then, click the Many Pages button to the right, and highlight the number of pages to display in the window. Click OK to see the new view.

6. Click the Zoom drop-down list on the Formatting toolbar, and choose a different view.

NOTE   If you select a 2 x 3 view and have only four or five pages, the first three pages will be displayed across the top row and the rest will be displayed in the bottom row. ∎

Access

Access is a powerful relational database program that is included with Microsoft Office Professional. You can use Access to store and organize data, search and retrieve information, *sort* and *filter* data, and create *reports*. Access lets you create data entry forms, and provides a flexible yet powerful reporting tool.

Action Queries: Append Query

An append query provides a method for adding records to one or more *tables*. This is useful when you want to transfer records from one table, or set of related tables, to another. You can also use the append query to write data to the same fields in matching records between two tables.

Steps

1. In the Query Design View, click the down arrow next to the Query Type button on the Standard toolbar, then select the Append Query option.

2. Enter the name of the source table and any related tables in the Table Name box. Click either Current Database or Another Database to specify the target table(s); then click OK.

3. Drag the fields from the field list that you want to *append* to the query design grid, along with any fields you will use for selection criteria.

4. Enter the criteria for creating the result set in the query design grid.

5. Click the View button in the toolbar to preview the records to be deleted. Click the Run button (!) to append the records to the table(s) you specified.

NOTE   If you want to automatically add new *AutoNumber* values in a *primary key*, don't drag the AutoNumber field onto the query design grid. To retain the AutoNumber values in the source table, drag the AutoNumber field onto the query design grid. For primary keys of this type, don't drag them onto the query design grid. ▪

Also, when fields have the same name, drag the asterisk for each table to the query design grid. ▪

After you run the query, your records are appended in the tables you selected.

Action Queries: Creating

An action *query* collects records that meet your search *criteria*, and changes the data contained in those records in a single step. Access allows four different action queries: delete, update, append, and make table query. A delete query removes the *groups* of records returned from your query from your *database*. An update query alters the information contained in your result set and writes the changes back to your *tables*. An append query adds the records in your result set to your tables. Finally, a make table query creates an entirely new table from your result set. The *records* in the result set may be read from, and written back to, one table or a set of related tables.

Before specifying an action query, you must first create your query and save it to disk. You can use one of Access' several Query wizards, or define your own query in the Query Design window.

Steps

1. Click the Queries tab in the Database window; then click the New button.

2. Select one of the Query wizards or click the Design View selection; then click the OK button.

3. Select the list of *objects* you want to select data from in the Show Table dialog box by double-clicking their names in the Table or Queries tab. Check that the tables are joined correctly in the query's data window.

4. Click the Close button; then add the *fields* from the field list to the query design grid by dragging them to the field list.

5. Enter criteria, add a sort order, create any calculated fields; then click the Save button or choose File, Save. Enter a name in the Save dialog box, then click OK.

TIP Double-click or drag the asterisk field to the field list to add all the fields in a table to a query.

Your query is saved to disk.

Action Queries: Delete Query

The delete query allows you to remove a like set of records from the table(s) you specified. Tables can be single tables or related tables in a one-to-one or one-to-many relationship. If deleting tables in a one-to-many relationship, where cascading deletes are required, then a delete query must be run twice: once to delete the *parent table* records, then again to delete the *child table* records.

Steps

1. Create the query required, then click the Query Type button on the Standard toolbar and select the Delete Query option.

2. Drag the asterisk from the tables in the data environment of the Query window that you want to delete records from to the Design grid, and they appear in the Delete cell.

3. Enter any criteria for deleting records, and they appear under Where in the Delete cell.

4. Click the View button in the toolbar to preview the records to be deleted.

5. Click the Run (!) button to delete the records from the table(s).

After closing the dialog box, the records in your result set are removed from the table(s) you specified.

Action Queries: Make Table Query

The make table query allows you to create a table for export, it provides the basis for a report, it provides a method for making backups, and it gives a snapshot of your data at a point in time. The make table query also allows you to improve the performance of your *forms* and reports by working from a set of records stored to disk that don't have to be retreived from a large data set.

Steps

1. Click the View button in the toolbar and select the Design View command.

2. In the Query Design view, click the down arrow next to the Query Type button on the Standard toolbar, then select the Make Table Query option.

3. Enter a name in the Table Name text box, select either the Current Database or Another Database radio button, then click OK.

4. Drag the fields that will be in the new table from the field list to the query design grid.

5. Enter the criteria for your result set, and any sort or show (filters) you want.

6. Click the View button to see your result set; then click the Run (!) button on the toolbar.

After dismissing the dialog box indicating that a new table will be created, Access writes your result set to disk as a table in the database you specified.

Action Queries: Update Queries

An update query can make global changes to selected records in a table or a set of related tables. This type of query is useful for replacing information quickly.

Steps

1. In the Query Design View, click the down arrow next to the Query Type button on the Standard toolbar, then select the Update Query option.

2. Drag the fields from the field list to the query design grid that will be in the new table. Enter the criteria for your result set, and any sort or show (filters) you want.

3. In the Update To cell, enter the expression or value to be used as a replacement for the field(s) selected.

4. Click the View button to see a list of records that will be updated. Then click the Run (!) button on the toolbar.

After closing the dialog box, Access replaces your old data with the new values in the result set you specified.

Briefcase: Replication of Databases

With the Briefcase Replicator you can reproduce an Access database, and transfer that file to or from another computer. The database is converted to a Design Master, and a *replica* is created. This method is used to work with a replica database on a laptop. When you connect the laptop with the replica to a network or computer with the original copy, you can synchronize the changes made in both copies so that the database is updated.

Drag the database into the Briefcase file on your desktop, a Design Master and the replica are created. On a server, the Briefcase may contain replicas for each use in the office.

Steps

1. Double-click the Briefcase icon on your desktop.

2. Click the replica icon of the database.

3. Choose Briefcase, Update Selection.

4. Click Update to begin synchronization.

Access does not create a new record until you actually enter some data into the first field of a new record.

Browsing: Finding a File Hyperlink

Access 97 has the capability to store *hyperlinks* as data in a special type of field. This new feature lets you display a description of your link while storing the address in a standard addressing convention.

Steps

1. Right-click an entry and select the appropriate shortcut menu command.

2. Select Hyperlink, Open That Link or Hyperlink, Open in New Window from the shortcut menu to go to the document referred to in the hyperlink.

Calculated Fields: Forms and Reports

You can create calculated fields in reports. Normally these fields are used to summarize a group of records using an aggregate function.

A calculated field in the query underlying the report will appear in the report using the expression you entered in the Query Design grid. If you want to enter an expression for a calculated field in a report, you can use the name of the field from the underlying query in the control. For an expression that is not based on a calculated field (for example, SUM or DSUM) in an underlying query, you must repeat the expression in the calculated control on the report.

Steps

1. Open a form or report in the Design View by selecting the form in the Form page of the Database window; then click the Design button.

2. Click the Textbox Object tool in the toolbox for the control you want to create. Click the design surface where you want to create your calculated control.

3. For a text box control, enter the expression for the calculation directly into the text box.

4. For any other control, click the Properties button on the Standard toolbar to open the Properties sheet.

5. Enter the expression in the ControlSource property box.

NOTE   Only controls that have *ControlSource* properties can take an expression with a calculated result. Expressions may be any valid Access function or operator, values, fields, or identifiers, and must start with an equal (=) sign. ▮

Calculated Fields: Queries

You can create a calculated field that is used to either select records or display a result in a query. To do this, enter an expression in the Field cell in the Query Design View. You can also create calculated fields that are displayed in reports or forms.

To create a calculated field in a query, enter the expression for the calculated field in the Field row underneath that field in the field grid of the Query Design window. Calculated fields in a query are not stored to disk, but are recalculated at the query's runtime.

Steps

1. Open the query in the Query Design View, then enter an expression in an empty field in the Field row using brackets for field names.

2. For group or *aggregate functions* like SUM, AVG, COUNT, MIN, MAX, STDEV, or VAR, click the Totals (Σ) button on the toolbar to view the Totals row.

3. Change the field that must be grouped on the Group By Row to **Expression**. Enter any additional criteria or sort expressions.

4. For the calculated field, click the Properties button on the toolbar and set the field properties.

When you run your query, the calculated field appears. If the calculation is based on a GROUP BY expression, then the calculated field calculates the value based on a group of records.

Controls: Changing a Control Type

If you want to change an existing control on a form or a report, Access offers you an easy way to do so. The Change To command can convert one control to another control. When doing so, the appropriate property settings are preserved. When a property exists, it is copied; when a property doesn't exist, it is ignored. If a property is left blank in the original control, Access sets it using the default control style.

Most often this is used to change one type of control to another of the same type (for example, a bound control to another type of bound control). Only appropriate choices are displayed in the Change To submenu when you select a particular type of control.

Steps

1. Open the form or report in Design View.

2. Select the control you want to change.

3. Select new control type from the available choices on the Format, Change To submenu.

Access changes the control type.

Controls: Creating a Bound Control

Controls are devices that display data. When a control displays data from a data source, it is called a *bound control*.

NOTE You can use the Control Wizard to create command buttons, list boxes, combo boxes, subforms, and option groups. A wizard can also create a control for a chart or a PivotTable. ■

Steps

1. Open a form or a report in Design View.
2. Click the Field List in the toolbar to display a field list.
3. Select the field(s) that your control is bound to.
4. Drag the selected field(s) to the form or report and position the upper-left corner of the icon where the upper-left corner of the control will be positioned, then release the mouse button.

Access creates the appropriate control for that field and sets *properties* of the control based on the data type and the DisplayControl property.

If the bound control isn't the one you want, click the control in the toolbox and click and drag the control onto the design surface. Then set the DisplayControl property. This property can be set for each field individually in the Table Design View.

Controls: Creating a Calculated Control

A calculated control displays the results of an expression on your form or report. You can't enter data into a calculated control, but you can control the nature of the calculation and the format of the control.

Steps

1. Open a form or a report in Design View.
2. Click the Textbox Box tool in the toolbox that will form your calculated control.

   Most calculated controls are created with text boxes.
3. Click, or click and drag the control on the form or report.

   A click places a standard control on your form, while a click and drag creates one of a custom size.

4. Type the expression into the control, starting with an equal sign. Or, for any control that has a ControlSource property (and can serve as a calculated control), click the Properties button on the toolbar and click the Build button (either on the toolbar or in the Properties sheet) to view the *Expression Builder*.

5. Create the expression (again starting with an equal sign) in the Expression Builder, and then close the Expression Builder.

Access creates the control of that type.

Controls: Creating an Unbound Control

The elements you add to a form or report are called *controls*. Controls can be graphics, text labels, pictures, and other static elements that do not change as you move from record to record. Controls can also be used to display or enter data, or perform and display calculations. Controls can be buttons that perform actions, and controls can be containers, like *subforms* (grids), or containers that point to objects, such as ActiveX custom controls.

In most instances, you add a control to a form or report using the toolbox in Form Design View or in Report Design View.

A control that is connected to a data source is called a *bound control*; one with no data source is called an *unbound control*; and one attached to an expression is called a *calculated control*. How you create a control, or add it to a form or a report, depends on the type of control it is.

Steps

1. Open a form or a report in Design View.

2. Click the tool in the toolbox for that unbound control.

   Typical unbound controls are text labels, pictures, lines, and so on.

3. Click and drag the control onto the form or report.

Access creates the control of that type.

TIP To lock a control in the toolbox so that you can create several of those controls, double-click the control tool before you create the control on the design surface. That tool stays selected until you select another.

Controls: Editing a Control

Controls are edited in the Design View for forms and reports. Some aspects of a control can be altered through manipulating the control's shape on the design surface, resizing the control, for example. Most aspects of controls are edited in the Property sheet for that control.

To view a control's property sheet, select the control and click the Properties button on the toolbar.

You can click either the All, Format, Data, Event, or Other page to see a subset of the properties for that control.

Steps

1. Click the Properties button in the toolbar to open the Properties sheet.

2. Click the Property you want to set; or navigate to it using the Up or Down arrow keys, or the Page Up or Page Down keys.

3. Enter or edit the value of the property.

4. If the property has a down arrow displayed, you can select the value from the drop-down list; or if the property displays a Build button, you can click that button and alter the expression in the Expression Builder.

5. Press the Enter key, or click outside of the row to establish your changes.

TIP If you need to open up a larger window for that property, press the Shift+F2 key to open a Zoom box. To get help for a particular property, press the F1 key while that property is current.

Controls: Modifying Appearance

You modify or adjust controls in the Design View of a form or report.

Steps

1. Click a control to select it. A selected control will show resize or reshape handles on it.
2. Resize the control by dragging the reshape handles; you can click and drag them to move them.
3. Open the control's Property sheet by right-clicking the control.
4. Select the Property command for that aspect of your control's appearance from the shortcut menu and make the appropriate changes.

What you can do to a control depends on the kind of control it is. For example, you can select the text in a text label and re-enter the text you want. In calculated field controls you can directly enter the expression you want to evaluate.

Data: Copying

Access can cut, copy, and paste data from a *datasheet* or a form through the Windows Clipboard. The Clipboard is an area of system memory or RAM set aside for transferring data between programs or between locations in files. Only one selection can be manipulated at a time, but a selection can include one piece of data or several pieces of data. All data types are supported.

When you copy a selection, the data is copied to the Clipboard and the original data is left intact.

Steps

1. Highlight the selection you want to copy.
2. Click the Copy button on the toolbar.
3. Paste the selection in the desired location (see also "Data: Pasting").

Data: Cutting

When you cut a selection, the data is copied to the Clipboard and the original data is deleted.

Steps

1. Highlight the selection you want to cut.

2. Click the Cut button on the toolbar.

3. If you want to move this selection to another location, see also "Data: Pasting."

Data: Exporting to a Dynamic HTML Page

Access 97 ships with HTML templates that you can use to create Web pages of a particular style. They are stored in the <path>\Program Files\Microsoft Office\Templates\Access folder by default.

Publishing dynamic HTML files to a Web server requires that you determine the format that your particular server requires. For Microsoft IIS, that format is IDC/HTX files; for ActiveX servers that format is ASP files.

Steps

1. Follow the previous Steps 1-3, and select either the Save As Type Microsoft IIS 1-2 (*.htx;*.idc) or as Microsoft ActiveX Server (*.asp) format.

2. Click Export.

3. In the HTML Output Options dialog box, specify the HTML template you want to use.

4. Specify the computer or data source used by the Web server, and a username or password if that data source requires it.

5. If you created an ASP file, enter the server URL of the location of the ASP file.

Access creates the HTML file and links it to the data source you specified.

You can create view forms that display records; data entry forms that add, modify, or delete records; or switchboard forms that navigate to other Web pages. The forms look very similar to the way they look in your database.

NOTE When you create a form, you can only output it as an ActiveX Server (.ASP) file. When a form is exported to HTML, most controls become *ActiveX controls* and all Visual Basic code that the controls have is ignored. All data types are output as unformatted text, and the Format and InputMask properties of the controls are also ignored. ▪

Data: Exporting to a Static HTML Page

You can export Access data and objects to an HTML format so that it can be read by Web browsers on your Internet/intranet site. Tables, queries, forms, and reports can all be exported in HTML format.

When you export a report, you create a static HTML document that doesn't change until you replace it. Datasheets and forms create either static or dynamic documents. When you export to HTML format, you create a single HTML page.

Steps

1. Click the table, query, or form you want to export in the Database window. Choose File, Save As/Export.

2. Click the To an External File or Database radio button; then click OK. Select the location you want to create the Web page to in the Save In list box.

3. In the Save as Type list box click the HTML Documents (*html;*.htm). Enter a name in the File Name text box.

4. Select the Save Formatted check box to save the datasheet in a tabular format. Click the AutoStart check box to display the HTML Output Options dialog box. AutoStart will display the page in your default Web browser when it is opened. Click Export.

   If you selected Save Formatted, then you see the HTML Output Options dialog box.

5. Select a template using the HTML Template to Use dialog box (accessed from the Browse button) or enter the file and its path directly; then double-click OK.

Access creates your static Web page with the name and style, and in the location you specified.

 TIP   Make sure you create your Web pages in byte-size chunks. While you certainly can create a Web page of almost any size, your readers will need to download that file, which can take some time. Divide your data into file sizes appropriate to the Internet or intranet application you have in mind.

Data: Exporting Using E-Mail

You can send Access data directly to a MAPI-compliant messaging application like Microsoft Mail or Microsoft Exchange. The process is relatively easy.

Steps

1. Select the object you want to send: a table or query in the Database window.

   Or, select any portion of a datasheet.

2. Choose File, Send.

3. In the Send dialog box, select the format of the data that will be attached to your message; then click OK.

   Access opens a mail form with your data attached.

4. Fill in your message form, and send your message.

Access allows data to be sent as HTML, ActiveX (.ASP), Excel (.XLS), IIS (.HTX or .IDC), MS-DOS text (.TXT), or Rich Text Format (.RTF) files.

Data: Pasting

When you paste a selection, the data is copied to the location of the insertion point in a field and the contents of the Clipboard are left intact.

ACCESS

Steps

1. Cut or copy selected text.

2. Position the insertion point where you want to paste the data.

3. Click the Paste button on the toolbar.

Data Types: Changing

When you create a table, you specify the data type for each field in the Table Designer. That *data type* appears as the DataType property in a field's property sheet. Access 97 supports the following data types: Text, Number, *Memo, Date/ Time,* Currency, AutoNumber, Yes/No, OLE Object, Hyperlink, and Lookup Wizard. You can see the DataType property in the Table Designer or in a field's Property sheet.

You can change a field's data type at any time. Depending on the data contained in your field, your data may be left untouched, truncated, or invalid.

CAUTION   You can change a field's data type, but, depending on the particular conversion, this process can lead to data loss.

Steps

1. Click the Tables tab of the Database window.

2. Click the table name and click the Design button.

3. Click the Data Type of the field, then select the data type of interest.

4 Click the Save button on the toolbar, or close the Table Designer to save your change.

Database: Backing Up

It is very important to back up your database in order to protect your data. Access automatically saves results to disk, and will overwrite data based on queries and other actions you perform. Often your backup is the only protection you have from data loss.

Steps

1. Close the database and have any open clients close their access to the database in a multi-user application as well.

2. Copy the database file using any of the following methods: Windows NT Explorer, Microsoft Backup, MS-DOS COPY command, or any other backup software that works with Windows 95.

NOTE To back up a database file that is larger than a single floppy disk, you must use backup software, or you must back up the file to a medium (like a removable disk drive) that can accommodate the larger file size. MS Backup can be installed as an option in Windows 95.

You should also back up the workgroup information file from time to time. ▤

Access does not create a new record until you actually enter some data into the first field of a new record.

Database: Compacting

Access stores all of its objects and data in a single file. As you add and delete information in tables, layouts, reports, and so on, not all of the space is reclaimed efficiently. Therefore, every so often you should compact your database to shrink its size, remove free space, and restore its data structures. During compacting, Access does data checks and database structure *validation*.

Steps

1. Close your current database, and have any connected users close their session to the database you intend to compact.

2. Choose Tools, Database Utilities, Compact Database.

3. Select the name of the database you want to compact in the Database To Compact From dialog box; then click Compact.

4. Enter the name, drive, and folder for the compacted database in the Compact Database Into dialog box; then click Save.

The database is compacted.

NOTE When you compact a database with serial number fields, Access resets the serial numbers so that the next record added takes the next incremented serial number for any AutoNumber field. ▓

Database: Creating a Blank Database

A blank database is a database file that contains no objects or data. It is an empty shell.

Steps

1. Choose File, New Database, or press Ctrl+N.

2. Double-click the Blank Database template in the General tab of the New dialog box; or click once to select it, then click the OK button.

3. Enter a name in the File New Database File Name text box, locate the file in the Save In drop-down list box, then click the Create button.

The Database Window for the new blank database appears on your screen. It is blank.

Database: Creating a New Database

Access creates the database for you with all of the tables and other objects that that database template contains. If you selected the Yes, Start the Database option, the database is opened for you.

Creating a blank database differs only in the selection of the Blank Database template in the New Database dialog box. When you select the Blank Database template, the Database Wizard does not run.

"Database: Creating a Blank Database" describes how to create a new database that is blank. Or, you can let the *Database Wizard* create one for you that contains the objects you specify for it. Both procedures begin the same way.

Steps

1. Launch Access and the introductory screen is displayed. Click Database Wizard. Click OK to open the Wizard.

   If you already have Access opened, click the New Database button on the Standard toolbar.

2. Select the database from the Databases tab of the New Database dialog box; then click OK.

3. Locate the database file in your file system using the Save In drop-down list box; enter a new name for the database in the File Name text box of the File New Database; then click the Create button. Access launches the Database Wizard.

4. Click Next to view the screen that lets you select additional fields and sample data.

   Sample data can help you learn how different features work in the sample database.

5. Click the check boxes next to the optional fields (in italics); click the check box next to the Yes, include sample data if you want that feature, then click Next.

6. Select the style you want for your database's appearance, then click the Next button. Select the style you want for your report's appearance, then click the Next button.

7. In the last step of the Database Wizard, click the check box Yes, Start the Database to view the open database, click the Display Help on Using a Database check box for assistance; then click Finish.

ACCESS

NOTE Access offers you the following database templates: Address Book, Office Tracking, Book Collection, Contact Management, Donations, Event Management, Expenses, Household Inventory, Inventory Control, Ledger, Membership, Music Collection, Order Entry, Picture Library, Recipes, Resource Scheduling, Service Call Management, Students and Classes, Time and Billing, Video Collection, Wine List, and Workout. ■

TIP You can click any button with an underlined letter in a dialog box by pressing the Alt key and that letter. For example, to press the <u>N</u>ext key, press Alt+N.

NOTE You can include a picture on your reports by clicking the Yes, I'd Like to Include a Picture check box, then click Picture to specify a picture file in the Insert Picture dialog box. Several graphic formats such as bitmaps, icons, the Windows Metafile, TIFF, PCX, PICT, JPEG, GIF, EPS, and so on, are supported. ■

Database: Encrypting

When you encrypt a database, you scramble the data and definitions contained therein using a utility that makes the file unreadable to anyone that doesn't have the password to open the file. Encryption also compacts the database file. When you decrypt a database, a reverse algorithm unscrambles the database and makes it available for use. In order to encrypt a database, you must have *exclusive* or single-user use of the database file.

Steps

1. Launch Access, but don't open a database in it.
2. Choose <u>T</u>ools, Security, <u>E</u>ncrypt/Decrypt Database.
3. Select the database you want to decrypt.

4. Or, select the database you want to encrypt and enter a name and location for that database.

When you supply the same name and location for the database you are encrypting, Access replaces the original database with the encrypted version.

5. Click OK.

Access encrypts or decrypts the database and posts a message indicating that the operation was successful.

When a user-level security has been assigned in a database, you must have a Modify Design permission for any and all tables in a database in order to encrypt or decrypt the database successfully.

Database: Exporting Data

Access can export selected records to different database file types, or to other data file formats. Single records, multiple records, tables, queries, forms, and reports can all be exported. Even macros and other objects can be exported.

Microsoft Excel and Microsoft Word can read Microsoft Access tables; Microsoft Exchange and Microsoft Mail, or any other MAPI-compliant (Messaging Application Programming Interface) application. Microsoft Excel and Word can also attach a table, query result, form, report, or a module to an e-mail message. The sections that follow describe some of the many ways of exporting data from Microsoft Access.

Steps

1. Click the table you want to export in the Tables tab of the Database window.

2. Choose File, Save As/Export.

3. Click the To an External File or Database radio button; then click OK.

4. Select the Access database you want to export to in the Save As Table <Tablename> In dialog box, then click Export.

5. In the Export dialog box, indicate whether you want to export just the table Definition Only, or the Definition and Data by selecting the appropriate radio button; then click OK.

Access copies the table definition, or the table with its data, to the database you indicated.

TIP Exporting tables in this manner works for all versions of Access. If you are exporting to version 7.0, which came with Office 95 Pro or later, you can use the same procedure to copy queries and macros from one Access database to another.

Database: Exporting Tables or Queries

Access creates a file in the format you specify. If a file doesn't support long table names, as is the case for FoxPro 2.5 for example, Access truncates the field names appropriately in the conversion.

Steps

1. Click the table or query you want to export in the Database window.

2. Choose File, Save As/Export.

3. Click the To an External File or Database radio button; then click OK.

4. Select the location of the file in the Save In list box. In the Save As Type list box, select the format you want to save the table or query in.

5. Enter a name in the File Name text box, then click Export.

When you export a table or query, Access offers you the following file formats as types: Access files, text files (.TXT) in either delimited or fixed width format; Microsoft Excel 3, 4, 5-7, 97; HTML files, dBASE III, IV and V; Microsoft FoxPro 2.x and 3.0; Microsoft Word Merge; Rich Text Format (.RTF); Microsoft IIS 1 and 2.0 (Internet Information Server); Microsoft ActiveX Server; and ODBC Databases. When you purchase the Office 97 ValuPack, a driver for conversion to Paradox databases versions 3.x, 4.x, and 5.0 is included.

NOTE When you select text files as your export type, Access opens the *Export Text Wizard*, which allows you to set the format of your text to Windows (ANSI), DOS, OS/2 (PC-8); date, time, and number format; and which fields get exported. This Wizard also lets you select whether you create a delimited or fixed width text file. ▪

Database: Opening

Access allows you to open one database at a time. If you have a database open in view and you open another database, Access closes the first one and opens a new one. That is, you do not have to close one database to open another.

Steps

1. Choose File, Open or press Ctrl+O.
2. Locate the database file in the Open dialog box and click the Open button.

Database: Optimizing

Because Access writes all of its data and design to a single file, as data and objects are deleted and created, free space and fragmented data structures are created. This is similar to what happens with your computer's file system. Over time, the database file grows larger than it needs to be and performance can suffer. To optimize performance, you can compact the database. Doing so creates a new file where all of the data is stored efficiently and in sequence. Compacting a database will improve its performance.

NOTE To compact the current database, see the topic "Database: Compacting." ▓

There are other things you can do to optimize the performance of a database:

- You can run the database in Exclusive mode by setting that check box in the Open dialog box when you open the database.
- You can install the database file to a local hard drive instead of to a network server.
- You can assign more memory to Microsoft Access, or close other programs or unnecessary system utilities like wallpaper, to free up additional RAM.
- You can add additional RAM to your computer, but do not set up a RAM disk as Access creates its own.
- You can defragment your hard drive using the Disk Defragmenter in the System Tools folder of the Accessories folder on the Start menu in Windows 95.
- You could improve your processor by upgrading your computer.

All of these will provide general performance improvement.

Oftentimes the performance of your database is limited by the design of the database itself. If you have tables with redundant data, you can have poorly constructed indexes, inappropriate data types, or the wrong join definition for relationships. Run the *Performance Analyzer* to see suggestions on optimizing database objects, and then perform the suggestions, as desired.

Steps

1. Click a tab in the Database window.

   Or, click the All tab to analyze performance for all database objects.

2. Choose Tools, Analyze, Performance.

Database: Repairing Closed Databases

You can also repair a database that isn't currently in view. The process is only slightly different than repairing an open database. Before another database can be repaired, Access closes your current database.

Steps

1. Close your current database.

2. Choose Tools, Database Utilities, Repair Database from the Database Utilities submenu or the Tools menu.

3. Select the database in the Repair Database dialog box.

4. Click the Repair button.

Access will perform data validation and other procedures and repair the database, if possible.

CAUTION   Access isn't always able to repair badly damaged database files. You should always maintain an active system for backing up your database so that you can revert to your last backup should your current file be unusable.

Database: Repairing Opened Databases

When you open, compact, encrypt, or decrypt a database that is damaged, Access will inform you of the damage and post a dialog box that offers to repair it. In instances when you find erratic behavior, you may want to initiate the procedure of repairing a database manually.

Steps

1. Open the database exclusively.

2. Select the Tools, Database Utilities, Repair Database command from the Database Utilities submenu or the Tools menu.

Database: Setting Startup Properties

You can specify a number of options that are set when a database starts up as a property of that database. For example, you can open a particular form, display and customize toolbars, and allow or disable shortcut menus.

Steps

1. Choose Tools, Startup with a database open.

2. Set the options you want in the Startup dialog box (see Figure 1).

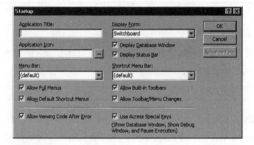

FIGURE 1
The Startup dialog box shows the advanced options.

Database: Splitting a Database

You can split a database into two files: one that contains the tables and another that contains all of the other objects in the database that act on the base tables (queries, forms, reports, macros, and modules). This is useful when you want to provide a means for users to access data while maintaining their own forms and reports or database interface.

For example, in a corporation that wants to maintain a separate and single data warehouse, you could distribute different versions of the database but maintain a single data set and data structure in a central location.

Steps

1. Choose Tools, Add-ins, Database Splitter.
2. Click the Split Database button.
3. Enter the name of your database in the Create Backend Database dialog box File Name text box, then click the Split button.

Access creates a new database based on your current data and structure.

You can also use the Database Splitter Wizard to perform the function of splitting an existing database into its data and other component objects.

Database: Using the Table Analyzer Wizard

You can also analyze your database table structure using the *Table Analyzer Wizard*. This Wizard checks for redundant data, and can create smaller related tables (normalization) or a single query, with no relationships to improve performance.

Steps

1. To run the Table Analyzer Wizard, choose Tools, Analyze, Table. Follow the wizard's prompts.

TIP   If you are finding and sorting records, creating an index specially composed for this purpose can often improve performance considerably. Access uses the FoxPro *Rushmore* query optimization engine; an understanding of how to compose indexes to use Rushmore can lead to extremely fast record selection and sorting.

Datasheet: Changing Appearance

There are numerous ways you can alter the appearance of your datasheet. You must have the datasheet for that table in view; these settings apply universally, and not to individual cells.

Steps

1. Double-click the table name in the Tables tab of the Database window to open its datasheet; or click the View button on the toolbar when a form is in view.

2. Select a new font, font style, font size, or color by choosing Format, Font.

3. Choose Format, Cells and change the gridline, gridline color, cell appearance, and cell background color in the Cells Effects dialog box.

4. Click the Close box to close the datasheet.

   Access remembers your settings the next time you open a datasheet for this table or form.

Additionally, you can change the width of a column or height of all rows in the datasheet using the Format, Column Width or Format, Row Height commands. Each column can have its own width, but all rows must be the same size.

You can also hide a column from view using the Format, Hide Columns command and return it to view using the Format, Unhide Columns command. One nice feature of a datasheet called freeze columns lets you have a column always appear on the left side of your datasheet regardless of how you scroll left and right through your columns. Use the Format, Freeze Column command to freeze a selected column; and the Format, Unfreeze All Columns command to return your columns to the naturally viewed order.

CAUTION Be careful when you hide columns from view that you don't neglect their data entry inadvertently.

Datasheet: Navigation

Navigating a datasheet uses techniques that are very similar to navigating most spreadsheets. You can move through columns (fields) and rows (records) using standard keystrokes.

Steps

1. Double-click a table name in the Tables tab of the Database window to open its datasheet.

2. Press the Tab key to move to the right; the Shift+Tab key to move to the left; or use the arrow cursor keys to move in any direction.

   When you move past the left field you move to the next record; and when you move past the right field you move to the previous record. See the following table for additional navigation information.

Datasheet View Navigation

To Navigate in Datasheet View	Do the Following
To advance a field to the right	Press Tab.
To move a field to the left	Press Shift+Tab.
To advance to the next record	Press the Tab key on the last field in a record.
To go back you are moved to the rightmost field in the previous record	Press Shift+Tab in the leftmost field of the current record.
To move to the first record	Click First Record in the Navigation section.
To move to the previous record	Click Previous Record.
To move to the next record	Click Next Record.
To move to the last record	Click Last Record.

continues

Continued

To Navigate in Datasheet View	Do the Following
To move to the first blank record	Click First Blank or New Record.
To move to a particular record	Double-click the Record Number text box, enter a record number, then press Enter.

If all else fails, you can always navigate by clicking an insertion point on any record or field in view. Move the scroll bars to view other records and click in any record or field of interest.

 TIP You may want to set some of the options on the Keyboard tab of the Options dialog box to change the behavior of the arrow and Enter keys during record navigation. Select the <u>O</u>ptions command from the Tools menu to view that dialog box.

Design View: Opening a Blank Form

Forms are one of the primary methods used to work with data, navigate, and perform actions in a database. You create, specify the contents of, and modify forms in the Design View. You work with forms and enter data into them in Form View. This construct separates the construction of your form from its use.

Steps

1. Click the Forms tab in the Database window, then click the <u>N</u>ew button. Select Design View in the New Form dialog box.

2. Click the Choose the Table or Query drop-down list and select the table or query that will be the data source.

3. Click OK or press the Enter key.

   Access opens the blank form in the Design View.

4. Click the Save button on the Form Design toolbar or choose File, Save.

5. Enter the name of the form in the Save As dialog box, then click OK.

Access creates the new form and saves it to disk.

Forms are used to:

■ Display and enter data into a database using a data entry form.

■ Select options via a form that looks like a dialog box.

■ Provide a method for launching or opening other elements of a database, such as forms and reports, through a form that looks like a switchboard.

All of these forms are created in the Design View, and some can be created with the Form Wizard. In Design View you can add graphic elements such as lines, boxes, text labels, and bound controls. Bound controls display data from underlying record sources like tables, queries, or calculations; or they contain the results of calculations based on data in your database.

When you work with forms in Design View, you add controls to the design surface of your form by clicking that control in the Toolbox and dragging it onto the form. You can add and delete sections from forms to control what appears on the form and where it appears.

Editing: AutoCorrect

Access 97 has a feature called AutoCorrect that can automatically capitalize names of days, correct typing errors, correct two capital letters in a row, correct the accidental use of Caps Lock, capitalize the first letters following a period and a space character (defined as a sentence), and correct text you type, such as replacing misspelled words. If you have used Word 7 or other Office 97 products, AutoCorrect may be familiar to you.

Steps

1. Choose Tools, AutoCorrect.

2. Make your selections in the AutoCorrect dialog box. Click OK

Editing: Spelling Check

You can check the spelling of your data in Datasheet or Form View; and check data in a table, query, or form in the *Database window.*

Steps

1. Select the data you want to check.

2. Click the Spelling button on the toolbar.

Editing: Undo Command

You can use the Edit, Undo command (Ctrl+Z), or the Undo button on the toolbar to remove your most recent change.

Steps

1. To remove edits to a record you have saved, choose Edit, Undo Typing.

If you move away from the record, or use a filter, Undo Saved Record or the Undo command will not be available to you.

Expressions: Using the Expression Builder

You can use the Expression Builder to create both simple and complex expressions for use in tables, forms, queries, and reports. Whenever a field, value, or control takes an expression, you will see a Builder button.

An expression takes a set of values, symbols, operators, or identifiers and evaluates it to produce a result. Often the result is a value, be it numeric, text, logical Yes/No, dates and times, and so on.

Expressions are evaluated based on *rules* of precedence, that is, the order in which the operations in an expression are carried out. The order is determined by the type of operation, its location in the expression from left to right, and whether the operation is surrounded by parentheses.

The syntax you use in an expression is also important. Most often an expression requires the use of a preceding equals sign, but not always. Text is often required to be surrounded by quotation marks. Many other rules are required for proper expressions.

Steps

1. Click the Builder button to view the Expression Builder.

2. Enter the expression of interest, or click the buttons in the dialog box to add operators, values, or formulas to the expression, then click OK.

Access checks the syntax of your expression when you close the Expression Builder to see if it violates any obvious rules; if it doesn't, it allows you to enter that expression. Just because the expression's syntax checks out, doesn't mean that you've created the correct expression. But at least you have an expression template interface to speed up your work, and to take much of the drudgery out of entering the symbols and data correctly.

The Expression Builder is an interface to the various database objects, functions, constants, operators, and expressions that are available in your current situation. When you select a function, for example, Access 97 creates the template that you can fill in to create your expression. You build your expression in the upper panel of the Expression Builder.

Fields: Editing

Access offers you several different methods for editing data: one field at a time, several fields at a time, one record, or many records at a time. The simplest method for editing data is to edit the data in a field of a datasheet, or a form in Form View.

Steps

1. Open a datasheet or a form in Form View.

2. Click the field you want to modify and select the portion you want to replace.

3. Enter the replacement text.

   Or, position the insertion point and begin to enter any new data, and delete any unwanted data.

   Or, select the entire field's value and enter a new value.

 TIP Some field types, like those in subforms, will display a plus pointer when you move the cursor to the leftmost part of the field. If you click at that point, the entire field will be selected.

When you enter or edit data in a multi-user situation, Access Record locks the record of the first user who accesses it. Other users can view the data, but cannot edit that data if you have edited the record. You will see a triangle in the record selector when a record is current (in a datasheet), a pencil icon when you are editing it and have a record lock on that record, and a circle with a slash (lock symbol) when someone else has a record lock on your current record. A locked record cannot be edited until the lock is released. Locks are released when the data is saved, or when the user with the lock moves off that record.

Fields: Editing Values

See also "Fields: Editing" before reading this section. To edit the values in a field, you must select the data in the field you want to edit. You can use your mouse to move to that field and select data by clicking and dragging the mouse over the data of interest; or you can navigate to the field using keyboard methods.

Steps

1. Open a datasheet or a form in Form View.

2. Click the field you want to modify and select the portion you want to replace.

3. Enter the replacement text.

   Or, position the insertion point and begin to enter any new data, and delete any unwanted data.

   Or, select the entire field's value and enter a new value.

Fields: Entering Descriptions

The Description property provides information about fields in tables, forms, and queries in the Database window. Descriptions can be up to 255 characters in length and appear in the Details View.

This property is set in the Table Designer for tables, in the Field Properties property sheet in the Query window for queries, and in the Description property for the control in the Form Design View.

When you create a control by dragging a field from a field list, Access copies the Description property to the control's StatusBarText property. It then displays that description in the status bar whenever the insertion point is entered into that field.

Steps

1. Click a table name in the Tables tab of the Database window, then click the Design button.

2. Click in the Description field of the field.

3. Enter a value for the description. You do not need to surround the description with quotation marks.

4. Click the Save button on the toolbar or the Close box to save your description.

NOTE When you use a linked table, the connection information is displayed in the Description property. ▨

Fields: Naming

You can change the name of a field in your database and your table's data is left unaffected. However, if you have used that field as a ControlSource in a bound control on a form, you must manually update that control to reflect the new field name.

CAUTION   Access does not check the properties of objects that depend on the field name of tables in the database.

Steps

1. Open a table in the Table Design View.
2. Click the name of the field and edit that name.
3. Save the table using the File, Save command.

Fields: Renaming in Datasheet View

To rename the field in a query, change the name of the field in the query design grid. That new name provides the column name for the field in Datasheet View, unless the Caption property has been set (there the caption is used). The renamed field also provides the name of the ControlSource for any control in a form or report that is based on that query.

Steps

1. Open the table in Datasheet View.
2. Click the column for the field of interest.
3. Choose Format, Rename Column.
4. Type the new name of the field.
5. Tab out of the column, or press Enter.

Access renames the field name.

Fields: Selecting

You can select fields in a datasheet in many different ways, using your mouse, menu commands, or with the keyboard.

Steps

1. Double-click the table name in the Tables tab of the Database window.

2. Click and drag on the data of interest, or click where you want to start the selection and press the F2 key to select an entire field's value. See the following table for additional selection techniques.

3. Click a column header to select all field data, or click a row selector to select all the data in a record. Extend your selection by pressing the Shift key and clicking at the end of your new selection range.

4. Choose Edit, Select All Records, or click the All Records selector to the left of the leftmost column header to select all the data in your datasheet.

5. Click the Save button on the toolbar, or click the Close button of the datasheet to save your changes.

Datasheet Selection Techniques

To Select this	Do this
Field data	Click and drag a selection, then release the mouse.
To extend a field selection	Hold the Shift key and click at the end of the new selection range.
An entire field	Move the pointer to the left edge of the field. When you see a plus sign cursor, click there.
An entire field	With the insertion point in that field press F2.

continues

Continued

To Select this	Do this
Adjacent fields	Drag the left edge of the current field to extend range of selection.
A column	Click the column header.
The current column	Press Ctrl+Spacebar.
Adjacent columns	Click the column header and drag over additional column headers to extend the range of selection.
A record	Click the record selector to the left of the row.
Multiple records	Click a record selector then drag down over additional record selectors.
Multiple records	Press Shift+Spacebar, and then Shift+Up arrow or Shift+Down arrow.
All records	Select All Records on the Edit menu, or click All Records selector to the left of the leftmost column header.
Adjacent fields	With a field selected, hold down the Shift key and press the appropriate arrow key.

Fields: Setting Default Values

You can set a *default value* for a field in the Table Designer on the General tab. When you enter a value or expression in that property, that default value is entered into the record at the time you create the record. You are free to overwrite the default value if you have write privileges for that field. At no other time does the database enter the default value into the field other than upon record creation.

Steps

1. Click the table name in the Tables tab of the Database window, then click the Design button.

2. Click in the Default Value text box, then enter your value. Or, enter an expression that evaluates to a value.

3. Click the Save button on the toolbar to save your new database value.

Because this default value is applied at the table level, the mechanism for entering the default value operates in a datasheet or form. During an append operation, default values are not added to the new records that are appended to the table. Nor are AutoEntered values (a form of default) applied to appended records.

 TIP   Creating default values is a great time-saver, and speeds up data entry. When you have a field that almost always has the same value entered into it, consider setting this property.

Validation rules are another property you can set in the Table Designer. When you move the focus off a field, Access will check a field's validation rule to see if the rule has been violated. For example, you could set a field's validation to "IS NOT NULL," and that would make it mandatory that your users enter a value into that field. You can set a range of values, a list of values, and so on.

Fields: Setting Properties

You can set many of the field properties in the Table Designer. Properties include name, data type, description, field length, validation rules, default values, and whatever you see on the General or *Lookup* tabs in the Table Designer. There are more properties available than those shown in the Table Designer.

Steps

1. Right-click the field in the Table Designer.

2. Select the Properties command from the shortcut menu to view the Properties sheet.

Fields: Setting Validation Rules

You can also create record validation rules. You do this to validate the data entered into two or more fields in a record. When you move off the record, Access checks that a record validation is not violated. You cannot leave the record without either removing the record's data or fixing a record so that it conforms to record validation. You set a record level validation rule in the ValidationRule property of a table's Property sheet.

Steps

1. Click the table name in the Tables tab of the Database window, then click the Design button.

2. Click in the Validation text box.

3. Enter an expression.

4. Click the Save button on the toolbar to save your new database rule.

   When you enter a value in that field, the value is allowed if the expression is evaluated as "True."

At the highest level, you can enforce *Referential Integrity* so that related records in tables get updated, deleted, or inserted appropriately with cascaded effects. You set RI rules by clicking a relationship in the Relationships window and setting the property there.

Filters: Advanced Filter/Sort

The most complex filters you can create let you both filter and sort records in a single operation for a single table or query. The Advanced Filter/Sort window is similar to the Query Designer in construction in that you work in a design grid where you specify the criteria used to filter your records and the sort order. The Advanced Filter/Sort feature can operate on tables or queries, but cannot provide related tables or a data environment.

Steps

1. Open a table, query, or form in the Datasheet View, or a form in the Form View.

2. Choose Record, Filter, Advanced Filter/Sort on the Filter submenu.

3. Enter the criteria and sort you want in the design grid.

4. Click Apply Filter on the toolbar.

Access returns the matching results set.

Filters: Filter by Form

If you want to select a set of records in a datasheet or a form, the simplest way to do this is to set a filter. A filter is a single set of criteria that can be applied to your data set. When you apply another filter to a result set from a previous filter, you narrow your result set even further.

Access remembers your last filter in a session and lets you reapply it at any time. If you apply a filter to a table or form, Access remembers that filter until you apply a new one. Filters applied to queries are not entered into the query grid, but can be applied later separately. You can also sort filtered records. You may find that filters provide much of the find and query capability you need in your work.

Steps

1. Open a table, query, or form in the Datasheet or Form View. Click the Filter by Form button on the toolbar to open a Filter by Form window.

2. Click the field you want to filter by and enter the selection criteria that records must match to be returned in a result set.

3. To enter a value to search for, select that value from the list in that field; or enter the value manually.

4. To enter a value of a check box, option (radio) button, or toggle button, click that button. Entering a value in two fields on the same line in the Look For tab (see the bottom of the window) requires both values to be matched in the result set.

5. To perform a filter based on alternative values, click the OR tab at the bottom of the window and enter additional criteria. Click the Apply Filter button on the toolbar to perform the selection.

Access returns the result set that matches your filter.

NOTE Check boxes display three states: checked (on), not checked (off), and not available (grayed). Make sure you place a check box into the condition you want. Also, you can select a field based on the conditions Is Null or Is Not Null. ■

You can reapply the filter by clicking the Apply Filter button at a later time. You can use the Remove Filter button to remove your current filter.

Filters: Filter by Selection

You can filter the records shown in a form, subform, or datasheet by applying a *filter by selection*. This procedure is very simple to use, but more limited than *filter by form*.

Steps

1. Select the value you want to select for a form, subform, or datasheet.

2. Select an entire field's contents to return matching fields.

   Or, select part of a field starting with the first character to return records where the value in that field also starts with those characters.

   Or, select any value after the first character in a field to return all or part of a value in that field with the same characters.

3. Click the Filter by Selection button on the toolbar.

Access returns a result set based on the values in the field you selected.

Filter by selection is very quickly applied, but not very flexible because you can only make one selection.

Filters: Filter for Input

Access lets you enter a filter directly into a field on your form or a datasheet as a filter request. This is called *filter for input*.

Steps

1. Open a table, query, or form in the Datasheet View, or a form in the Form View.

2. Right-click a field and enter a value or expression in the Filter For text box; then press Enter.

   Or, press the Tab key to apply the filter but leave the shortcut menu displayed to enter additional criteria.

Access, by successively filtering, can narrow your result set.

Forms: Adding and Removing Sections

The sections of a *form* or a report allow you to set up a page for display, or to provide a particular kind of layout. Through proper use of sections, you can provide information that appears on every page at the top or bottom, at the beginning or end of a form or report, repeats for each record, repeats for each group of records, and so on.

Forms contain the following sections: Form headers, Page header, *detail section*, and Page footer.

You can also create sections in subforms that appear inside forms: headers, detail sections, and footers.

Reports can contain all of the same sections as forms do (although they are called Report headers, and so on), but a report can also contain bands for grouped records. When a record set is sorted by a sort key, each value in that sort key becomes a group of records. Each group will appear in its own detail section, and can be preceded by a Group header and followed by a Group footer. Grouping allows you to place calculated fields or controls on a report that provides statistical information on the aggregate of those grouped records. This is in addition to statistical information like Running Counts that can be done sequentially through a set of records.

Steps

1. Click the form or report name in the Database window, then click the Design button.

2. Choose View, Page Header/Footer or View, Form Header to add those items to view for a form.

3. Choose those commands again to remove the check mark and eliminate them from your form or report.

4. Click the Save button to save your changes.

You can set properties for sections that make them hidden, or set their height to 0 if you don't want one to appear.

Forms: Changing Tab Order

The order in which you move through fields on a form is called the tab order. By default, the tab order is for fields going from left to right across the screen, and top to bottom. You can change the tab order to suit your purpose, even leaving fields out of the tab order to aid in speeding up data entry when a field has data entered into it infrequently.

Steps

1. Open the form in Design View. To switch to Design View, click the View button on the Standard toolbar and select the Design View option.

2. Choose View, Tab Order. To keep or return to the default tab order, click the Auto Order button.

3. For a custom tab order, click the control selector to place it in the tab sequence; then drag the selector into the position in the order you want and click OK.

4. To test the tab order, switch to the Form View of your form. Switch to Form View by selecting the Form View option on the View button menu on the Standard toolbar.

The new order is installed in your form.

Forms: Creating with Form Wizard

Access 97 contains a Form Wizard that can create many different kinds of forms based on your input. Even if you intend to create a custom form, the Form Wizard can be a good starting place from which you can make modifications.

Steps

1. Click Form Page in the Database window, then click New. Select Form Wizard in the New Form dialog box. Click Choose the Table or Query drop-down list and select the table or query that will be the data source. If you don't select a table or query, your current table or query is used. Click OK or press the Enter key.

2. In the first step of the Wizard, select the fields you want to see on your form from the Available Fields list box by moving them onto the Selected Fields list.

3. For any related tables, select that table from the Tables/Queries list box, then add the fields of interest to the Selected Fields list box; then click Next.

If you are building a form based on a relationship, in Step 2 of the Wizard you can specify the parent table used to control the view of your data.

4. Select also whether the child table appears in a Form with subform(s) (grid) or is a Linked form linked through a button to a new window; then click Next.

For a single table or a query, Steps 6-8 are not performed.

5. Select the layout desired, Tabular or Datasheet; then click Next.

6. Select the style for your form, then click Next. Enter a name for the form in the Form text box, or a name for the subform derived from the related or linked tables, as appropriate.

7. Select either the Open the Main Form to View and Enter Data or the Modify the Design of the Forms radio button, then click Finish.

8. Click the Save button on the Form Design toolbar, or choose File, Save. Enter the name of the form in Form Name text box of the Save As dialog box, then click OK.

Access creates the new form and saves it to disk.

There are a number of other wizards you can use to create forms automatically, but with fewer options than the Form Wizard. AutoForm Wizards exist for Columnar, Tabular, and Datasheet form views.

Forms: Creating with New Form Dialog Box

The New Form dialog box is your key to creating forms. There you can create forms from scratch, or use one of the different form wizards to create forms based on your input.

Steps

1. Click New on the Forms tab of the Database window.

2. Choose a wizard from the New Form dialog box.

3. Follow the wizard's prompts and instructions.

NOTE With a table or query selected in the Database window, choose Insert, AutoForm; click New Object on the toolbar; and select the AutoForm command to bypass the New Form dialog box and create a form directly. ▪

When you open the New Form dialog box, you must select a table or a query to base your form on.

Among the choices you have in the New Form dialog box are the following:

- *Design View.* This selection opens a blank form that you can build from scratch.
- *Form Wizard.* This Wizard runs you through several steps that enable you to select the tables, *relationships*, controlling table, form style, and other features you want your form to have.
- *AutoForm Columnar.* This columnar report is one where fields are stacked vertically with text labels on the left and text boxes on the right. Each record appears on a single page.

NOTE Some databases refer to tabular layout as columnar layouts. ▧

- *AutoForm Tabular.* This Wizard creates forms in which you see several records repeat themselves on every page.
- *AutoForm Datasheet.* This Wizard creates a spreadsheet-like display for your form where records repeat in rows, and fields in columns.
- *Chart Wizard.* The Chart Wizard creates a form with an attached chart. This is an optional installation.
- *PivotTable Wizard.* A PivotTable is an interactive table where data is summarized by field. Access uses the Microsoft Excel PivotTable Wizard to create these types of forms.

When you run an auto wizard, the wizard runs with default choices and without your intervention, creating a form. In all cases you will need to save your form to disk using the Save button on the toolbar.

Group Calculations: Adding to Queries

You can add group calculations to queries and reports. These calculations provide information on groups of related records. In order to summarize or calculate a value from a group of records, those records need to be sorted in a query. When the calculations involve all records browsed, then they do not need to be sorted.

You can calculate expressions based on groups of records in a query. To do so you must establish the grouping by entering the field in a Group By expression in the Query Design grid. Then you create an expression using an aggregate function like SUM, AVG, COUNT, MIN, MAX, STDEV, or VAR.

Steps

1. Enter a name for the expression in the field row of the Query Design grid.

2. Enter the expression in the Group By row.

For simple sums, the Simple Query Wizard lets you enter the fields you want to sum. You can also calculate different types of totals in the Total row of the Query Design grid using an aggregate function. You do not need to enter an equal sign at the start of an expression in the Query Design window.

A calculation is not stored, but is evaluated and displayed each time the query is run. There is no way to update calculated results, but you can use the results of a group calculation to update records in an Update Query.

Group Calculations: Adding to Reports

To calculate an expression for a group of records on a report, you must add a control on that report and set the ControlSource property.

Steps

1. Open the report in Design View.

2. Click the tool in the toolbox and create the control.

3. To sum or average a group of records, add a text box or bounded text box to the group header or footer.

4. To sum or average all records, add a text box to the report header or footer.

5. With the text box control selected, click the Properties button on the Standard toolbar to open the Properties sheet.

6. Enter the expression starting with an equal sign in the ControlSource property box.

   Or, click Build and create the expression in the Expression Builder.

To count the number of records in each group, set the Name property to RecordCount, the ControlSource to =1, the Visible property to No, then place the text box. The text box control should be in the group header or footer part.

To create a running sum, set the RunningSum property to Over Groups (resets at 0 after a group) or to Over All (runs throughout the report). The text box should be added to the group footer. The ControlSource property in this case should be the name of the control in the detail section that tracks the total (for example, =[RecordCount]).

Help: Context Sensitive

Microsoft Access contains several different types of help, with different amounts of information. You will find access to various help methods on the Help menu, or by using the What's This? button on the right of a window's title bar.

Steps

1. Press the F1 key, or choose Help, Microsoft Access Help.

   Access opens the Help system and displays the topic it most closely associates with your current condition or position in the program.

2. Or, choose Help, Contents and Index to open the online Help system.

3. Enter keywords and phrases on the Index page of the Help system.

   Access displays a list of matching topics.

4. Double-click a topic or procedure to view it in the help system.

The What's This? button at the right of many Windows system windows and dialog boxes turns your cursor into an arrow and a question mark. If you click anything in the Database window that has a help topic associated with it, the Help system opens to that topic. Any window with a What's This? button in the title bar (a button at the right of the title bar with a question mark in it) will activate this feature when you click it.

The Microsoft on the Web command lists a variety of resources on the Internet related to Microsoft Access. If you select one of the commands on this submenu, Windows opens your browser and attempts to locate this Web page. In order for the Web page to be loaded, you must have an active connection to the Internet, otherwise the page won't be found.

Help: Microsoft Office Assistant

Microsoft *Office Assistant* is another feature that provides context-sensitive help, based on questions that you select. You can also enter a question in words or sentences that the Office Assistant will attempt to answer.

Steps

1. Click the Office Assistant button at the right of the toolbar.

   The assistant appears and provides context-sensitive help.

2. Select one of the task-oriented questions.

Hyperlinks: Copying

A *hyperlink* field stores a description of an address as either an URL (Uniform Resource Locator) for a Web address or an UNC (Universal Naming Convention) for an intranet address. The actual address is stored internally, with a description that is browsed by others. The procedure describes how to copy these values in your database.

Steps

1. Right-click a hyperlink field.

2. Choose Hyperlink, Copy Hyperlink on the shortcut menu to copy it to the Clipboard.

You can paste that hyperlink along with its description to any cell in any other hyperlink field. If you paste a hyperlink to a field of another data type, only the description is pasted into the cell.

Hyperlinks: Creating Fields to Store Hyperlinks

You can use hyperlinks in forms and datasheets to jump to the location described in that hyperlink. Locations can be other objects in Access databases, documents created by Word, Excel, or PowerPoint, and documents on the Internet or an intranet.

Access 97 now contains a new data type called a hyperlink field. A hyperlink field contains the text and numbers that comprise a hyperlink address, which is the path to the object, document, or Web page. A hyperlink address can also be an URL (Uniform Resource Locator) for an Internet or intranet address. Access recognizes a hyperlink address from the entered syntax.

Steps

1. Open the table in the Datasheet View by selecting it in the Database window on the Table page and clicking the Design button.

2. In the field list enter the field name for the new hyperlink field.

3. Tab to the Data Type column and select the hyperlink data type.

4. Click the Save button on the toolbar, or choose File, Save.

Access creates the new field, and saves any other design changes you made.

Hyperlinks: Entering a Hyperlink

Your table contains the hyperlink description as underlined text. When you click that link, you open your browser or the appropriate application and bring that document into view.

Steps

1. Open the table or query in the Datasheet or Form View.

2. Move the insertion point into the hyperlink field.

3. Enter the text you want to display for the hyperlink, if you want to provide an explanation of the underlying address.

4. Click the Insert Hyperlink button on the toolbar. Enter the UNC path or URL address into the Link to File or URL text box.

5. Or, enter the location in the Named Location in File (optional) text box; then click OK.

NOTE   To enter a hyperlink based on the location of the current file, and not on an absolute path, check the Use Relative Path for Hyperlink check box. ▓

Importing: Data

When you import data, you store the data in an Access table. When you import a text file or spreadsheet, you can append the data directly to a table. When you import from a database table you must first create a new table. Then you can use an Append query to add the data to another table in your database.

Steps

1. Open a database.

2. To import the data, choose File, Get External Data, Import.

3. In the Import dialog box, select the file format of the data of interest from the Files of Type list box.

   For example, you could select FoxPro 2.x, dBASE III, IV, or V, and so on.

4. Locate the file of interest using the Look In list box, then double-click the file.

5. If the file is a database file, Access creates the table and prompts you to select the appropriate index file that matches that database; then click Close, or Cancel if there are no indexes.

6. In the Select Unique Record Identifier dialog box, select the index that is the primary or candidate *key* that will be used to update data in queries with *joins*.

   If the file is a spreadsheet or text file, the import occurs automatically without requiring Steps 5 and 6.

Access imports the table or data source you specified.

Importing: HTML Files

When you import data you create a copy of the data in a table in your Access database, but you leave the original data source intact. You can import (read-only) an HTML table or list data source.

Steps

1. Open a database.

2. To import the data, choose File, Get External Data, Import.

   Imported data is copied into your database and can be altered. Imported data is an independent copy of the original data.

3. In the Import dialog box, select HTML Documents (*html;*.htm) from the Files of Type list box.

4. Locate the file of interest using the Look In list box.

   The Import HTML Wizard runs.

5. Use the Wizard, or its Advanced feature, to edit the import of each table or list.

Indexing: Creating Based on a Single Field

You can index a single field to serve as a method for ensuring unique values, to sort your data, or to speed up search and retrieval operations.

Steps

1. Click the field in the Table Designer and set the indexed property in the General tab to Yes (No Duplicates).

2. Click the Field Name cell in the Indexes window and select the field of interest.

   Enter an index name, and the properties you desire in the Indexes window.

TIP Double-click the Field Name in the Indexes window to move through the list of fields in that table. Double-click the Index Properties options in the bottom section of the Indexes window to cycle through the available list of index types. (This is a general feature of Property sheets.)

Indexing: Creating a Composite Index

Access allows you to create indexes based on two or more fields in your table, up to a limit of 10 fields. You can specify that a composite index is unique and use it as a primary key, or use that composite index for sorting or searching through your data. Access does not allow you to index on expressions.

Steps

1. Enter the first field in the index on a line in the Indexes window.

2. Name that index.

3. Add additional fields below that line, without naming another index, up to 10 fields.

To remove an index, click again the Primary Key button, removing the indexed property, or deleting the index in the Indexed window.

Indexing: Setting Index Properties

Indexes are listings of values or expressions in a field or combination of fields. An index in a database operates just like the index in a book. Indexes point to where something is found.

Indexes are particularly valuable in a number of database operations. They can provide a fast method for finding something, for sorting your table, and for providing a view of your data. Indexes are necessary to match the data in a field of one table to a field in another, and thus provide the means for relating one table to another.

Steps

1. Open the table in the Table Designer.

2. Click the Index button on the toolbar.

In the Indexes window you can set index properties: the Index Name (which by default takes the field(s) name but can be changed), the Sort Order, and whether the index is Primary, Unique, or Ignores Nulls.

Indexing: Setting the Primary Key

A primary index is the index used to uniquely identify records in a table. Every table must have one primary index, although other unique indexes may be defined (as so-called candidate indexes). Often the primary index is used to establish a relationship with a child table.

Steps

1. Click the field in the Table Designer.

2. Click the Primary Key button on the toolbar to make that single field's index the primary key.

 TIP You can also select multiple fields (in the order they will appear in the key), and click the Primary Key button to create a primary composite key based on the index constructed in the order the fields were added to the composite key.

To remove a primary key, with that field selected in the Table Designer, click the Primary Key button on the toolbar again, or delete the index from the Indexes window.

Linking: Data

Access lets you import and link to a wide variety of data sources. The previous section described these processes for HTML files; this section describes the situation for other data sources such as delimited text files, and database and spreadsheet data files. You can import or link to Excel, dBASE, FoxPro, Paradox, ODBC databases, and other data sources.

When you link an external data source, even a table in another Access database, that linked data source appears in the Tables section of the Database window and takes an identifying icon such as: a black table for a linked Access table, a Px symbol for a Paradox table, a dB symbol for a dBASE table, and so on. Linked tables or spreadsheets show an arrow symbol next to them.

Steps

1. Open a database.

2. To link the data, choose File, Get External Data, Link Tables on the Get External Data submenu of the File menu.

3. In the Link dialog box, select the file format of the data of interest from the Files of Type list box.

For example, you could select FoxPro 2.x, dBASE III, IV, or V, and so on.

4. Locate the file of interest using the Look In list box; then double-click the file.

5. If the file is a database file, Access creates the table and prompts you to select the appropriate index file that matches that database; then click Close, or Cancel if there are no indexes.

6. In the Select Unique Record Identifier dialog box, select the index that is the primary or candidate *key* that will be used to update data in queries with *joins*.

   If the file is a spreadsheet or text file, the link occurs automatically without requiring Steps 5 and 6.

Access links the table or data source you specified.

Linking: HTML Files

When you link data, you store a reference to that data object in its original location, and generally you can modify or update the data from within Access.

Steps

1. To link the data, choose File, Get External Data, Link.

   Linked data is viewed by reference in your database from its original location, and cannot be altered in Access.

2. In the Link dialog box, select HTML Documents (*html;*.htm) from the Files of Type list box.

3. Locate the file of interest using the Look In list box.

   The Link HTML Wizard runs.

Access imports or links to each table or list in an HTML file as if it were an individual table. You will need to repeat this procedure if your HTML file contains two or more tables or lists in it.

Mailing Labels: Creating

A mailing label is a special type of report formatted to repeat across or down a page. You have control over the contents of your mailing label through the placement of bound controls displaying your field data, text labels, graphics, and so on. You can also control the size of the labels and their repetition pattern.

Through the use of queries you can specify which records will have labels printed for them. The Label Wizard makes it particularly easy to create mailing labels.

Steps

1. Click the Reports tab in the Database window; then click New.

2. Click Label Wizard in the New Report dialog box. Select the table or query that will supply the data for the labels in the Select Table or Query drop-down list box; then click OK.

3. Select the standard Avery label you want, or click Customize and specify the label size and type; then click Next.

   To create a custom size label, click Customize and enter the size and page setup specification.

4. Select the font, size, and color of your text, then click Next.

5. Create a prototype label by moving any desired fields from the Available Fields list box to the Prototype Label text box; then click Next. To move fields, first select them and then click the Move button. Type any text you want to appear on the label (spaces, commas, and so on), then press Enter to start a new line. When your prototype label is complete, click Next.

6. Select the fields you want to sort your records, with the top field being the last field sorted (the primary sort key).

7. Finally, name your label in the last step of the wizard, then preview it and save it to disk.

If you select the Modify the Label Design radio button, then your label opens up in the Report Designer.

 TIP You can sort by any field in your underlying table or query, even those that do not appear on your prototype label.

Previewing: Layout Preview

Access 97 offers you two different types of previews: Print Preview and *Layout Preview*. In the former instance you see everything that will print to your printer, each page and all of the data contained therein. For long print jobs, it may take a while for your computer to process this information. If you want to view a small group of your records in preview, you can see an example layout in the Layout Preview mode. In this mode you see just enough data to get a feeling for all of the sections of a report.

Steps

1. With your report in Design View, click the View button on the toolbar.

2. Select the Layout Preview command.

CAUTION Layout Preview can be misleading because you don't get a view of all of your data. If you are using a *parameterized query*, for example, Layout Preview will not detect this and show you a truly representative data set. For reports that don't take a long time to process, you are better off using the Print Preview view to see your reports.

Printing: Using Dot Matrix Printers

Many people print labels to dot matrix printers using tractor feed stock. The best way to do this is to create a printer file that contains the page setup appropriate to this task.

Steps

1. Choose Start, Settings, Printers.

2. Right-click the printer you will use, then select the Properties command from the shortcut menu.

3. Click the Paper tab, and in the Paper Size section click the Custom icon.

4. Enter the size of your label in the User Defined Size dialog box.

   The width measurement extends from the left edge of the leftmost label to the right edge of the rightmost label. The length is measured from the top of the first label to the top of the second.

5. Double-click OK.

A label layout is a report layout that has no header or footer, only a detail part. If you are creating a label from scratch, then open the Page Setup dialog box from the File menu and set the following:

■ Set the Page tab to the Use Specific Printer you will use; the printer Source to User-Defined Size; and the source for label stock to Tractor, Cassette, AutoSelect tray, or whatever is appropriate.

■ Set the Columns tab to Same as Detail in the Column Size section.

■ For a layout with more than one label across on the Columns tab enter: the number of labels across in the Number of Columns text box, the amount of space between the bottom of one label and the top of another in the Row Spacing text box, the space between the right edge of one label and the left edge of the next in the Column Spacing text box, and specify whether the Column Layout is Down, then Across or Across, then Down.

■ For a dot matrix printer, specify the paper size as a User-Defined Size as described in the Numbered list above.

Printing: Using Print Preview

The Print Preview mode provides a view of your datasheet, form, query, or report as it would print to your current printer. It is always a good idea to preview your printed output rather than wasting paper.

Steps

1. Open a table, query, form, or report in either Design, Form, or Datasheet View.

2. Click the Print Preview button on the toolbar, or choose File, Print Preview.

3. Use the toolbar buttons to switch your preview view, and click the page to switch between multiple or zoomed view and single page 100% view.

If you preview a form from Design or Form View, your preview is in Form View. If you preview a form from the Datasheet View, then your preview is in the Datasheet View. If you preview a form selected in the Database window, then the DefaultView property controls the view you see in the preview mode.

The following table shows you how to perform various tasks in the Print Preview View.

To Do this	Press this
To open the Print dialog box	P or Ctrl+P
To open the Page Setup dialog box	S
To zoom in or out on a part of the page	Z
To cancel Print Preview or Layout Preview	C or Esc
To move to the page number box; then type the page number and press Enter.	F5

continues

continued

To Do this	Press this
To view the next page (when Fit To Window is selected)	Page Down or Down arrow
To view the previous page (when Fit To Window is selected)	Page Up or Up arrow
To scroll down in small increments	Down arrow
To scroll down one full screen	Page Down
To move to the bottom of the page	Ctrl+Down arrow
To scroll up in small increments	Up arrow
To scroll up one full screen	Page Up
To move to the top of the page	Ctrl+Up arrow
To scroll to the right in small increments	Right arrow
To move to the right edge of the page	End or Ctrl+Right arrow
To move to the lower-right corner of the page	Ctrl+End
To scroll to the left in small increments	Left arrow
To move to the left edge of the page	Home or Ctrl+Left arrow
To move to the upper-left corner of the page	Ctrl+Home

The Layout Preview command on the View menu allows you to see some representative data in preview mode prior to printing. Layout Preview is only available on the View menu for reports and only when they're open in Design mode. From the preview window you can merge data with Word, publish to a Word document, or analyze data with Excel. These three options are available as toolbar buttons.

NOTE   The preview mode has been substantially reworked in
Access 97 and Office 97. ■

Publishing: Web Publishing Wizard

Most people will begin their foray into database publishing to
the Web by visiting the new Web Publishing Wizard. This
wizard guides you through the process of Web page and site
creation. You start the Web Publishing Wizard by choosing
File, Save As HTML. The Web Publishing Wizard can output
datasheets, forms, and reports as static or dynamic Web documents using template files. It can create a home page or default page. You can use the Web Publishing Wizard to copy the
files and folder created to your Web server.

TIP   Microsoft Office contains a Web Fast Find Search page
that you can use to search for files on an intranet. You can locate
files by keywords. Consider including this page in any site you
create with the Web Publishing Wizard. Consult your administrator
to get a copy, or learn about the location, of this page on your
intranet.

Steps

1. Choose File, Save As HTML with a datasheet, query,
   form, or report open.

2. Click the I Want to Use a Web Publication check box,
   and select that publication if you already have created a
   Web page or set of pages in the format you want using
   the Wizard (if you don't have any Web pages already
   created, this option will be grayed out). Click Next.

3. Click either Select or Select All in the check box to select
   the table(s), query(s), form(s), or report(s) you want to
   publish. Click Next.

4. Select the HTML template document you want to use,
   then click Next. You can select the type of document you
   want to create: Static HTML, Dynamic HTX/IDC, or
   Dynamic ASP; then click Next.

5. Enter the location of the folder that you want to save your files to.

6. Click the Yes, I Want to Create a Home Page check box if you want that feature; name that page (Default is the default); then click Next.

7. On the final page of the Wizard, select the Yes, I Want to Save the Answers to the Wizard check box if you want to create a Web publication profile; enter a Profile Name; then click Finish.

Access creates the pages you specified from each object, and creates the publication profile if you specified that.

Queries: Creating a New Query

Queries are recipes for finding, selecting, sorting, and filtering data in tables. Access stores the definition of a query, runs the query, and returns a result set when the query is requested. Queries can be used as the underlying data set for forms and reports. Queries can also be used to select, append, delete, and update records in the database (see the appropriate "Action Queries" sections).

You create a new query using either the Query Wizard or the Query Design window. Both are relatively easy to use, though the Query Wizard will walk you through the process step-by-step. The Query Design Wizard provides you with additional options.

NOTE You can select records by applying a filter and sorting those records. Access 97 remembers the last filter you applied without you having to re-enter it. This is an alternative to running some queries. ■

Steps

1. Click Query Page in the Database window, then click the New button.

2. Select Design View in the New Query dialog box; then select the table(s) you want from the Show Table dialog box and click OK.

If you add related tables, Access will use the permanent relation in the Data Environment of the Query.

3. To create a relationship between two tables, drag the index of the parent tables to the related field of the child table.

4. Click the field cell in the Query Design Grid, then select the field you want to use in your query, or select the asterisk field to add all fields to your query.

5. Press the down arrow key and select the sort order for any field that you want to sort.

   Fields are sorted in their order from right to left, the left field being the primary sort key. To re-order the fields, click and drag the column header.

6. Click the Show check box for any field you want to see in the query.

   Fields can be used in queries that do not appear in the query output.

7. Enter any filter in the Selection criteria cell for that field, and additional AND statements in the same cell; enter OR statements (expanding the range of selection) into an OR clause, or on the next line beginning with the row label OR.

8. Click Save in the Query Design toolbar, or choose File, Save. Enter the name of the form in the Query Name text box of the Save As dialog box, then click OK.

Access creates the new query and saves it to disk.

TIP   You can drag a field from the Data Environment window onto the grid to have it appear, or just double-click that field.

You can also use one of the Query Wizards to create a new query. You can choose from the *Simple Query Wizard*, Crosstab Query Wizard, Find Duplicates Wizard, and Find Unmatched Query Wizards in the New Query dialog box.

ACCESS

When you run a query, the data you see reflects the data that conforms to your query at runtime. You can update, delete, or append the data in a result set.

Queries: Sorting Query Results

You can apply a sort order to the result set of a query in either Form or Datasheet View. You can also sort the result set of a filter or an advanced filter/sort.

Steps

1. Click the column(s) or field(s) you want to sort on.

2. Click either the Ascending Sort or Descending Sort buttons on the toolbar.

   Or, use the Advanced Filter/Sort window to enter those sorts.

The primary sort key is the leftmost sorted column in the Query Design grid. A sort order is saved with the datasheet or form and reapplied when you open it.

Queries: Specifying Properties

There are a number of useful properties that you can set as part of a query. These properties help you control the number of records returned in your view of the result set, optimize performance, and specify other useful options.

Steps

1. Open a query in Design View.

2. Click a field in the field row, a field list in the data environment, or elsewhere on the Design View window to select the query.

3. Click the Properties button on the toolbar to display the Property sheet for the selected object, or choose View, Properties.

4. Add your properties or expressions; then close the Property sheet.

Queries: Specifying Query Criteria

You can enter selection criteria into filters and into queries. Queries are more generally useful in that they can work with related tables of records and direct the output of the result set to several different places. Filters apply only to the current table or query and cannot be used elsewhere.

Steps

1. Enter the criteria into the design grid of the Query Designer.

2. Criteria on the same line are AND expressions that must be true for each field to be returned in the result set.

3. Enter OR expressions on two or more criteria rows in the Query Design grid.

Access allows for a wide range of values and expressions, and the Query Designer is a powerful tool for composing queries and applying criteria for selection. Access translates the query into *Structured Query Language* and applies it to the appropriate data sources (tables and grids) that the query operates on.

Records: Copying and Cutting

You can select data from one or more fields, and even one or more entire records in a datasheet or a form and move them elsewhere.

Steps

1. Open the datasheet, or a form in Form View, then select the record(s) you want to copy or move.

2. Click the Copy button on the toolbar to copy records; click the Cut button to move records.

3. Open the datasheet that is the target for these records and set up the datasheet by moving fields so that the fields match up to the records on the Clipboard. You can click and drag column headers to change the order of fields in a datasheet.

4. Select an appropriate range of records by clicking the record selector for the first record, holding the Shift key, and clicking the record selector for the last record in the range.

5. Click the Paste button on the toolbar.

   Access replaces the records you selected with the contents of the Clipboard.

   Or, to add the records at the end of the datasheet, choose Edit, Paste Append.

The same procedure can be used to paste records into forms. In order to replace records in Form View, you must be able to select a group of records that matches the number of records on the Clipboard. Also, the *tab order* or, as a minimum, the *data types* of the fields in a form's tab order, should match the contents of the Clipboard. Using the Paste Append command adds the records on the Clipboard to the end of the that file(s).

CAUTION   Getting the tab order in a form to match the data type order of fields in records on the Clipboard can be difficult. It's much easier to cut, copy, and paste data in the Datasheet View.

Records: Deleting

You can delete records one at a time manually, or delete groups of records simultaneously using the delete queries.

Steps

1. In Datasheet or Form View, select the record(s) to be deleted.

2. Click the Delete Record button on the toolbar.

> **CAUTION**   When you delete a record in the Datasheet View from a
> table involved in a relationship with another table, make sure that
> either you are enforcing Referential Integrity or that you take care of
> cascade deletions. Do not delete a parent record and leave orphaned
> child records behind.

You can use delete queries to delete groups of records in a
single operation. See also "Action Queries: Delete Query."

> **NOTE**   You can set a property in the Design View called
> AllowDeletions that controls whether users can delete records in
> a form. You can also set a property called AllowAdditions that
> controls whether records can be added. ■

Reports: Creating with Report Wizard

Reports are a display of the results of a query or the contents
of the data in data source(s) when the report is run. The data
displayed in a report cannot be modified in the data source.

Access provides a report writer or report formatting tool that
allows you to create a report format suitable to your purpose.
Reports are created in a Design View, and the results can be
previewed in either the Layout Preview or Print Preview
modes. You can switch between these views using commands
on the View menu, or by selecting these commands from the
View button's drop-down menu on the Report toolbar.

Steps

1. Click Report Page in the Database window, then click
   New.

2. Select Report Wizard in the New Report dialog box.
   Click the Choose the Table or Query drop-down list and
   select the table or query that will be the data source.
   Then click the OK button or press the Enter key.

If you don't select a table or query, your current table or query is used; or you can select the tables or queries that underlie the report in the next step.

3. In the first step of the Wizard, select the fields you want to see on your report from the Available Fields list box by moving them onto the Selected Fields list. For any related tables, select those tables from the Tables/Queries list box, add the fields of interest to the Selected Fields list box, then click Next.

4. If you are building a report based on a relationship, specify the parent table used to control the view of your data, then click Next.

5. Select the field(s) used to group your data, position them in a priority order, then click Next.

    Grouped fields are sorted and can be summarized by fields that calculate aggregate functions for that group (sums, averages, and so on).

6. Select the sort field(s) of your data with the top sort field being the primary sort key; click the Sort button to specify ascending or descending sorts; then click the Next button.

    Grouped fields are already sorted, and are not on the list of fields to be sorted.

7. Click the Summary Options button to open the Summary Options dialog box.

8. Click the types of summaries you want to see in the check boxes on the Summary Options dialog box and their placement in either the Detail and Summary parts or the Summary part alone; then click OK, followed by Next in the Report Wizard.

9. Select a layout and orientation for your report, then click Next. Select a presentation style for your report, then click Next.

10. Enter a title for the report, and click either Preview the Report or Modify the Report's Design in the last step of the Report Wizard; then click Finish.

Access creates the new report and saves it to disk. If you selected the Preview, Access opens the report in the Layout Preview mode; otherwise it appears in the Report Design window.

To switch between views of your report select the appropriate command from the View menu, or from the View button's drop-down menu in the Report Design toolbar.

Access offers you additional Report Wizards that you can try: AutoReport (Columnar), AutoReport (Tabular), Chart Wizard, and the Label Wizard. You can also create a report from scratch by selecting Design View from the New Report dialog box.

Reports: Modifying

To modify a report, you must switch to the Report Design View. In Design View you can add and remove sections or controls, format the report or any object contained therein, adjust properties, and so on.

Steps

1. In the Database window, click the report name in the Report tab you want to modify.

2. Click the Design button to open the report in Report Design View.

3. Remove or add controls (using the toolbox); change properties in the appropriate Property sheet; remove or add sections using commands on the View menu; format objects using the Formatting toolbar; and generally have a good time.

4. When done modifying your report, choose File, Save.

   Or, to save the resulting report as a different file, choose File, Save As; name and locate your file in the file system using the Save As dialog box; then click OK.

Access saves your report to disk. If you create a new report, that report's name appears in the Report tab of the Database window.

Reports: Sorting and Grouping

Your reports are based on tables or queries. When you change the basis of the query and how it is grouped and sorted, you change the grouping in a report based on that query. Reports allow you to sort and group records through their setup and layout.

Steps

1. Open the report in Design View.
2. Click the Sorting and Grouping button on the toolbar.
3. In the Sorting and Grouping dialog box, click and drag the row selector for the field or expression you want to move in the report.

Access rearranges Group header and footer sections appropriately but does not move the controls that those sections contained. That you must do manually.

Security: Limiting User Input

Access provides you with a number of different options for securing a database. To limit user input you must create and define user-level security in your database. This provides password access based on a username through a challenge/response mechanism.

You can use the User-Level Security Wizard to define which features and database objects can be used by which users. After that point, only users with an Administer permission level can perform the most sensitive functions such as database replication, password creation, and so on. Information about user group permissions, accounts, and access privileges are stored in the workgroup information file, and are opened when you log on.

Steps

1. Open the database, then choose Tools, Security, User and Group Permissions.

2. Click users or groups on the User/Group Name list on the Permission tab to select who you want to apply an access privilege or restriction.

3. Click the type of object in the Object Type drop-down list box, then click the name of the specific object in the Object Name box.

4. In the Permissions section, click on or off the permissions you desire; then click Apply.

5. When you are done adding or removing permissions, click OK.

NOTE See also "Security: Securing a Database" to learn how to control overall access to your database. ▨

Security: Securing a Database

You can secure a database by creating a password that allows the user full access to the database file. When password access is on, a user supplies a password in order to open the file. The password is encrypted and secure.

CAUTION If you set a password for opening a database, you must remember the password. If you forget that password you will lose access to your file.

Steps

1. Close the database and end any other user sessions in a multi-user Access database.

2. Create a backup copy of the database by either copying the database file in the Windows Explorer or on the Windows Desktop, or by choosing Tools, Replication, Create Replica.

3. Choose File, Open Database (Ctrl+O), or click the Open button on the toolbar; click the Exclusive check box; then click the Open button.

4. Choose Tools, Security, Set Database Password.

5. Enter your password in the Password text box, then enter it again in the Verify text box. Click the OK button.

If the two passwords match, Access enters the password for overall database file access and requires it the next time you open the file.

CAUTION   If you set a password for opening a database, you will not be able to synchronize databases using replication.

You can also create user-level security that limits the particular objects in a database that a user or group of users can read or write to. Here a user account is created and a username and password is associated with it. Groups of users can be given specific privileges, and users can be associated with accounts. This information is stored in a workgroup information file.

Microsoft Access has two built-in groups: the Admins group and a Users group, for administrators and users respectively. You assign permissions to groups such as access to tables, forms, fields, reports, and so on. One group of users (usually Admins) must have complete access to your entire database.

Security: Setting User-Level Security

To help you set user-level security for your database, Access offers you the User-Level Security Wizard. This Wizard will help get you started defining accounts and privileges.

Steps

1. Join a secure workgroup or create a new workgroup information file.

2. Choose Tools, Security, User and Group Accounts.

3. Select the Admin user account on the Users tab. Then click the Change Logon Password tab.

4. Click the New Password text box, enter a password, then enter that same password in the Verify text box. Click OK.

5. Choose Tools, Security, User-Level Security Wizard.

   The Wizard creates a new database, exports the objects from your current database to it, revokes all permissions for access to the objects, and then encrypts the new database file. The Admin group has access, but the Users group has no access to the database.

6. Choose Tools, Security, User and Group Permissions.

7. Click the User or Groups radio button and select the user or group you want to modify in the User/Group Name list box of the Permissions tab.

8. Select the kind of object from the Object Type drop-down list box. Select objects in the Object Name list box, or hold the Ctrl key and select multiple objects.

9. Select the permissions you desire in the Permissions section, then click Apply. Repeat Steps 6-9 as required; then click OK.

Access sets the permissions you indicated when you exit the User and Group Permissions dialog box.

Sorting: Datasheet View

You can sort by the values in a field or by the values in two or more fields. The last field used to sort is called the primary sort key and is always fully sorted. Sorts can be either ascending or descending, and can be performed at any time.

Steps

1. Click the Sort Ascending or Sort Descending button on the toolbar to sort by the current field, or on a group of selected fields (columns).

2. To change the sort order, click and drag the field (column) to the left.

   The leftmost selected sorted column is the primary sort key.

You can also apply an Advanced Filter/Sort using that command from the Filter submenu of the Records menu.

Choose Records, Remove Filter/Sort to remove a filter and sort and return your records to their natural order (as well as view your entire set).

Subreports: Adding to Reports

A subreport is a report that is embedded inside another report. The main report can be bound or unbound to a table, query, or an SQL statement.

Unbound reports serve as container devices into which subreports can be placed when the subreports are unrelated to one another and derive their data from different sources. You use a bound main report when you want to use subreports that use the main report's data source in different ways.

Steps

1. Open the main report in Design View; and click the Control Wizards tool in the toolbox, if necessary.

2. Click the Subform/Subreport tool in the toolbox. Make sure that the table relationships are correct before proceeding.

3. Click the location of the subreport.

4. Follow the directions in the Subform Wizard.

When you finish, a subreport control is added to your report. The Wizard also creates a separate report that is displayed as the subreport.

Tables: Adding New Records

You add new records to tables in either the Datasheet or Form View in Access.

Steps

1. Open the table or related tables in either the Datasheet or Form View.
2. Click the New Record button (>*) on the toolbar.
3. Enter the data you want in the first field, then press the Tab key to advance to the next field.
4. At the end of the record (the last field), press the Tab key to advance to the next record.

Access does not create a new record until you actually enter some data into the first field of a new record.

Tables: Creating in Datasheet View

In order to create a new table, you first have to open the database that the table will belong to. You can create a new table in several different ways:

- ▓ By entering data directly into a blank datasheet
- ▓ By running either the Database Wizard or the Table Wizard
- ▓ By designing the table in the Table Designer from scratch
- ▓ By specifying that a query be output to a new table
- ▓ By duplicating and renaming a preexisting table

Which method you use depends on whether you want to create a blank table, or one that contains existing data already. The most general method to create a table uses the Design View.

You can open a blank table as a datasheet and enter data into it. You can also open the Design View and create your table structure. When you are done designing your table, you can switch to the Datasheet View and all of the cells will be blank. If you select the Table Wizard, then it can create a structure for a set of suggested table(s), and they too will be blank when you open them.

Steps

1. Click the Tables tab in the Database window; then click the New button.

2. In the New Table dialog box, click Datasheet View; then click OK.

Access creates a datasheet with default field names that is blank on your screen. Enter data, and save the file to your disk.

Tables: Creating in Design View

A convenient place to create the structure of your database tables is the Table Designer. This is the only place where you can add and remove fields, and serves as a very convenient place to get an overview of the properties associated with your fields and tables.

Steps

1. Click the Tables page in the Database window, then click New.

2. Select Design View in the New Table dialog box, then click OK.

3. Enter a name for a field in the Field Name column, then tab and enter the data type in the Data Type column.

4. Proceed to enter into the Description column the information that is displayed in the status bar when the insertion point is in that field in the table. Enter Field Size (number of characters), Format and *Input Mask* (display and allowable characters), Caption (for the Datasheet view), Default Values, Validation rules, and other properties in the General section.

5. Click the next blank line of the field grid and create the next field in your database; then repeat Step 4. To *insert* a field, click the Insert Rows button on the Table Design

toolbar, or select the Insert Rows command on the Insert
menu.

6. To select the field you want to use to create a primary
   key, click the field selector to the right of the field name.
   Or, select multiple fields for a compound primary key by
   holding the Ctrl key and clicking each field selector; then
   click the Primary Key button on the toolbar.

7. Click Save on the Table Design toolbar or choose File,
   Save; enter a name for the table in the Table Name text
   box of the Save Table dialog box and click OK.

Access creates the new table and saves it to disk.

NOTE   You don't have to assign a primary key, but it is
recommended. Make sure that the order of a compound primary
key is correct. You can change the order by clicking the Indexes
button on the toolbar and reordering the field names in the index
that comprises the Primary Key. ▓

Tables: Creating a New Table by Importing

Microsoft Access can import tables from other Access databases and from data created in several other databases and
spreadsheets that save their data to standard file formats.
Among the programs that Access can import data from are:
Microsoft Excel, dBASE, Microsoft FoxPro, Paradox, Lotus
1-2-3, and many others.

If what you want to do is to read and write to the source table,
see also "Tables: Creating a New Table by Linking."

Steps

1. Open the database that will contain the linked table, and
   view the Database window.

2. Choose File, Get External Data, Import.

3. In the Import dialog box select the appropriate file
   format in the Files of Type drop-down list; then locate
   the table or spreadsheet of interest using the Look In
   list box.

4. Select the table or spreadsheet, then click Import.

5. You can repeat the process to import additional tables.

Access adds the imported table to your database and displays its name in the Database window as an Access file.

Tables: Creating a New Table by Linking

The process of linking to a table in Access is similar in operation to importing a table. In the former case, the original table serves as the data source and only a reference to that table is contained in your Access database. When you link to a table, you can view and often also modify the data in that table. Access takes care of the details of opening the table and saving it in the appropriate data format.

When you import a new table, a copy of the table is created in the Microsoft Access format. The source table is left intact. When you link to a table in Access, you see different icons for the tables in the Tables section of the Database window. A dBASE table shows the dB symbol, Paradox at Px symbol, and other Access tables show a datasheet icon.

By comparison, when you import a table, you create a copy of that table in your database, and Access converts the table into its own format and incorporates the data inside an Access database file.

Steps

1. Open the database that will contain the linked table, and view the Database window.

2. Choose File, Get External Data, Link Table.

3. In the Link dialog box select the appropriate file format in the Files of Type drop-down list; then locate the table or spreadsheet of interest using the Look In list box.

4. Select the table or spreadsheet, then click the Link button.

What happens next depends on the data source you selected.

- For Access, unencrypted Paradox tables, or spreadsheets, Access tables and spreadsheets are imported directly.

- For FoxPro or dBASE, if you have selected a FoxPro or dBASE table, then a dialog box appears asking you to associate that table with the corresponding index (.CDX or .IDX) file; for dBASE you would associate the table with an .MDX or .NDX file.

  Select the index(es), then click Close or Cancel if no index exists.

  Enter the index that identifies each record in the Select Unique Record Identifier dialog box.

  Normally that index is the primary index, but it can also be candidate indexes for these two databases.

- For encrypted Paradox tables, Access prompts you for the password; enter the password and click OK.

- For data in HTML files select the HTML file in the Import dialog box and the Link HTML Wizard appears.

  Follow the steps in the Link HTML Wizard.

Access adds the linked table to your database and displays its name and an appropriate icon in the Tables page of the Database window.

Tables: Creating with Table Wizard

The Table Wizard is a very fast way of creating tables. It lets you structure tables based on fields in existing tables, create rudimentary table relationships, and specify a primary key.

Steps

1. Click Tables Page in the Database window, then click New.

2. Select Table Wizard in the New Table dialog box, then click OK.

3. Click the Business or Personal radio button to view a set of sample tables.

4. Select the table(s) you want to view fields from in the Sample Tables list box; then move the fields of interest from the Available fields list box to the Fields in My New Table list box; click Next.

   Use the Rename Field button to rename any selected field you added. Use the same data type for your fields when you rename a field.

5. Enter a name in the text box; select either Yes, for the Wizard to set a primary key, or No because you will set the primary key radio button; click Next.

6. Select any desired relationships in the My New <Tablename> Table Is list box; then click the Next button.

7. Enter the name of the table and select from one of the following: Modify the table design; Enter data directly in the table; or Enter data into the table from a form that the Wizard creates for you. Click Finish.

Access creates the new table and saves it to disk. If you selected to modify the table design, you end up viewing the Design window. For the Enter Data Directly selection in the last step, you see a Datasheet window. For the form selection, a form is created for you.

Tables: Creating Using Datasheet View

The datasheet method is a very fast method for creating tables, but is limited in its capabilities. It is best used for small tables where you will add features later to the table design. It does not create table relationships, nor does it provide for data validation or database rules.

Steps

1. Click Tables Page in the Database window, then click the New button.

2. Select Datasheet View in the New Table dialog box. A datasheet with 20 columns and 30 rows appears with default field names.

3. Rename the column headings by double-clicking them and entering your field name(s); press Enter or click another column or value in the datasheet.

4. Enter data into the datasheet; each column is a field and each row is a record.

5. Click Save on the Table Datasheet toolbar, or choose File, Save. Enter the name of the table in the Table Name text box in the Save As dialog box, then click OK.

   An alert box is posted asking you if Access can create a primary key; click Yes if you haven't created a field with unique values that can identify each row of your datasheet (records in the table), or No if you have created such a field.

NOTE Use a consistent style of data for dates, times, numbers, and so on, so that Access can create a data type and display format based on the values it sees you enter. ▪

TIP If you need more than 20 columns, click a column to the right of your new field, then choose Insert, Column.

Access creates the new table and saves it to disk. When you have Access create the primary key, it creates an AutoNumber field that has sequential numbers entered into it.

Tables: Locating Data

There are several ways of locating data in Microsoft Access. If you are interested in locating data in groups of records, then you should apply a filter or a query to your data set. For locating a particular value, one occurrence at a time, you can use the Find dialog box.

Steps

1. Open a table, query, or form, and position the insertion point in the field you want to search (optional).

2. Choose Edit, Find, or press Ctrl+F to view the Find dialog box.

3. Enter the string or value you want to search for in the Find What text box, and select the Search range: All (default), Up, or Down.

4. Enter the Match criteria: Any Part of a Field, Whole Field, or Start of Field. Select the Match Case check box if you want the search to be case-sensitive.

5. Select the Search Field as Formatted check box when you want to search a field that has data entered into it one way and displayed another (such as a date field where 1/1/96 was entered, but you want to search for Jan 1, 1996). Leave the Search Only Current Field to limit your search, or click this check box off to search the entire data set.

6. Click Find First to go to the first match; then Find Next to go to the next match. Click Close when you are finished with your search.

Tables: Modifying

To modify a table, you must select that table in the Database window and open the table in the Table Design View. In this view you can add or remove fields; change field names; change a field's data type; and add, modify, or delete descriptions, field validations, and table rules.

Steps

1. Open the database and select the table name in the Tables tab of the Database window.

2. Click the Design button.

3. Make your changes or additions in the Table Design View.

4. Choose Insert, Rows to add fields, or Edit, Delete Rows.

5. Choose View, Indexes to create or modify table indexes, or View, Properties to add or alter field or table properties.

6. Enter any General field properties like Captions, Default Values, Format, Input Masks, Validation Rule, Validation Text, Allow Zero Length, Required (mandatory data entry), and so on, that you want.

7. When done modifying your table, choose File, Save. Or, to save the resulting table as a different file, choose File, Save As; name and locate your table in the file system using the Save As dialog box; then click OK.

Access saves your table to disk. If you create a new table, that table's name appears in the Table tab of the Database window.

TIP   You can use the buttons on the Table Design toolbars to perform these functions.

CAUTION   Pay particular attention to modifying the data type of an existing field. When you change data types, you have the potential for data loss due to data type mismatch. Your previous field's data may be truncated or discarded completely. Once it is gone, it is gone forever (except in the backup you just recently made prior to this operation).

Tables: Replacing Data

You can use the Replace command to find and replace all or some of the occurrences of a particular value in your tables or queries. You can use the Datasheet or Form View for this purpose.

In the Replace dialog box you specify the value or string that you will replace your match with, and you can use the Replace All button to perform a single replacement for all matches. You can also replace values one at a time using the Find Next button and then the Replace button in sequence.

NOTE   If you want to find and replace *nulls* or zero length strings, you have to manually enter the replacement values as you find them. ■

Steps

1. Open a table, query, or form in Datasheet or Form View.

2. Choose Edit, Replace.

3. Enter the value to find in the Find What text box and the value used to replace it in the Replace With text box.

4. Click the Find Next button followed by the Replace button to replace the next occurrence. Or, click the Replace All button to replace all matches.

5. Click Close when you are done.

Tables: Setting Relationships

When you define a relationship between two tables, you match the values in one table to one or more values in another table. In order to create a relationship, one or both of the tables requires that the values used in the match be unique. Normally an index in the controlling or parent table is used, and a field or index in the child table is matched.

Steps

1. Click the Relationship button on the toolbar to open the Relationship window.

2. Click and drag a relationship between a field or index onto the parent table and the field in the child table.

Relationships are objects; you can click them to select them, right-click them to view their shortcut menu, and open their Property sheet by selecting the Property command from the shortcut menu. You can also select a relationship and press the Delete key to remove it.

Tables: Setting Table Properties

A number of important table properties can be specified that affect the way in which data is stored and accessed. Two different groups of properties can be accessed.

Steps

1. Right-click the table in the Table tab of the Database window and select the Properties command from the shortcut menu.

2. Enter the description and whether the table is hidden.

   Or, right-click the fields selection box in the Table Designer (to the left of the leftmost column header of the field grid), and select the Properties command in the shortcut menu there.

   There you can set validation rules and validation text, description, and a few other general properties.

Of the two different types of Properties sheets, the latter is more useful and used more often.

Toolbars: Customizing

When you are displaying a datasheet or are in Design View for a form or report, you can display the formatting toolbar by choosing View, Toolbars. This toolbar contains a number of shortcuts for formatting your data and the controls on your reports or forms.

The Table Design toolbar normally appears when you open the Table Designer to modify an existing table or to create a new one. If that toolbar is not in view, you can bring it into view by choosing View, Toolbars, Table Design. The condition of the toolbar, and which buttons are active, is determined by the current state of the Table Design window.

Steps

1. Choose View, Toolbar, Customize.

2. Click a toolbar check box to bring that toolbar into view.

3. Click the Properties button and make your selections from the Toolbar Properties dialog box; or click the Restore Defaults button to return to the default toolbar condition.

4. Click the Close buttons in both dialog boxes to close them and make your changes.

   Or, click the Reset button to restore Access' default toolbar behavior.

Toolbox: Using a Tool

You see the toolbox normally when you are in the Form or Report Design View. The toolbox contains buttons that let you create and manage controls.

Steps

1. Click the Toolbox button on the toolbar to bring it into view.

2. To use a tool in the toolbox, click the button for that tool. To use a tool repeatedly, double-click the tool first. That tool stays locked until you either click another tool or press the Esc key.

Excel

Excel is the powerful, full-featured spreadsheet program that comes with Microsoft Office. Excel is a versatile tool that can be used for simple applications or complex financial planning.

You can use Excel to create charts of your financial data, such as bar charts, area charts, and pie charts. In addition, the data mapping feature enables you to view the relationships between numbers and geographical data. Excel also can help you organize data, using some common database features such as sorting, extracting, and finding data.

Alignment: Aligning Cell Entries

Excel automatically aligns entries within a cell, according to the data you enter. When you enter text in a cell, Excel horizontally aligns the data to the left of the cell. When you enter numbers, Excel aligns them to the right. You can specify how you want data aligned: to the left, to the right, centered, justified within a cell, or centered across a range of cells.

By default, Excel aligns text and numbers at the bottom edge of a cell. You also can change the vertical *alignment* of cell data so that the data is displayed at the top edge or centered in a cell or justified between the top and bottom edges. In addition, you can change the orientation of cell data, or you can wrap text within a cell.

Steps

1. Select the cell or range containing data you want to align.
2. Choose Format, Cells. Click the Alignment tab.

3. Select one of the alignment options in the Horizontal drop-down list; then select one of the alignment options in the Vertical drop-down list.

4. In the Orientation area, change the text orientation, if desired.

5. Select one or more of the Text Control options, if desired: Wrap Text, Shrink to Fit, and Merge Cells. Click OK.

 TIP You can quickly align data by selecting a cell or range and then clicking one of the following buttons on the Formatting toolbar: Align Left, Center, Align Right, or Merge and Center.

Auditing: Displaying the Auditing Toolbar

Excel's *auditing* tools help you trace errors in your worksheets. To use these auditing tools, you must first display the Auditing toolbar. Unlike the Standard and Formatting toolbars, the Auditing toolbar doesn't automatically appear on-screen.

Steps

1. Choose Tools, Auditing.

2. Select the Show Auditing Toolbar option.

Auditing: Locating Errors in a Worksheet

Excel enables you to set up relationships among the various cells in the worksheet. However, if you run into an error in the worksheet, you may need to trace those various relationships to find the error. You can use the Auditing toolbar when you need to trace an error.

Steps

1. Click the cell containing the error.

2. Click the Trace Error button on the Auditing toolbar. An arrow or arrows appear showing the source of the error.

3. Correct the error.

4. To remove the arrow(s), click the Remove All Arrows button on the Auditing toolbar.

Auditing: Tracing Formulas

You can display *tracer lines* to find *precedents* (cells that are referred to by a formula), *dependents* (cells that contain formulas that refer to other cells), and errors in any cell. Most of the time, you probably want to trace the precedents to a formula to find out what other cells contribute to the formula in that cell.

Steps

1. Click the cell whose precedents you want to trace.

2. Click the Trace Precedents button, located on the far left end of the Auditing toolbar. An arrow or arrows appear showing the precedents.

3. To remove the arrow(s), click the Remove Precedent Arrows button, the second button from the left end of the Auditing toolbar.

NOTE The tracer lines show the flow of data through the worksheet by connecting the active cell with related cells. The line ends with an arrow pointing to a formula. ■

TIP Double-click the arrow to go directly to the cell the arrow points to. Double-click the arrow a second time to highlight the formula precedents. This feature works as a toggle.

AutoComplete: Entering Duplicate Data

The *AutoComplete* feature makes it easy to enter repeated text items in a column. Instead of typing the same text items over and over, you only need to type the entire entry once in a column. The next time you want to type the same text in the column, you can type the first few letters of this entry. Excel completes the rest of the entry for you.

In a business expenses worksheet, you might have categories for Travel, Lodging, Entertainment, and so on. You must type the complete name, such as Travel, the first time you enter these items in a column. The next time, however, you might only have to type the letter **T** to enter the word Travel.

Steps

1. Type a complete entry into a cell and press Enter to move down one cell.

2. Begin typing the same entry in the next cell of the same column; Excel automatically inserts the rest of the entry.

3. Press Enter to accept the entry that Excel suggests, or keep typing if you want to enter a different text item. Press Enter when you finish typing the entry.

TIP To see a list of possible cell entries in a column, right-click a cell in that column and choose Pick from List from the shortcut menu. Click an item in the list to insert the entry; or press Esc to clear the list without inserting an item.

NOTE You can use an apostrophe to reject an autocorrected entry that you don't want. For example, if one column entry is Titles, and you want to enter the letter T below it, you can't just type **T** and press Enter as you normally would. First, type the apostrophe, then type **T**, and then press Enter. ■

AutoFormats: Applying

AutoFormats are 15 different pre-defined format styles for data. They combine a smaller list of formatting controls: font size, patterns, data alignment, and table borders and lines, creating special visual effects. Several formats present a green-bar look; others create effects commonly seen in the Internet and intranet applications.

Steps

1. Highlight the range of data to apply the AutoFormat to.

2. Choose F<u>o</u>rmat, <u>A</u>utoFormat. The AutoFormat dialog box appears.

3. As you click the pre-defined formats shown in the <u>T</u>able Format list box, the layout and formatting elements can be seen in the Sample frame to the right.

4. To use only selected formatting elements, click the <u>O</u>ptions button. The Formats to Apply group is available at the bottom of the AutoFormat dialog box. Click in the different check boxes to define the format elements to apply to the selected data range.

5. Click OK to close the dialog box and apply the AutoFormat.

Charts: Changing Chart Types

At any point, you can change the *chart type* to represent another type of data. You can change to any of the chart types that Excel offers: bar charts, line charts, pie charts, or special custom charts like floating bar charts. When you switch chart types, Excel retains the data used to create the chart.

Steps

1. Right-click a blank area of the chart, and choose Chart Type from the shortcut menu.

2. In the Chart Type dialog box, click the Standard Types or Custom Types tab.

3. Select the chart type you want, and then click OK. Resize the chart, if necessary.

NOTE Make sure you use an appropriate chart type for the data you want to graph. Bar charts illustrate individual values at a specific point in time. Line charts illustrate changes in a large number of values over a period of time. Pie charts show the relationship of each part to the whole. ■

EXCEL

CAUTION   In some cases, data may be more effective when presented in a table or text chart. Don't overwhelm your charts with a large number of data points. You can make your charts more effective by combining data into logical units.

Charts: Changing Fonts and Styles

You can change fonts and styles in charts just as you change them in worksheets. First, select the elements you want to change and then make the changes.

Steps

1. Click the text element you want to format.

2. If you want to format only individual characters within a text element, select those characters.

3. Click a button on the Formatting toolbar for the format you want to change. For example, click the Font button to change the font, or click the Italic button to italicize the text.

Charts: Changing Object Colors, Patterns, and Borders

Excel provides many options and commands that enable you to enhance your chart objects. You can easily add or change the colors, patterns, and borders of objects in a chart. Excel 97 includes several new patterns, including interesting gradients and textures, that you can use in your charts.

Steps

1. Right-click the chart object and choose Format from the shortcut menu.

2. In the Format dialog box, click the Patterns tab.

3. In the Border group, select the desired border options. In the Area group, select the desired color.

4. To select a fill effect (pattern), click Fill Effects. Click one of the tabs and choose the pattern you want; then click OK to return to the Format dialog box. When you are finished, click OK.

 TIP If you want to change the color or pattern for the chart background, right-click any edge of the chart and choose Format Chart Area from the shortcut menu. Make your desired selections and click OK.

Charts: Creating Picture Charts

Excel charts can use pictures as markers in place of columns, bars, or lines. You can use this feature to make picture charts that draw attention and then communicate the information.

You can use the Picture tab in the Fill Effects dialog box to select a graphic file that is stored on your computer and use it to replace the data markers for the selected data series.

Steps

1. Right-click the data series in the chart that you want to replace with a picture, and choose Format Data Series. You can also select the plot or chart area and fill in the background with a picture.

2. In the Format Data Series dialog box, click the Patterns tab. Then, choose Fill Effects and click the Picture tab.

3. Choose Select Picture and change to the drive and folder where the image is stored in the Look In box. Select the file for the picture you want to insert and click OK.

4. Choose other options on the Picture tab, as desired. Experiment with various options to see which effect (Stretch, Stack, or Stack and Scale) looks best on your chart.

5. For 3-D charts, select the options you want from the Apply To group; click OK twice to return to the worksheet.

EXCEL

Charts: Creating Using Chart Wizard

Charts enable you to present worksheet data in graphical form so that your viewers can more easily understand the information. When you create a chart, the worksheet data used to create the chart is linked to the chart. When the worksheet data changes, the chart is updated to reflect those changes. You can change chart types and elements within a chart such as colors and fonts.

In Excel, you can create charts quickly using the *Chart Wizard*. You can add a chart directly to the worksheet, or you can create a separate chart sheet.

Steps

1. Select the data that you want to chart, and then click the Chart Wizard button in the Standard toolbar.

2. Select the type of chart you want in the Chart Type list; then choose Next.

3. Verify the chart data range and specify whether you want to plot the series in rows or columns; then choose Next.

4. Choose the appropriate tab, then enter chart options (as desired) for titles, axes, gridlines, legend, data labels, and data table; then choose Next.

5. Select whether you want the chart to appear as a new sheet or as a chart object in one of the existing worksheets. Choose Finish. The chart appears in the worksheet (or as a separate sheet).

 TIP To move a chart object, select it, then drag an edge of the chart to the desired location. To change the size or proportions of the chart, drag one of the black handles along the borders until the chart is sized and proportioned the way you want.

Charts: Formatting Axes

When you create a chart, Excel uses the default settings for the axis style, tick marks, and scaling. You can customize the axis, changing the style of the line used for the axis, the tick marks, the positioning of the tick-mark labels, and the scaling of the axis.

Steps

1. Right-click the axis line you want to customize, and choose Format Axis from the shortcut menu.

2. In the Format Axis dialog box, click the Patterns tab and then select one of the Axis options.

3. Select the desired options from the Major Tick Mark Type and Minor Tick Mark Type areas.

4. Select an option in the Tick Mark Labels area to specify where the tick-mark labels should be positioned.

5. Check to see if the line in the sample box looks the way you want, and then choose OK.

Charts: Formatting Data Series

You can enhance the presentation of your data by adding error bars or data labels to a data series. You also can change the gap width between the columns in a column chart, and make other formatting changes. You access these options from the Format dialog box.

Steps

1. Right-click the data series you want to format, and choose Format Data Series from the shortcut menu.

2. In the Format Data Series dialog box, click the tab containing the options you want to change (such as Error Bars, Data Labels, Series Order, or Options).

3. Select the options you want to change. Click OK when you are finished.

Charts: Formatting Numbers

You can format the numbers in a chart just as you format the numbers in a worksheet. You can, for example, add dollar signs to the numbers on the value (Y) axis or change the format of numbers used as data labels.

If the numbers in the worksheet you used to create the chart are formatted, the numbers used in the value axis in the chart are formatted the same way. You can override this formatting, however, or add formatting if the numbers in the chart are unformatted.

Steps

1. Right-click the object whose numbers you want to format, and then choose Format from the shortcut menu.

2. In the Format dialog box, click the Number tab, then select the number format you want from the Category list.

3. The Format dialog box changes to display options that relate to your category choice. Change any of these options, as desired. A sample of what the format looks like appears at the top of the dialog box. Click OK.

TIP   To return the formatting to the numbers in the source worksheet, select the Linked to Source option in the Format dialog box.

Charts: Formatting Titles and Labels

For some text objects in charts, such as titles, you can change both the horizontal and vertical alignment, as well as the orientation of the text. For other objects, such as the labels on the axes, you can change only the orientation. You can rotate axis titles or text boxes that contain explanations.

Steps

1. Right-click the text object, and choose Format cells from the shortcut menu.

2. In the Format dialog box, click the Alignment tab.

3. Select the desired alignment options from the Horizontal and Vertical drop-down lists.

4. Drag the pointer in the Orientation box up or down to change the orientation of the text, or specify a value in the Degrees spin box between 90 and -90 degrees. Click OK.

TIP To quickly select a stacked orientation, reading top to bottom, click the box to the left of the Orientation gauge.

Charts: Saving

A chart that you embedded in a worksheet is saved when you save the workbook that contains the worksheet. A chart in its own sheet also is saved when you save the related workbook.

Steps

1. Modify the chart, as desired.

2. Click the Save button on the Standard toolbar.

3. If the Save As dialog box appears, type a name for the workbook that contains the chart, and then click Save.

NOTE When you format and enhance a chart in Excel 97 and save it as an earlier version file, you may lose some of the formatting or enhancements. This is due to incompatibilities between Excel 97 and earlier versions of Excel. ■

Colors: Adding a Pattern or Color

Just as fonts and attributes can enhance your worksheets, patterns and colors can help clarify meaning and help make important data stand out by differentiating parts of the screen. With Excel, you also can change the color of fonts. If you have a color printer, you can print these colors.

Steps

1. Select the cell or range to which you want to add color or a pattern (or both).

2. Choose Format, Cells.

3. Click the Patterns tab, and select the main color for your pattern from the Color grid.

4. Select a pattern from the Pattern drop-down list.

5. If you want the pattern to appear in color (instead of black), select a background color from the lower portion of the Pattern drop-down list. Check the Sample area at the bottom-right corner of the dialog box to see the color and pattern. Click OK.

TIP You can use the Format, *Conditional Formatting* command to format cells in a color or pattern you choose, depending on whether or not specific conditions in the cell are met. In a sales worksheet, for example, you can format a cell so that data appears in red if the value in the cell falls below a lower limit, or blue if the cell's value exceeds an upper limit.

Colors: Using Buttons on the Formatting Toolbar

You also can use buttons in the Formatting toolbar to change the color used for the cell background or the text in the cell.

Steps

1. Select the cell or range you want to format.

2. To change the background color, click the down arrow next to the Fill Color button on the Formatting toolbar; or, to change the font color, click the down arrow next to the Font Color button. You see a palette of colors.

3. Click the color you want to use.

TIP Another way to add shading is with the Light Shading and Dark Shading buttons. These buttons can be found in the Formatting category in the Commands tab of the Customize dialog box. You can add them to any toolbar. To use a shading button, just select the cells you want shaded and then click the button.

Columns: Changing Width

You can improve the appearance of your worksheet by adjusting the width of columns to fit the data contained in those columns. Adjusting column widths can also help you fit more data on-screen or in a printout. If a column is not wide enough to display a number, date, or time, Excel lets you know by displaying # characters in the cell.

Steps

1. Select multiple adjacent columns by dragging the pointer across the column letters. Select non-adjacent columns by pressing Ctrl and clicking the letter in each column's header.

2. Move the pointer onto the column separator directly to the right of the column heading. To change the width of column B, for example, move onto the line between the B and C headers. The pointer changes to a two-headed, horizontal arrow.

3. Drag the column left or right until the shadow is where you want it; then release the mouse button. All selected columns adjust to the same width.

 TIP To fit the column to its widest entry using the mouse, double-click the column heading separator (the vertical line between column headings) on the right side of the column you want adjusted.

Columns: Displaying Hidden Columns

If one or more column letters appear to be missing in the worksheet frame, this is because the columns have been hidden from view. You can easily redisplay a hidden column if you need to see or edit data in that column.

Steps

1. In the worksheet frame, drag across a range of columns that spans the hidden column.

2. Right-click one of the selected columns.

3. From the shortcut menu, choose Unhide.

Columns: Hiding

Excel also enables you to hide confidential data within a column. When you generate a worksheet for multiple users, you may not want to print all the information that you enter. You can hide columns temporarily so that they do not print or appear on-screen.

Steps

1. Right-click the column heading of the column you want to hide.

2. From the shortcut menu, choose Hide.

Customizing Excel: Displaying Formulas

You may at times prefer to see the formulas in your worksheets (such as =8-6) rather than the results of the formulas (such as 2). Perhaps you want to evaluate the structure of a worksheet to see that the formulas are correct.

Steps

1. Choose Tools, Options.

2. Click the View tab.

3. In the Window Options area, select the Formulas check box. Click OK.

If you change your mind and want to see the results of the formulas, repeat the steps and deselect the Formulas check box.

Customizing Excel: Hiding Row and Column Headings

If you are working with a small number of rows and columns, you may not need to refer to the column and row headings (sometimes referred to as the worksheet frame) as you work. You may also choose to remove these headings from the screen to increase the visible workspace on the screen.

Steps

1. Choose Tools, Options.
2. Click the View tab.
3. In the Window Options area, clear the Row & Column Headers check box.

NOTE There are other parts of the Excel worksheet that you can hide from view. Some of these options appear on the View tab when you choose Tools, Options. For example, you can hide the Formula Bar, the Status Bar, the Sheet Tabs, and the Horizontal or Vertical scroll bars. ■

Customizing Excel: Hiding Workbooks

Workbooks can become quite cluttered as you work with them. To simplify your workspace, you can hide the entire workbook. (See also "Customizing Excel: Hiding Worksheets.")

Steps

1. Place the mouse pointer in the workbook you want to hide.
2. Choose Window, Hide.

(See also "Customizing Excel: Restoring Hidden Workbooks.")

CAUTION When you hide a workbook, it remains hidden after you quit Excel and then try to open the workbook again. If you will not be using your workbook for some time, or if others need to access the same workbook, you may forget that you have hidden the workbook. You should remember to unhide workbooks each time you finish using Excel.

Customizing Excel: Hiding Worksheets

You may want to hide only selected worksheets in a workbook. Perhaps you have three sheets and want to work with just two of them. (See also "Customizing Excel: Hiding Workbooks.")

Steps

1. Click the sheet tab for the worksheet you want to hide.
2. Choose Format, Sheet.
3. Select the Hide option.

TIP   You can hide more than one worksheet in a workbook. Click the first sheet tab, then hold down Ctrl and click the other sheets you want to hide. (The sheets do not need to be adjacent.) Then follow the steps above to hide the selected worksheets.

NOTE   If your workbook includes just one worksheet, you cannot hide that worksheet. To get around this problem, insert a new worksheet in your workbook; then hide the other worksheet. ■

(See also "Customizing Excel: Restoring Hidden Worksheets.")

Customizing Excel: Placing a Workbook on the Start Menu

If you use the same Excel workbook every day, such as a sales data workbook, you can place that workbook on the Windows 95 Start menu. Then, when you click the workbook icon on the Start menu, both Excel and the workbook open automatically.

Steps

1. Open Windows Explorer, and find the workbook you want to open each time you start Excel.
2. Drag the icon to the Start Menu folder (normally located in the Windows folder).

3. Windows 95 places an icon for the workbook on the Start menu. Click the icon to start Excel with your workbook open.

Customizing Excel: Restoring Hidden Workbooks

If you need to modify or view a hidden workbook, you will first need to restore the workbook.

Steps

1. Choose Window, Unhide.

2. In the Unhide dialog box, select the name of the workbook you want to display. Click OK.

Customizing Excel: Restoring Hidden Worksheets

If you need to modify or view a hidden worksheet, you will first need to restore the worksheet.

Steps

1. Choose Format, Sheet.

2. Select the Unhide option.

3. In the Unhide dialog box, select the name of the worksheet you want to display. Click OK.

Customizing Excel: Setting Startup Switches

You can set a number of switches to control how Excel starts. For instance, you might not want to see the Excel startup screen and a new, blank workbook each time.

Steps

1. In Windows Explorer, find the Microsoft Excel shortcut icon (open the Windows folder, then open the Start Menu folder and click the Programs folder).

2. Right-click the Microsoft Excel icon, and then click Properties.

3. Click the Shortcut tab.

4. In the Target text box, place the cursor after the path to Microsoft Excel, type a space, then type the switch you want to use. If you type /e, for instance, the startup screen and blank workbook won't appear. Setting Excel to start this way makes it load more quickly than with a file.

 TIP For information on additional startup switches available in Excel, search for the topic "switches" in Excel Help.

Customizing Excel: Starting Excel with a Group of Workbooks

You may have a group of workbooks that you use together, such as sales profiles from a number of different districts. Through the use of a workspace file, Excel enables you to open multiple workbooks at a time when you start the program.

Steps

1. Open all the workbooks that you want to open together each time you start Excel.

2. Position the workbooks as you want them to appear.

3. Choose File, Save Workspace.

4. Type a name for the workspace file, and then choose Save.

5. Save the workspace file in the XLStart folder in the Microsoft Excel folder.

 TIP You don't have to use XLStart as your startup folder. To specify a different startup folder, choose Tools, Options, and then click the General tab. In the Alternate Startup File Location text box, type the name of the alternate folder.

> **CAUTION**   If you do set up an alternate startup folder, limit the number of workbooks in it to just those you want. Excel will attempt to open every file in the folder.

Data Mapping: Adding and Formatting Text Labels

You can add text labels with the size and font you want anywhere on your map.

Steps

1. Double-click the map to activate it.
2. Click the Add Text button in the toolbar.
3. Click the insertion point in the map where you want the text to appear and type the text; then press Enter.
4. Repeat Step 3 for each additional label you want to add.

TIP   You can drag text anywhere in the map. To format it, right-click the text, select Format Font from the shortcut menu, and then make your formatting selections from the Font dialog box.

Data Mapping: Adding New Map Data

You can add new data to an existing data map at any time. You can either insert data within existing categories, or add entirely new categories (columnar data) to display in the map.

Steps

1. In the worksheet, type the new data in its own column (adjacent to the existing columns of data).
2. Double-click the data map to activate it.
3. Choose Insert, Data.
4. When the Microsoft Map dialog box appears, drag across the entire data range you want to map (existing data and new data); then click OK.

5. The Microsoft Map Control now includes additional buttons that correspond to the data you have added. Drag the new column buttons into the working area to add the data to the map.

TIP Double-click the column buttons at the top of the Microsoft Map Control to see the source for the data.

(See also "Data Mapping: Changing the Column Source.")

Data Mapping: Changing the Column Source

You can use the Microsoft Map Control to plot different columns of data and watch the map change.

Steps

1. Double-click the map to activate it.

2. If the Microsoft Map Control doesn't appear, click the Show/Hide Microsoft Map Control button in the toolbar.

3. Drag a column button from the top of the Microsoft Map Control down on top of a column button in the working area (the white box inside the Microsoft Map Control).

4. The dropped column button replaces the column button in the working area, and the map redraws to show the new column of data. If necessary, click the Map Refresh button to update the map.

Data Mapping: Creating a Basic Data Map

Excel provides the capability to present geographical data in map form. Just as charts enable you to see trends and the relationships between numbers, *data mapping* enables you to see the relationships between numbers and geographic features.

Why Use Maps?

Maps can be used for many common business applications that involve geographical data. For example, you can create a map that shows how sales and commissions are distributed by region.

Maps Provided with Excel

The following are geographical maps that come with Excel: Australia, Canada, Europe, Mexico, North America, Southern Africa, U.K. Standard Regions and ROI, United States (with AK and HI inset), United States in North America, and World Countries.

The Data Map feature is an Excel add-in written by MapInfo Corporation. Although the maps and data that come with Excel may suit your needs, you can also purchase add-in maps, data, and feature extensions from MapInfo. These maps include census data and feature data such as roads, cities, and airports. For more information on how to contact MapInfo and purchase these items, activate a data map and choose <u>H</u>elp, How to Get More <u>D</u>ata.

Steps

1. Select the range containing the geographic identifiers and associated data that you want to map. The geographic identifiers should appear in the first column, with data column(s) appearing to the right. Include the headings at the top of the columns.

2. Click the Map button in the Standard toolbar, then drag across the area where you want the map to appear (make the map frame as large as possible). Release the mouse button.

3. If the Data Map feature cannot determine a unique map to use when it analyzes the left column of data, it displays the Multiple Maps Available dialog box. Select the map you want to use and then click OK to display the map.

4. Use the Microsoft Map Control dialog box to specify the column of data and which type of map you want. The gray buttons at the top of the dialog box represent the columns in your selected data range. The six buttons on the left side of the dialog box enable you to change the map type.

The default map created is a value-shaded map using the first column of data. To change the data in the map, drag the column and format buttons you want to use into the working area (the white box inside the Map Control).

5. Size and format the map, as desired.

NOTE The data you plan to map must include geographical data, such as country, state, city, or county names; or postal codes. For more information on the types of data you can map and the abbreviations accepted by Excel, see the file named Mapstats.xls. This worksheet also contains sample population sizes and forecasts you can use to experiment with. To find Mapstats.xls on your computer, click the Start button and choose Find, Files or Folders. Then type the file name and click Find Now. ■

(See also "Data Mapping: Changing the Column Source.")

Data Mapping: Customizing Map Formats

You can customize each of the map formats to use different symbols, dots, and so forth. For example, you can change the color and symbols used with a graduated symbol format. Or you can change the dot density by specifying how many units each dot represents.

Steps

1. Double-click the map to activate it.

2. From the Map menu, choose the appropriate option command from the bottom of the menu. Commands for map formats only appear on the menu when that format is in use in the current map. Examples of these options include: Category Shading Options, Value Shading Options, and Dot Density Options.

3. Each map format has a different dialog box and a different set of options. Choose the desired options from the displayed dialog box. Click OK when you are finished.

TIP A quick way to display the customizing options for a map format is to double-click the appropriate button in the work area.

NOTE When the map does not display the correct colors or symbols, even though the Microsoft Map Control includes the appropriate format button, choose the Map menu. From the bottom of the menu select the appropriate map format option command. When the map Format Properties dialog box appears, select the Visible check box and then click OK. If the Visible check box was already selected, try clicking the Map Refresh button on the toolbar to refresh the map. ■

Data Mapping: Entering Map Titles

Your data map already includes a main title as soon as you create the map. This title appears in a bordered box at the top of the map. You also can add a subtitle to your map.

Steps

1. Double-click the map to activate it.

2. Choose View, Subtitle. (If your map doesn't have a main title, choose View, Title if you want to display it.)

3. To edit the text in the subtitle (or the main title) click it to select the title, and then click where you want the insertion point.

4. Use standard Windows editing techniques to modify the text in the title; then press Enter.

Data Mapping: Formatting Map Titles

You can enhance the appearance of your map titles by changing the font, font styles, and font color used for the titles.

Steps

1. Double-click the map to activate it.

2. Right-click the title and choose Format Font from the shortcut menu.

3. Select the options you want to change in the Font dialog box, such as Font, Font Style, Size, and Color; then click OK.

TIP You can drag the title (or subtitle) to a new location by clicking the title once, then dragging it by the border. To remove a title or subtitle, select it, and then press the Delete key.

Data Mapping: Inserting Data in an Existing Map

The Data Map feature enables you to easily insert new data in your map.

Steps

1. Select cells in the middle of the current data range; then choose Insert, Cells.

2. Select the Shift Cells Down option and click OK.

3. Enter the new region name and data where you inserted the cells.

4. Double-click the map to activate it, and then click the Map Refresh button on the toolbar to update the map.

Data Mapping: Zooming in on a Data Map

Data maps cover a lot of geographic area, but you may only be interested in a few states or countries. You can magnify maps and reposition them so that they show only the area in which you are interested.

Steps

1. Double-click the map to activate it.

2. Click the Zoom Percentage of Map drop-down list in the toolbar, and select or type a magnification.

3. Press Enter or click the map to see the map magnify.

4. If you can't see the map or want to return to the default size, click the Display Entire button on the toolbar. If you want to move the magnified map within the map window, click the Grabber button in the toolbar and drag the map. To return to the previous view of your map, choose View, Previous.

TIP If you prefer a magnification different from those in the list, type in a magnification. To increase magnification greater than the default enter a number greater than 100. To decrease magnification enter a number less than 100.

Databases: Creating

One of the most common uses of Excel is to help manage databases (or lists) of information. A *list* is information that contains similar sets of data, such as a client database. In an Excel list, the information in one row (such as all the information for one client) is known as a *record*. In each row, individual items are stored in *fields*—each field is a column in the worksheet. An example of a field in a client database would be the client's name; another would be the address of the client. When information is organized in a list, you can easily sort, filter, and summarize data.

With the *Template Wizard*, Excel also enables you to create professional-looking data-entry forms that make it easier for others to enter data into an Excel database.

Steps

1. Type the field names in a single row. These field names (such as Name, Address, Phone, and so on) appear as column headers in your database.

2. Select all the field names and apply a style to them, such as boldface. This makes the field names stand out from the records of your database.

3. Type the records of your database, such as information on each client, directly below the field names, one record per row. Do not leave a blank row after the field names.

NOTE   Your Excel database is actually just a special type of Excel worksheet. You can still use all the familiar worksheet commands to modify your database. ■

Databases: Returning a Sort to the Original Order

When you want to sort a list or database but later return it to the original order, you need to add a record index to the list. A record index can assign a number to each record according to the record's position or its date and time of entry. You can insert a column or cells to make room for an index.

Steps

1. Insert a column adjacent to the list or database. (If you named the list or database range, you need to redefine the name to include the new cells.)

2. Type a number, such as **1**, in the top cell of the column (beside the first database record). Type **2** in the second cell.

3. Select the cells containing 1 and 2 and drag the fill handle (the small black square in the corner of the selected range) down the length of the list. When you release the mouse button, a series of numbers fill in next to each row. These are the index numbers.

When you sort, always make sure that you include the column containing the index numbers. When you want to return the database records to their original order, select the column of index numbers in the Sort By list and select <u>A</u>scending.

Databases: Sorting

Excel enables you to organize the data in a list to serve your needs. You can sort data either alphabetically or numerically, in ascending or descending order.

Steps

1. Select any cell in the database.

2. Choose Data, Sort.

3. In the Sort By box, select the field you want to sort on.

4. Select either Ascending or Descending sort order.

5. If you want to sort on additional fields, select the fields in the Then By text boxes, and then select the sort order for each field; click OK to perform the sort.

TIP To quickly sort the database on a single field, select any cell in that field. Then click either the Sort Ascending or Sort Descending button in the Standard toolbar.

NOTE Excel sorts date fields using the serial number created by dates and times entered in cells. Sorting works correctly only on dates and times entered with a date and time format that Excel recognizes. If you enter dates and times that Excel does not recognize, Excel normally stores them as text and sorts them in text order. (See also "Dates and Times: Entering Dates" and "Dates and Times: Entering Times.") ■

Dates and Times: Entering Dates

When you enter a date, Excel converts your entry to a serial number. If Excel recognizes your entry as a valid date format, you see the date on-screen.

Steps

1. Select the cell in which you want to enter the date.

2. Type the date into the cell using any of these formats: 11/6/97, 6-Nov-97, 6-Nov, Nov-97, 11/6/95 09:45. Then press Enter.

NOTE You can also enter the dates as 11/6, 11/06/97, Nov-97, or November 6, 1997, but Excel formats the number using one of the preceding formats. If Excel does not recognize your entry as a valid date or time format and you type a text date, such as **Nov 6 97**, Excel treats the entry as text and, in an unformatted cell, aligns it to the left. ■

Dates and Times: Entering Times

When you enter a time, Excel converts your entry to a serial number. Time is recorded as a decimal fraction of a 24-hour day. If Excel recognizes your entry as a valid time format, you see the time on-screen.

Steps

1. Select the cell in which you want to enter the time.

2. Type the time into the cell using any of these formats: 16:32, 16:32:45, 4:32 PM, 4:32:45 PM, 11/6/97 16:32. Then press Enter.

NOTE The first two examples are from a 24-hour clock. If you use a 12-hour clock, follow the time with a space and A, AM, P, or PM (in either upper- or lowercase). Be sure that you leave a space before the AM or PM. Do not mix a 24-hour clock time with an AM or PM. As the last format shows, you can combine the date and time during entry. ■

TIP To quickly enter the current date in a cell, select the cell and press Ctrl+; (semicolon). To enter the current time in a cell, press Ctrl+: (colon).

Dictionaries: Creating Custom Dictionaries

You may need a custom dictionary with your worksheets so that you are not frequently prompted to verify the spelling of client names, abbreviations, product codes, industry terms, and so on. When Excel checks spelling, it looks first in the standard dictionary. If Excel doesn't find the word there, it checks the custom dictionary.

Unless you specify otherwise, words you add go into the dictionary named Custom.dic. This name appears in the Add Words To drop-down list in the Spelling dialog box. You can build your own custom dictionaries and select them from the list. You can have as many custom dictionaries as you like, but only one can operate at a time with the standard dictionary.

Steps

1. Click the Spelling button on the Standard toolbar.

2. When the spelling checker finds a word that you want in the new dictionary, type the dictionary name in the Add Words To text box.

3. Click Add to add the current word to the new dictionary.

At any time when the Spelling dialog box is open, you can change to a different custom dictionary by selecting the dictionary from the Add Words To list.

To add words to your custom dictionary, start the spelling checker. When you want to add a word to a custom dictionary, select the dictionary from the Add Words To list and choose the Add button.

Dictionaries: Using the Standard Dictionary

With Excel's dictionary, you can check the spelling of one word, the entire worksheet, or even a chart. Microsoft Office applications all use the same spelling checker and dictionaries.

EXCEL

Steps

1. Select a single cell if you want to spell check the entire contents of a worksheet, or select a range, embedded chart, or object to limit the spelling check to the selected item.

2. Click the Spelling button on the Standard toolbar. If a word cannot be found in the dictionary, the Spelling dialog box appears.

3. Accept or edit the word in the Change To text box; and then choose the Change button. Or choose the Change All button if you want to change this word throughout the document.

   Alternatively, select one of the words from the Suggestions list, and then choose the Change or Change All button.

   You can also choose from the options in the table that follows this procedure.

4. If prompted, choose Yes to continue from the top of the document.

5. When an alert box tells you that the entire worksheet has been checked, click OK.

Spelling Check Options

Option	Description
Ignore	Ignore this word and continue.
Ignore All	Ignore this word throughout the document.
Add	Add this word to the current dictionary.
Suggest	Suggest some alternatives from the dictionary.
AutoCorrect	Add this misspelling and the correction to the list of AutoCorrect entries. When you make this same mistake again, Excel automatically replaces the misspelling with the correct spelling.

Option	Description
Undo Last	Undo the most recent correction in the spell check.
Cancel	Stop the spelling check.

NOTE If no misspelled words are found, the Spelling dialog box never appears. A dialog box appears and tells you that the text in the formula bar or the document has no misspelled words. ■

Editing: Directly in a Cell

When you need to edit a cell entry, you can either edit the text in the cell itself, or in the formula bar. For worksheets built like data-entry forms, the users often expect to type and edit directly in a cell.

Steps

1. Double-click the cell containing the text you want to edit.

2. Move the cursor to where you want to edit, and click the left mouse button.

3. Type the new data. If you want to delete text, use Backspace to delete text to the left of the cursor or use Delete to remove text to the right of the cursor.

4. Press Enter to accept your changes, or press Esc to leave the cell contents unchanged.

Editing: In the Formula Bar

In addition to editing data directly in the cell, you also can edit data from within the formula bar. If you frequently use the formula bar, you may prefer to edit data in the formula bar.

Steps

1. Select the cell containing the text you want to edit.

EXCEL

2. Move the pointer over the text in the formula bar, until it changes to an I-beam. Move the I-beam pointer to where you want to edit the text, and then click the left mouse button.

3. Type the new data. If you want to delete text, use Backspace to delete text to the left of the cursor or use Delete to remove text to the right of the cursor.

4. Press Enter to accept your changes, or press Esc to leave the cell contents unchanged.

TIP To replace part of a cell entry, click and drag the I-beam pointer to highlight the characters you want to replace. Then, type the new data and press Enter.

Editing: Pasting Formats, Values, or Transposed Data

With the Edit, Paste Special command, you can copy and paste part of a cell's attributes, such as the format or value, but not both. This command also enables you to transpose data by switching rows of cells to columns, and columns to rows. The command also enables you to combine the attributes of cells by pasting them together.

Steps

1. Select the cell or range of cells you want to paste; then click the Copy button on the Standard toolbar.

2. Select the cell in the upper-left corner of where you want to paste the data. Be sure to select an area where you won't overwrite existing cell data.

3. Choose Edit, Paste Special. The Paste Special dialog box appears. In the Paste area, select the characteristics you want transferred: All, Formulas, Values, Formats, Comments, Validation, or All Except Borders.

4. In the Operation area, select how you want the transferred data combined with the cells you are pasting into:
   None, Add, Subtract, Multiply, or Divide.

5. Select the Skip Blanks check box if you do not want to
   paste blank cells on top of existing cell contents. Select
   the Transpose check box to change rows to columns or
   to change columns to rows. Then click OK.

 TIP To quickly copy formats, select the cells with the formats
that you want to copy. Click the Format Painter button on the
Standard toolbar. Then select the range to copy the formats to.

Editing: Pasting Multiple Copies

You can save a great deal of data-entry time with Excel's Copy
and Paste commands and other shortcuts. Rather than typing
each formula in a worksheet, you can type a few formulas and
copy or fill them into other cells. You can even copy the formula and format at the same time.

Steps
1. Select the cell or range of cells you want to copy.

2. Click the Copy button on the Standard toolbar.

3. Select only the cells in the upper-left corner of where you
   want each of the duplicate ranges to go.

4. Click the Paste button on the Standard toolbar.

Editing: Pasting Non-adjacent Multiple Copies

You can paste multiple copies of data even if the areas into
which you are pasting are not adjacent.

Steps
1. Select the cell or range of cells you want to copy.

2. Click the Copy button on the Standard toolbar.

3. Click the cells in the upper-left corner of each range where you want to paste the data. Hold down the Ctrl key as you click each cell.

4. Click the Paste button on the Standard toolbar.

Editing: Using Ctrl+Enter to Fill Cells

You can use Ctrl+Enter to quickly fill cells as you enter data or formulas. When you use Ctrl+Enter, formulas and values fill into all selected cells just as though you used a Fill or Copy and Paste command. This method also works with non-adjacent multiple selections.

Steps

1. Select the adjacent cells or ranges you want to fill.

2. With the range(s) still selected, type the formula or value in the active cell.

3. Press Ctrl+Enter to enter the formula or value (instead of Enter).

Formatting: Adding Borders and Lines

You can place borders around cells or use borders as lines and double lines under cells to add emphasis, to define data-entry areas, or to mark totals and subtotals. When combined with shading, borders make your documents easier to read and add flair. You can use the Borders button on the Formatting toolbar to quickly add borders to selected cells.

Steps

1. Select the cell or range you want to add a line or border to.

2. Click the down arrow next to the Borders button on the Formatting toolbar. A palette of border selections appears.

3. Click the desired border.

TIP You can access additional border options and line styles by using the Format Cells dialog box. First, select the cell or range you want to add a border to. From the Format menu, choose Cells. Then click the Border tab and select the options you want. If you want to add a color to your line or border, click the Color drop-down list and select a color from the palette.

Formatting: Using AutoFormat

Excel's AutoFormat feature lets you create professional-looking tables with the click of a few buttons. No matter what your level of expertise with Excel, you can use AutoFormat to apply a set of pre-defined formatting choices to reports, tables, and lists without resorting to complex formatting operations.

Steps

1. Select the range you want to format.

2. Choose Format, AutoFormat.

3. In the Table Format list, select the desired format. A preview of your selection appears in the Sample box.

4. Click OK. The range you selected now displays the AutoFormat you chose.

NOTE When you need to apply only parts of an AutoFormat, choose the Options button in the AutoFormat dialog box. Clear formats in the Formats to Apply group that you do not want applied. For example, if you don't want AutoFormat to change your row heights or columns widths, clear the Width/Height check box. ■

 TIP If the format does not appear as you expected, immediately choose Edit, Undo AutoFormat to restore the table to its previous format.

Forms: Adding Check Boxes for TRUE/FALSE Responses

A check box is linked to a cell so that the result of the check box status appears as TRUE or FALSE in the linked cell. Selecting the check box makes the cell TRUE. Deselecting the check box makes the cell FALSE.

Steps

1. Draw a check box in the worksheet by clicking the Check Box button and dragging where you want the check box; then right-click the check box and choose Format Control from the shortcut menu.

2. Click the Control tab.

3. Select the default value of the check box, Unchecked for FALSE result, Checked for TRUE result, or Mixed for #NA result. Choose the 3D Shading check box to add depth to the check box.

4. Select the Cell Link edit box, and then click the cell that you want to hold the results of the check box. Click OK.

Forms: Adding List or Combo Boxes

A list box or combo box restricts users to choosing from a defined list of items. Restricting user selections prevents them from typing a mistake, entering incorrect data, or using old data.

List boxes and combo boxes produce the same result, but the appearance of these lists differs. A list box shows multiple items in the list, while the list stays the same height. A combo box is only one item high and has a drop-down arrow to the right side. Clicking the drop-down arrow displays the list. Combo boxes usually are used when not enough room exists for a list box.

Steps

1. In the worksheet, enter a vertical list of items you want to appear in the list. Enter one item per cell.

2. Click the List Box or Combo Box button on the Forms toolbar and draw the control in the worksheet. Make a list box wide enough to see the entries in the list, and tall enough to see multiple items. A combo box only needs to be tall enough for one item.

3. Right-click the list and choose Format Control; then select the Control tab.

4. Select the Input Range edit box; then drag across the range of cells in the worksheet that contain the data for the list. This list appears in the list box or combo box.

5. Select the Cell Link box and click the cell that receives the results of the list. If you are using a combo box, enter in the Drop Down Lines box the number of lines displayed when the list appears. Click OK.

NOTE The cell you specify in the Cell Link box returns a value that represents the *number* of the selected list item, not the actual list item itself. However, you can use this number in a formula to return the selected item in the list. If a combo box is linked to cell B5 and the input range for the list is in the range C5:C10, for example, the following formula returns the value from range C5:C10 based on the selection from the combo box:

=INDEX(C5:C10,B5) ∎

TIP Choose Data, Sort to sort the list data in a worksheet (before you create the list) if you want the list to appear sorted within a control.

Forms: Adding Option Buttons

Option buttons are used most frequently when you need to make a single choice from a group of choices. Option buttons are round buttons that come in groups.

If you just draw option buttons on a worksheet, all these buttons belong to the same group, which means that you can select only one option button at a time. You can have multiple groups of option buttons, however, by enclosing each group in a group box drawn with the group tool.

Steps

1. Draw a group box by clicking the Group Box button and dragging where you want the box. While the box is selected, type a title to replace the default box title.

2. Click the Option Button tool and draw an option button inside the group box. Type a title while the option button is selected.

3. Right-click the option button and choose Format Control; then select the Control tab. Select the value for the option button: Unchecked or Checked.

4. Select the Cell Link edit box; then click the worksheet cell that you want to contain the results from the group of option buttons.

5. Click OK and then repeat Steps 2 through 4 for each additional option button you want to include. When you are finished creating option buttons, click a cell outside the group box.

NOTE   When you create additional option buttons, you don't have to enter a cell reference for the Cell Link. Only one linked cell exists for all option buttons in a group. ■

Forms: Adding Scroll Bars

Scroll bars enable users to enter a number within a wide range, while getting a visual impression of where their entry lies within the range. To enter a number, you can click the top or bottom arrow, click the gray part of the scroll bar, or drag the square button in the scroll bar.

Steps

1. Draw a scroll bar control in the worksheet by clicking the Scroll Bar button and dragging where you want the scroll bar; then right-click the control and choose Format Control from the shortcut menu.

2. Select the Control tab.

3. In the Current Value edit box, enter the amount you want the linked cell to have when the worksheet opens.

4. Enter the lowest value you want the scroll bar to produce in the Minimum Value box. Enter the highest value you want in the Maximum Value box. Set the amount of change for each click of the control in the Incremental Change box. In the Page Change edit box, enter the amount of change you want when the user clicks the gray part of the scroll bar.

5. Select the Cell Link edit box and then click the cell in the worksheet you want to receive the scroll bar result. Click OK.

Forms: Adding Spin Boxes

Spin boxes are controls that show two arrow heads. Each click of an arrow head increases or decreases the amount in the cell linked to the spin box. Holding down the mouse button on a spin box causes the number to change continuously.

Steps

1. Draw a spin box control in the worksheet by clicking the Spinner button and dragging where you want the spin box; then right-click the spin box control and choose Format Control from the shortcut menu.

2. Select the Control tab.

3. In the Current Value edit box, enter the amount you want the linked cell to have when the worksheet opens.

4. Enter the lowest value you want the spin box to produce in the Minimum Value box. Enter the highest value you want in the Maximum Value box. Set the amount of change for each click of the control in the Incremental Change box.

5. Select the Cell Link edit box and then click the cell in the worksheet that you want to receive the spin box result. Click OK.

EXCEL

Forms: Creating a Data-Entry Form with Template Wizard

After you create a data-entry form on a worksheet, be sure to save the worksheet. The Template Wizard guides you through the process of converting your worksheet into a data-entry form.

Steps

1. Open the workbook that contains the data you want to use for the form.

2. Choose Data, Template Wizard. If you don't see the Template Wizard option, you need to install the Template Wizard with Data Tracking add-in before you can continue. Search for "Template Wizard" in Excel Help for more information.

3. Follow the steps in the Wizard.

4. Click Finish when you are done creating the template.

NOTE To enter data using the data-entry form you have created, you open a new workbook based on the template you created with the Template Wizard. Opening a new workbook based on a template is different from opening a workbook. When you open a new workbook from a template, the original template remains untouched and a copy of the template is opened. This new workbook contains all the formatting, formulas, and data contained in the template, but it must be saved using a different name. ■

Forms: Creating Your Own Form on a Worksheet

Before you can create a data-entry form using the Template Wizard, you need to create a worksheet that is the basis for your form. Excel has many features that enable you to create nice-looking and easy-to-use data-entry forms.

Using Excel formatting techniques, you can make worksheets appear more like a paper form. You probably want to start by having the form in the same workbook as the worksheets that do the calculations, which makes it easier to create and maintain links from the controls on the form to the worksheets using the data.

Steps

1. Choose Tools, Options.
2. Select the View tab.
3. Select from the options in the Window Options group to affect the appearance of only the active window. Refer to the table following this procedure for information on specific options you can choose.
4. Enter the text labels you want to include in your form; enter these labels in cells above or to the left of the cells that contain the data input.
5. To enhance the appearance of the form, format the workbook data as desired. Remember to print the form to see how the printed copy looks.

Window Options

Option	Effect
Page Breaks	Deselect so automatic page breaks do not show.
Formulas	Deselect so results show, not formulas.
Gridlines	Deselect so gridlines do not show.
Row & Column Headers	Deselect so row and column headings are hidden.
Outline Symbols	Deselect unless your form is built in an outline.
Zero Values	This is optional. Deselect to hide zeros.
Horizontal Scroll Bar	Deselect to hide the scroll bar at the bottom.

EXCEL

continues

Continued

Option	Effect
Vertical Scroll Bar	Deselect to hide the scroll bar on the right edge.
Sheet Tabs	Deselect to hide the worksheet tabs.

TIP Color the background area of a form with light gray to give it a more pleasing appearance. Use the Shadow button on the Drawing toolbar to give pictures, charts, or text boxes a more three-dimensional appearance.

Forms: Drawing a Control

Excel enables you to place on a worksheet the same type of data-entry controls as you can place in a dialog box run by a macro or Visual Basic procedure. *Controls* are data-entry objects commonly used in *forms*, such as scrolling lists or check boxes. When you enter a value in a control or make a selection from a control, the entry appears in a worksheet cell.

Steps

1. Display the Forms toolbar by right-clicking in the toolbar area and choosing Forms.

2. Click the button in the Forms toolbar that represents the control you want to draw. To create a check box control, for example, click the Check Box button. The pointer changes to a cross-hair.

3. Move the cross-hair to the top-left corner of where you want the control to appear and drag down and to the right to where you want the control's opposite corner.

4. Release the mouse button. The control appears in the worksheet. If you created a button control, the Assign Macro dialog box appears when you release the mouse button. Select the macro you want to assign to the control, and then click OK.

5. Hold down Ctrl and then click the control to select it. When a control is selected, handles appear around the object. You can then move, resize, or change the properties of the selected control. Drag an edge of the control to move it. Resize the control by dragging one of the handles.

To deselect a control, click a cell or object outside the selected control. To delete the control, select it and then press Delete.

 TIP Double-click a selected control to display the Format Object dialog box. To change the format of the control, select the options you want from the available tabs.

Formulas: Entering

Formulas enable you to enter calculations in a worksheet. Once you enter a formula, you can change the values in the referenced cells; Excel automatically recalculates values based on the cell changes.

You can save a great deal of data-entry time with Excel's Copy and Paste commands and other shortcuts. Rather than typing each formula in a worksheet, you can type a few formulas and copy or fill them into other cells. You can even copy the formula and format at the same time.

Steps

1. Select the cell where you want the formula to appear.
2. Type = to start the formula.
3. Type or click the first cell reference in the formula.
4. Type the operator, such as a plus sign (+).
5. Type or click the next cell reference, and then press Enter.

The result of the formula appears in the cell. When you select the cell containing the formula, the formula appears in the formula bar.

Formulas: Unprotecting and Hiding

Cell protection prevents someone from accidentally entering data on top of a formula and prevents unauthorized users from changing your formulas. You also can specify whether a cell's contents are visible in the formula bar. Even when the cell contents are hidden from the formula bar, the cell's value or formula results still appear in the worksheet.

Steps

1. Select the cell or range that you want to unprotect, or whose contents you want to hide from the formula bar.

2. Choose Format, Cells.

3. Click the Protection tab.

4. Clear the Locked check box to mark the cell or range as one that can be changed, or select the Hidden check box to mark the cell or range as one whose contents do not show in the formula bar. Click OK.

You can continue to change all cells in the worksheet and see any cell contents until you turn on protection for the worksheet. Protection and hiding do not take effect until you use the Tools, Protection command. After you enable cell protection, you cannot change the cell contents or the cell format.

Functions: Entering

Functions are pre-defined formulas that perform a specific operation, such as determining loan payments or calculating investment returns. Excel provides several categories of functions, such as financial, logical, and engineering functions.

Functions accept information, referred to as arguments, and return a result. In most cases, the result is a calculation, but functions also return results that are text, references, logical values, arrays, or information about the worksheet.

Steps

1. Select the cell where you want the function to appear.

2. Type **=** to start the function.

3. Type the function name, such as **AVERAGE**, and a left parenthesis.

4. Select the range of cells for the argument.

5. Press Enter. Excel automatically adds the closing parenthesis and enters the function.

TIP To enter more complex functions that require the use of multiple arguments, use the Paste Function button on the Standard toolbar.

Functions: Using AutoCalculate

If you need to find a quick total in a worksheet, but you don't want or need to include that total in the worksheet, you can use the *AutoCalculate* feature. For example, you may want to sum a list and then use that sum in a formula. You could grab a calculator and add up the figures using the calculator. Or you can use Excel's AutoCalculate feature.

Steps

1. Select the range you want to sum. The AutoCalculate button in the status bar automatically displays the sum of the selected range.

2. Right-click the AutoCalculate button in the status bar.

3. From the pop-up menu that appears, select the function you want to use, such as Average or Count. The result of the function you selected appears in the status bar.

If you select additional ranges, Excel uses the most recent function you selected on the AutoCalculate button.

Functions: Using AutoSum

The SUM function totals the numeric value of all cells in the range(s) it references. An *AutoSum* button, which you can use to sum adjacent columns or rows automatically, appears on the

Standard toolbar. In addition to entering the SUM function automatically, the AutoSum button selects the cells in the column above or in the row to the left of the current cell.

Steps

1. Select a cell below or to the right of the values you want to sum.

2. Click the AutoSum button in the Standard toolbar.

3. To accept the formula that AutoSum supplies, press Enter. Or, if the formula is incorrect, select a different range to sum, and then press Enter.

NOTE If you select a range of cells and then click the AutoSum button, Excel automatically enters the formula results for the entire range. ■

Functions: Using the Paste Function

The *Paste Function* displays a list of functions from which you can choose the function you want, based on a description that appears when you select a function. The Paste Function also assists you in building the function, and explains the purpose of each argument in a function.

Use the Paste Function if you want to enter a complex function that requires multiple arguments, or if you are unsure of the syntax required for a specific function. (See also "Functions: Entering.")

Steps

1. Select the cell where you want to enter the function, then click the Paste Function button in the Standard toolbar.

2. Select the type of function you want from the Function Category list. If you are unsure of the category, select Most Recently Used or All.

3. Choose the specific function that you want from the Function Name list box. Read the description in the

lower part of the dialog box to verify that this is the function you want.

4. Click OK. A pop-up dialog box appears under the formula bar.

5. Enter the arguments in each argument text box. You can type the cell references or numbers, click the cell to enter, or drag across multiple cells to enter. Click OK to complete the function and insert it in the cell.

Numbers: Entering

Numbers are constant values containing only the following characters:

0 1 2 3 4 5 6 7 8 9 + - ( ) , / $ % . E e

You can enter integers, such as 24 or 973; decimal fractions, such as 908.37 or 0.72; integer fractions, such as 3 1/4 or 2/3; or scientific notation, such as 5.87137E+3.

Steps

1. Select the cell in which you want to enter the number.

2. Type the number into the cell. To type a negative number, precede the number with a minus sign. Press Enter.

Numbers: Formatting

By default, numbers are right-aligned and appear in the General number format. You can change the existing format to any Excel format you choose.

Steps

1. Right-click the cell that contains the number.

2. Choose Format Cells from the shortcut menu.

3. Click the Number tab.

4. Select the desired format from the Category list, then choose from any additional options that appear. Click OK.

NOTE A cell filled with # signs indicates that the column is not wide enough to display the number correctly. In this case, you need to change the numeric format or widen the column. ■

TIP To enter a fraction, type an integer, followed by a space, and then the fraction. If you are entering only the fractional part, type a zero, a space, and then the fraction; otherwise, Excel may interpret the entry as a date. Excel reduces fractions when you enter them; if you enter **0 4/8**, for example, Excel converts the entry to 1/2. The formula bar displays the decimal equivalent of the fraction (0.5, in this example).

Outlines: Creating Manually

Outlining enables you to expand or contract worksheets or reports so that you see more or less detail. In a sales report, for example, you might need to display various levels of detail depending on who reads the report. With the outline feature, you can hide or display up to eight levels of detail in rows or columns.

Excel can create an outline for you, or you can manually create the outline. Manual outlining is necessary if the data is organized in a way that Excel doesn't understand. (See also "Outlines: Using Automatic Outlining.")

Steps

1. Select cells in the rows or columns that you want to change. Select up to, but not including, the cell that contains the summary formula. If the rows or columns include only the data to outline, you can select the rows or columns to group.

2. Choose Data, Group and Outline, Group to group items on a level. The Group dialog box appears.

3. In the Group dialog box, select Rows or Columns, depending on what you want to group. If you selected an entire row or column, you don't see this dialog box.

Excel groups the data by rows if you have rows selected, or by columns if you have columns selected. Click OK.

4. Repeat Steps 1 through 3 for each section you want to outline.

TIP If you make a mistake or if you want to undo a grouping, you can use the Ungroup command. Select the section you want to ungroup. Choose Data, Group and Outline, Ungroup. Select either Rows or Columns and then click OK.

Outlines: Displaying or Hiding Outline Levels

You use the outline symbols to select which levels in an outline you want to display or hide. When you create an outline, the outline symbols appear automatically in a gray area to the left of the row numbers. You can also choose whether or not you want to display the outline symbols.

Steps

1. If outline symbols do not appear, press Ctrl+8. This key combination works as a toggle to display or hide the outline symbols.

2. Display or hide levels of detail in specific rows or columns with one of the following actions:

 * Expand a specific row or column by clicking the related Display (+) symbol.

 * Expand to an entire level by clicking the appropriate Level number button. The Level number buttons appear at the top of the gray area that displays the outline symbols. To display all levels, click the highest numbered button.

 * Collapse a specific row or column by clicking the related Hide (-) symbol.

 * Collapse to a level by clicking the appropriate Level number button. To collapse all levels, click the lowest numbered button.

Outlines: Formatting

If you are creating a new outline, you can apply outline styles when Excel creates the outline. You also can apply outline styles to an existing outline.

Steps

1. If you are formatting an existing outline, select the cells to which you want to apply the outline styles. Otherwise, begin with Step 2.

2. Choose Data, Group and Outline, Settings. The Settings dialog box appears.

3. If you are formatting an existing outline, choose Apply Styles. Otherwise, select Automatic Styles and then click OK.

Outlines: Using Automatic Outlining

You can have Excel create an outline for you automatically, instead of creating the outline manually. Automatic outlining is useful if you haven't created an outline before or your outline has a consistent layout. (See also "Outlines: Creating Manually.")

Steps

1. If you want to outline data within a part of the worksheet, select the range you want to outline. If you want to outline the entire worksheet, select a single cell.

2. Choose Data, Group and Outline, Auto Outline.

If Excel can determine a consistent direction of summarizing, it creates an outline. If Excel doesn't create an outline, it displays a warning message. If this occurs, you need to adjust the layout of your data or manually create an outline.

TIP To remove a portion of an outline, select cells in the row or columns at the level you want removed, and then choose Data, Group and Outline, Clear Outline. To clear the entire outline, select a single cell in the worksheet and choose Data, Group and Outline, Clear Outline.

PivotTables: AutoFormatting

You can select from any of 16 pre-defined table formats to automatically apply to a PivotTable. The Number, Border, Font, Patterns, Alignment, and Width/Height formatting elements can be applied automatically.

Steps

1. Choose Format, AutoFormat. The AutoFormat dialog box is displayed.

2. In the AutoFormat dialog box, select the desired format from the Table Format drop-down list box.

3. Click the Options button to disable or enable the Number, Border, Font, Patterns, Alignment, or Width/Height format settings for the previously selected table format. Click OK to close the AutoFormat dialog box.

NOTE Any manual formatting you apply to the PivotTable, before or after you format, automatically takes precedence over formatting applied with the AutoFormat command. ■

PivotTables: Changing Field and Item Names

When data is brought into a PivotTable from another source, the field names are derived from the field name in the source data. Item names are set by default to the data in the source fields. When you change the field or item name in the PivotTable, the source data is not affected.

Steps

1. Open the PivotTable in which changes are to be made.

2. Choose View, Toolbars, PivotTable.

3. From the PivotTable menu, open the PivotTable drop-down list.

4. Choose Select from the submenu.

5. Click Enable Selection. Double-click the field or item name to be changed. Type the new name into the cell or formula bar.

EXCEL

PivotTables: Creating

PivotTables are interactive worksheet tables that quickly summarize large amounts of data using the format and calculation methods you choose. They are called PivotTables because you can rotate the row and column headings around the core data area to give you different views of the source data.

A PivotTable organizes your data by putting the fields you choose as row, column, and page headings, and then summarizing data elements for those row, column, and page intersections according to the summarizations and calculations you choose.

NOTE Before you format a PivotTable in a file created in an earlier version of Microsoft Excel, save the workbook as a Microsoft Excel 97 file. Choose File, Save As. The Save As dialog box appears. Click Microsoft Excel Workbook (*.xls) in the Save as Type drop-down list box. ■

Steps

1. Choose Data, PivotTable Report. The PivotTable Wizard opens at Step 1 of 4.

2. Select the source of the data to be used for the PivotTable from the Microsoft Excel List or Database, External Data Source, or Multiple Consolidation Ranges radio buttons. Click the Next button to proceed to Step 2 of the PivotTable Wizard.

3. If you have already selected the range on your worksheet, click the Next button to proceed . You see the range of data highlighted. Click the Next button to proceed to Step 3.

4. In Step 3 of 4, drag and drop the field buttons on the right of the window into the boxes on the left. Click the Next button to proceed to Step 4.

5. In Step 4 of 4, specify either a data range in the existing worksheet or a new worksheet to contain the results of

the PivotTable. Click the Finish button to see the
PivotTable you have created.

NOTE Click the Options button in Step 4 of the PivotTable
Wizard to change the default name of the PivotTable or to change
Format and Data options. ■

PivotTables: Editing PivotTable Data

Editing your PivotTable consists of two tasks: Editing the data
from which your PivotTable is drawn, and editing the layout of
the database from which your PivotTable is drawn.

Remember, the formatting of the data source is not automatically reflected in the PivotTable.

TIP To apply formatting to all pages of the PivotTable, select All
for each page field and then apply formatting.

Steps

1. Open the PivotTable you want to edit. Choose View,
   Toolbars, PivotTable.
2. From the PivotTable submenu, choose PivotTable to
   open the PivotTable menu bar.
3. From the PivotTable menu bar, choose Select, Enable
   Selection.
4. To apply the formatting changes you want, use the
   buttons on the Formatting toolbar and the commands
   on the Formatting menu.
5. From the PivotTable menu, choose PivotTable, Refresh
   Data.

PivotTables: Formatting Numbers

To retain formatting changes when you refresh or change the
layout in a PivotTable, you must choose the Enable Selection
button on the PivotTable menu of the PivotTable toolbar.

EXCEL

Steps

1. Choose View, Toolbars, PivotTable to open the PivotTable menu bar.

2. From the PivotTable menu bar, choose PivotTable.

3. Click Select, Enable Selection.

4. Choose Format, Cells. The Format Cells dialog box appears.

5. Click the Number tab to bring the Number sheet to the front. Select the type of formatting to apply from the Category list box. Set any additional formatting options that appear when you select different types in the Category list box. Click OK to close the dialog box.

Printing: Creating Headers and Footers

You can create custom *headers* and *footers* for your reports using the Page Setup dialog box. With one of 18 built-in headers, and a Footer Designer, you can create informative page notes included in the printouts.

Steps

1. Choose File, Page Setup. The Page Setup dialog box is displayed.

2. Click the Header/Footer tab to bring the Header/Footer sheet to the front.

3. Click the Header and Footer drop-down list box arrows in the Header/Footer sheet to select from the predefined options for headers and footers.

4. To create individualized headers and footers, click the Custom Header or Custom Footer button and follow the instructions in the Header or Footer dialog box displayed.

Printing: Previewing the File

You can check a printout before you actually print it, seeing the results with all formatting and other effects in place. (See also

"Printing: Creating Headers and Footers" for formatting page information.)

Steps

1. Choose File, Page Setup. The Page Setup dialog box is displayed.

2. Enter the data range of the area to be printed in the Print Area text box. You could also click the Collapse Dialog button at the right end of the Print Area text box, opening the Page Setup - Print Area dialog box where you can use your mouse to select the data range.

3. With the data range specified in the Print Area field, click the Print Preview button. The page is displayed as it would appear in a printout.

3. To exit Print Preview, click the Close button on the menu bar.

Printing: Reducing and Enlarging Prints

You can control the scale of the final printout on the paper through the Page Setup dialog box. The printout can be reduced to accommodate a border on the paper or other situation. If enlarged, the report would be printed on several pages to handle the larger size.

TIP If you have a postscript-capable or other multi-page-handling printer, you could also use the 2 Up or 4 Up printout property to place multiple pages on one sheet of paper.

Steps

1. Choose File, Page Setup. The Page Setup dialog box is displayed.

2. Click the Page tab to bring the Page sheet to the front.

3. In the Scaling group, select desired size in the Adjust to: % Normal Size spin box.

4. Click the Print button to close the Page Setup dialog box and open the Print dialog box where you can make other print job decisions.

Printing: Selecting a Print Area

Before you can print or preview your worksheet, you need to select the area or data range of the sheet(s) that contains the material for output. This area can include any charts, graphics, or other material as well as traditional spreadsheet data with any specified formatting in that area.

Steps

1. Highlight the area in the worksheet to be printed.

2. Choose File, Print Area.

3. Choose Set Print Area from the submenu. The previously selected area is defined as the print area. A dotted line will be displayed around the data range until you select and set a new print area, or select Clear Print Area from the Print Area submenu.

Printing: Setting the Paper Margins

Excel uses default margin settings of Top: 1", Bottom: 1", Left: .75", and Right: .75". You can change these settings in the Page Setup dialog box to control the appearance of the specified print area on the page(s). The Margins sheet of the dialog box is also used to set the position of headers and footers, and the centering of the data horizontally and vertically on the page.

Steps

1. Choose File, Page Setup. The Page Setup dialog box is displayed.

2. Click the Margins tab to bring the Margins sheet to the front.

3. Set the Top, Bottom, Left, and Right margins in the appropriate spin boxes.

Totals: Creating a Subtotal

Subtotals are a quick and easy way to summarize data in an Excel list. Suppose you have a list of sales information that includes the date, account, product, unit, price, and revenue. You can specify that you want to see subtotals by account, or subtotals by product, and so on.

With Excel's Subtotals command, you don't need to create the formulas. Excel creates the formula, inserts the subtotal row(s), and outlines the data automatically. The resulting data is easy to format, chart, and print.

Steps

1. Sort the list as desired.

2. Click a cell in the column that you want to subtotal.

3. Choose Data, Subtotals.

4. In the Subtotal dialog box, make any desired changes. To create subtotals for more than one column, for example, select additional columns in the Add Subtotal To list.

5. Click OK. Excel creates the subtotals; a grand total appears at the bottom of the list.

TIP To quickly remove the subtotals from your list, select a cell in the list. Then choose Data, Subtotals, Remove All.

CAUTION Excel lists work best when Excel can readily distinguish the column labels and data entries in the list. Include a row of column labels across the top and, with no blank rows, place your data in the appropriate columns just below the labels.

Totals: Creating Nested Subtotals

If you want additional subtotals within each group (a nested subtotal), you can create two sets of subtotals. For example, you might want to total all accounts and also include subtotals for each product within an account.

Steps

1. Sort the list by the two or more columns that you want to contain subtotals. Click a cell in the first column you want to subtotal.

2. Choose Data, Subtotals; then click OK to insert subtotals for your first sorted column.

3. Click a cell in the second column you want to subtotal.

4. Choose Data, Subtotals; then choose the options for the second group.

5. In the At Each Change In drop-down list, select the column for the second set of subtotals. Then clear the Replace Current Subtotals check box. Click OK.

Totals: Using Multiple Summary Functions

In addition to the SUM function (used for creating subtotals in Excel lists), a number of Excel functions are useful in lists as well. For instance, you may want to use COUNT to summarize the number of items in the list, AVERAGE to give the average values in the list, and MAX to give the largest value in a list.

Steps

1. Choose Data, Subtotals.

2. Select the first function in the Use Function drop-down list, and then click OK. Excel inserts the subtotal rows.

3. From the Data menu, choose Subtotals.

4. Select another function from the Use Function drop-down list.

5. Clear the Replace Current Subtotals check box, and then click OK. Excel inserts an additional subtotal row with the new calculation.

Rows: Changing Height

Row height can be changed within individual worksheets. A
row can also be hidden within a worksheet.

NOTE If a range has already been defined as a print area, it
can be selected from the Name box of the formula bar. Even
when selected, the area will be hidden. ■

Steps

1. Point your mouse icon to the numbered row headings on
   the left side of your worksheet until the cursor turns into
   a horizontal bar with an arrowhead on either side. As
   soon as you click the separator bar, the height is displayed to the upper-right in a message such as, Height:
   12.75, the default row height.

2. Drag the boundary below the row heading until the row
   is the desired height.

TIP To change the row height for multiple rows, select the rows
you want to change. Drag a boundary below a selected row
heading. To change the row height for all rows on the worksheet,
click the Select All button (the gray rectangle in the upper-left
corner of a worksheet where the row and column headings meet),
and then drag any row in the document to the desired height. All
of the rows in the document are changed.

Rows: Hiding

If you do not want a data range or area of a worksheet to
be seen, highlight the area and hide it. The area can be
returned to view at any time unless the worksheet is password protected.

Steps

1. Select the range that you want to hide.

2. Choose Format, Row, Hide. The rows are no longer
visible, and the row numbers move up, but do not
reincrement.

 TIP   To unhide rows in a worksheet, choose Format, Row,
Unhide.

Scenarios: Adding

When performing what-if analysis, it is handy to have reusable
sets of data to apply to your business set. These reusable sets
of data are referred to as scenarios and can be defined and
saved with different business scenarios to run through a business plan.

Steps

1. Choose Tools, Scenarios. The Scenarios Manager is
displayed. Click the Add button to open the Add Scenario
dialog box.

2. Enter a name for the scenario in the Scenario Name
text box.

3. Enter the cell addresses of the cells that you want to
change in the Changing Cells text box.

4. In the Protection group at the bottom of the dialog box,
select the options you want. Click OK to close the Add
Scenario dialog box and open the Scenario Values
dialog box.

5. In the Scenario Values dialog box, type the values for the
changing cells in each of the text boxes. Click OK to
close the dialog box and return to the Scenario Manager.
Click the Show button to apply the scenario to the data
range, or click the Close button to close the Scenario
Manager.

Scenarios: Editing

An advantage of using a scenario is the ability to easily change the data set for a what-if analysis without changing the formulas and other supporting data.

Steps

1. Choose Tools, Scenarios. The Scenario Manager is displayed.

2. Click the name of the scenario that you want to edit in the Scenarios list box.

3. Click the Edit button to open the Edit Scenario dialog box.

4. Make the desired changes and click OK to close the dialog box, opening the Scenario Values dialog box.

5. Enter the desired values for the changing cells in the appropriate text boxes. Click OK to close the dialog box and save your changes.

TIP To return to the Scenario Manager dialog box without changing the current scenario, press Esc or click the Cancel button.

Scenarios: Switching Between Scenarios

The advantage of using scenarios to do what-if analysis is the ability to quickly change the data affecting the results. Use the Scenario Manager to switch between previously defined data sets.

Steps

1. Choose Tools, Scenarios. The Scenario Manager appears.

2. Click the name of the scenario that you want to apply in the Scenarios list box and click the Show button to apply the new data to the worksheet.

3. Click the Close button to close the Scenario Manager.

EXCEL

Solver: Creating a Report

Solver is a mathematical tool that you can use to analyze data on worksheets. You can then create a report to see the results of your analysis. Solver is an optional component that is not automatically installed. Use online help to install it.

Steps

1. Choose Tools, Solver. The Solver Parameters dialog box appears. In the Set Target Cells text box, enter a cell reference or name for the target cell. The target cell must contain a formula.

2. For the value of the target cell to be as large as possible, select the Max radio button in the Equal To group. For the value of the target cell to be as small as possible, select the Min button in the group. For the value of the target cell to be have a specified value, select the Value Of radio button and enter the specific value in the text box to the right.

3. Enter a name or address for each adjustable cell, separating non-adjacent cell references with commas in the By Changing Cells drop-down list box. The Solver will propose the adjustable cells based on the target cell if you click the Guess button to the right of the drop-down list box.

4. Enter any constraints to be applied in the Subject to the Constraints list box.

5. Click the Solve button to run the Solver and close the dialog box.

Solver: Saving and Loading Solver Data

Before proceeding with this section, see "Solver: Creating a Report." Solver is useful for performing what-if analysis on your data. This tool simplifies what-if analysis by allowing you to create and save specific sets of data. The Solver Parameters dialog box stores the last settings used to solve a problem. You can save those settings for use at a later time to run Solver using the same conditions.

Steps

1. Choose Tools, Solver. The Solver Parameters dialog box appears.

2. In the Solver Results dialog box, click Save scenario.

3. In the Scenario Name box, type a name for the scenario.

4. To load solver data, open the scenario in which it is contained.

Styles: Creating

When you define styles for worksheets, Excel saves these settings with your worksheets. The styles can be applied to any selected data, immediately accomplishing the formatting effect. Creating a style sheet is easier than deciding what the style will be.

Steps

1. Choose Format, Style. The Style dialog box appears.

2. Select the Style Name text box and type in the name of the style sheet you want to create. Click the Modify button to open the Format Cells dialog box and start defining your style sheet.

3. In the Format Cells dialog box, click each of the Number, Alignment, Font, Border, Patterns, and Protection tabs, selecting the desired format elements. Click the OK button to return to the Style dialog box.

4. Click the Add button to add the defined style to the list of other styles. To apply this or any other style to the currently selected cells, click the OK button. Otherwise, click the Close button to close the Style dialog box without adding the selected style sheet to any cells in the open worksheet.

EXCEL

Styles: Deleting

Deleting styles is a three-step process, but it affects all worksheets in the workbook. When you delete a style sheet, all cells in worksheets in the current book that are formatted using this style revert back to the default normal style.

Steps

1. Choose Format, Style. The Style dialog box appears.

2. Select the style from the Style Name list box.

3. Click the Delete button in the Style dialog box. All affected cells are immediately reformatted to the settings in the normal style sheet.

4. Click OK to return to the current worksheet.

CAUTION　Undo cannot restore the formatting of a deleted style sheet.

Styles: Redefining the Default (Normal) Style

Redefining the default normal style sheet affects all of the areas of worksheets in the current workbook that are not formatted using other style sheets. The redefined normal style sheet is only saved with the current workbook, not making automatic changes to other worksheets in other books.

Steps

1. Open a workbook with the style sheet to be redefined.

2. Choose Format, Style. The Style dialog box appears.

3. Select Normal in the Style Name text box. Click the Modify button to open the Format Cells dialog box.

4. In the Format Cells dialog box, click the Number, Alignment, Font, Border, Patterns, or Protection tab and make the desired format changes for the normal style.

Click OK to return to the Style dialog box.

5. Click the Add button to add the redefined normal style to the list of other styles. The format change is immediately seen in all cells that are not currently formatted using a different style sheet. Click OK to return to the current worksheet.

Styles: Redefining with Format Commands

Redefining a style sheet is as easy as creating a new style sheet. Any changes made to a style sheet are immediately seen in all cells in all worksheets of the current workbook.

Steps

1. Open a workbook with the style sheet to be redefined.

2. Choose Format, Style. The Style dialog box appears.

3. Select the style that you want to modify from the Style Name text box. Click the Modify button to open the Format Cells dialog box.

4. In the Format Cells dialog box, click the Number, Alignment, Font, Border, Patterns, or Protection tab and make the desired format changes. Click OK to return to the Style dialog box.

5. Click the Add button to add the redefined style to the list of other styles. The format change is immediately seen in all cells using this format. Click OK to return to the current worksheet.

Templates: Creating and Saving a Workbook Template

When you create and save a workbook template, you specify to use the template as the default for all new workbooks, or as a template to be selected by choice. Templates also include page formatting, print area settings, and calculation options. You can

EXCEL

also define toolbars, macros, hyperlinks, ActiveX controls, and other workbook definitions to be included.

Steps

1. Open a workbook with one worksheet included.

2. Create the look you desire in the worksheet and place any desired text or data in the appropriate locations.

3. Define any style sheets that you anticipate using in workbooks that use this template.

4. Choose File, Save or Save As. The Save (or Save As) dialog box appears.

5. Enter the name you want to use for the new template in the File Name text box.

6. From the Save as Type drop-down list, choose Template. Click the Save button to save the template with the new name in the specified folder.

NOTE When you select Template from the Save as Type list, the default folder changes to Templates in the Microsoft Office folder. ■

Templates: Editing

Templates are designed to make creation of documents easy. Templates can be edited at any time to change any elements and then saved as the same template or as a new template.

Steps

1. Choose File, Open. The Open dialog box appears.

2. Select Templates in the Files of Type drop-down list box to display all templates. If necessary, change the folder, using the Look In drop-down list box to move to the appropriate folder.

3. When you have located the desired template, double-click the file name to open it in the Editing window.

4. A warning dialog box may appear if there are macros in the template. Click Enable Macros to open the template.

5. Make the desired changes to the template. If you want to save the template with the same name, press Ctrl+S. To save the template as a new template, choose File, Save As. Enter the new file name in File Name text box, and click the Save button.

NOTE Changes made to templates only affect workbooks and worksheets that are created after the template used to create the new workbooks is modified. Existing workbooks are not changed when a template is edited. ■

Text: Entering

Excel treats all data as text. Cells can be previously formatted to accept data, declaring it text, numeric, date, or whatever. The data in the cells is text, regardless of the applied formatting.

Steps

1. Move the insertion tool to the cell that you want to enter text in. Type in your text and press Enter.

2. To change the format, choose Format, Cells. The Format Cells dialog box appears.

3. Click the format folder's tab that you want to modify. Make the desired changes, selecting from the different format elements. Change desired elements in other folders.

4. Click OK to close the Format Cells dialog box and apply the formatting changes to the selected text.

5. To make a font change to selected text in a string in a cell, select the cell and click in the formula bar with the mouse. Highlight the text to be changed in the cell or in the Text Edit field in the worksheet toolbar.

EXCEL

6. Choose Format, Cells. The Format Cells dialog box
appears with only a Font folder. Make your font selections and click OK to close the dialog box and apply the
changes to the highlighted text.

NOTE Format changes made in the Format Cells dialog box
override previously made changes with a style sheet. ■

Workbooks: Automatically Saving

Excel includes the ability to automatically save your workbooks as you are working. The AutoSave add-in, if installed,
can ensure that you always have a work-in-progress copy of
your workbook at all times. You determine how often to save
and whether the setting is for the open workbook or all workbooks.

Steps

1. With a selected workbook open, choose Tools, AutoSave.
The AutoSave dialog box appears.

   If AutoSave does not appear on the Tools menu, choose
Tools, Add-Ins. Mark the check box to the left of
AutoSave in the Add-Ins Available list box. Click OK to
close the dialog box and add the AutoSave option to the
Tools menu.

2. In the AutoSave dialog box, make sure that the Automatic Save Every check box is checked and enter the
time interval for saving in the Minutes text box.

3. To autosave all workbooks when open, click the Save All
Open Workbooks radio button. Otherwise, click the Save
Active Workbook Only radio button.

4. If you want to be prompted to save the workbook, mark
the Prompt Before Saving check box.

5. Click OK to close the dialog box and start the autosave
timer.

Workbooks: Changing Drives and Folders

Organizing your workbooks can include moving the files to different folders on your hard drive or company network. The new file structure could reflect your corporate organization. Whether opening or saving files, moving through your drives and folders is as simple as several clicks of your mouse button.

Steps

1. Choose File, Open. The Open dialog box appears.

2. The current or last folder you accessed appears in the Look In drop-down list. Clicking the arrow to the right of the drop-down list opens the desktop tree. Move up the drive tree or select a different drive from the expanded tree, and click with the left mouse button.

3. When you click a different folder, all folders below the folder and files appear in a large list box below the Look In drop-down list.

4. Double-click the folders shown in the large list box to open their contents.

5. When you have located the desired file, double-click the file name to close the Open dialog box and open the workbook in Excel.

NOTE   You can click the Up One Level button to the right of the Look In drop-down list to move up one folder level at a time. ■

Workbooks: Copying a Worksheet

Worksheets can be copied from one workbook to another. With proper care, the links can also be maintained.

Steps

1. Open the workbook that you are copying the worksheet from, and then open the other workbook. Bring the original workbook to the front by selecting the workbook from the Window menu.

2. Click the tab of the worksheet that you want to copy.

3. Choose Edit, Move or Copy Sheet. The Move or Copy dialog box appears.

4. Select the name of the workbook where you want to insert the worksheet in the To Book drop-down list box. From the Before Sheet list box, select the destination sheet that the new sheet will appear before in the workbook. Click the Create a Copy check box to place a copy of the original worksheet in the selected workbook, leaving the original in its original workbook.

5. Click OK to close the dialog box and copy the worksheet from the original workbook to the selected workbook. The destination workbook appears at the front of the desktop.

Workbooks: Closing

When you have finished working with a workbook or several open workbooks, closing the workbooks takes just a couple of keystrokes. You can close just the current workbook or all open workbooks at once.

Steps

1. Bring the workbook that you want to close to the front of the desktop.

2. Choose File, Close.

3. If you have made any changes to the workbook since it was opened or since you last saved it, a dialog box appears and asks if you want to save the changed workbook. If you click the Yes button, the workbook is saved and then closed. Clicking the No button closes the workbook without saving any changes, while clicking the Cancel button returns you to the open workbook.

NOTE You can choose to close all open workbooks by holding down the Shift key on your keyboard and choosing File, Close All. Answer the warning dialog box to save or not save the workbooks.

Holding down the Shift key toggles the File menu option from
Close to Close All. ■

Workbooks: Inserting a Worksheet

When you move or copy a worksheet, by default, the original
worksheet is placed as the first worksheet in the workbook. If
placement of worksheets is important to the organization of
your workbook, you can specify the worksheet to be placed
before the original worksheet.

Steps

1. Open the workbook that you are moving the worksheet
   from and then open the other workbook. Bring the
   original workbook to the front by selecting the workbook
   from the Window menu.

2. Click the tab of the worksheet that you want to move.

3. Choose Edit, Move or Copy Sheet. The Move or Copy
   dialog box appears.

4. Select the name of the workbook where you want to
   insert the worksheet in the To Book drop-down list box.
   From the Before Sheet list box, select the destination
   sheet that the new sheet will appear before in the
   workbook.

5. Click OK to close the dialog box and move the
   worksheet from the original workbook to the selected
   workbook. The destination workbook appears at the
   front of the desktop with the original worksheet inserted
   in the workbook.

Workbooks: Opening

Opening your workbooks can be accomplished with a couple
of mouse clicks.

Steps

1. Click the Open button on the Standard toolbar. The
   Open dialog box appears.

EXCEL

2. Select Microsoft Excel Files in the Files of Type drop-down list. If you do not see the desired file in the current folder, use the Look In drop-down list to navigate to the desired location.

3. Double-click the file name in the large list box below the Look In field to open the workbook in the desktop.

Workbooks: Opening a Protected Workbook

A workbook can be protected so that a password is required to open a workbook and/or to modify the contents of the workbook. The protection is set using the Save Option dialog box.

Steps

1. Choose File, Open. The Open dialog box is displayed.

2. Choose the name of the workbook to be opened in the list box below the Look In drop-down list box. Click the Open button to close the Open dialog box.

3. The Password dialog box is displayed. Enter the password in the Password text field. Click the OK button to open the workbook.

Workbooks: Password Protecting

To prevent other users from opening or modifying a workbook, you can password protect the workbook.

CAUTION If you forget a password, you cannot open a password protected document. Passwords are case-sensitive.

Steps

1. Choose File, Save As.

2. Click the Options button. The Save Options dialog box appears.

3. In the Save Options dialog box, enter your passwords in the Password to Open text box and the Password to Modify text box. Click OK to close the Save Options dialog box. The Confirm Password dialog box is displayed.

4. Reenter the password(s) in the Reenter Password to Proceed text box in the Confirm Password dialog box.

Workbooks: Protecting a Worksheet

You can assign password protection to just selected worksheets in a workbook, rather than to the entire workbook.

Steps

1. Choose Tools, Protection, Protect Sheet. The Protect Sheet dialog box is displayed.

2. Place a check mark in the Contents, Objects, and Scenarios check boxes to protect the contents of the current worksheet.

3. Enter the password in the Password text box. Click OK to close the Protect Sheet dialog box. The Confirm Password dialog box appears.

5. Reenter the password in the Reenter Password to Proceed text box. Click OK to close the dialog box and apply the password protection to the worksheet.

Workbooks: Saving

Saving your work is the most important command you can use on the computer. Saving your workbook while you are working provides you with a certain peace of mind if the power goes out in your office.

Steps

1. Bring the workbook that you want to save to the front of the desktop.

EXCEL

2. Choose File, Save. The workbook is saved without any other input.

3. If you want to save the open workbook with a different name, choose File, Save As. The Save As dialog box appears.

4. Type the new name in the File Name text box, select a different folder through the Look In drop-down list if you want, and click OK to close the dialog box and save the workbook.

Worksheets: Clearing, Inserting, or Deleting Data

The data in cells or defined ranges of data can be cleared, deleted, or inserted anywhere in the worksheet. Care should be taken when you delete cells from a worksheet. Not only do you delete data, but the cells themselves are removed and adjacent cells are moved.

Steps

1. Open the workbook that contains the worksheet.

2. Click the tab of the worksheet that contains the data you want to clear or delete. Select the data range.

3. Choose Edit, Clear. Click the All, Formats, Contents, or Comments option in the Clear submenu to specify what to clear from the range. Clicking All completely clears the cells.

4. Choose Edit, Undo Clear to return the data range to its original state.

5. Choose Edit, Delete. The Delete dialog box appears. Because the cells themselves are deleted, select which direction to move adjacent cells or rows of cells. Click OK to close the dialog box, delete the cells and their contents, and move adjacent cells from the specified side to fill the empty region of the worksheet.

Worksheets: Moving a Sheet

Worksheets can be moved from one workbook to another.
With proper care, the links can also be maintained.

Steps

1. Open the workbook that you are moving the worksheet
   from and then open the other workbook. Bring the
   original workbook to the front by selecting the workbook
   from the Window menu.

2. Click the tab of the worksheet that you want to move.

3. Choose Edit, Move or Copy Sheet. The Move or Copy
   dialog box is displayed.

4. Select the name of the workbook where you want to
   insert the worksheet in the To Book drop-down list box.
   From the Before Sheet list box, select the destination
   sheet that the new sheet will appear before in the workbook.

5. Click OK to close the dialog box and move the worksheet from the original workbook to the selected
   workbook. The destination workbook appears at the
   front of the desktop.

NOTE If you want to leave the original worksheet in place and
just place a copy in the new workbook, click the Create a Copy
check box, toggling between the Move and Copy functions. ■

TIP To place a worksheet in a new workbook without first
opening a workbook, select (new book) in the To Book drop-down
list box in the Move or Copy dialog box. A new workbook opens
on the desktop with the moved or copied worksheet.

PowerPoint

Microsoft PowerPoint 97 is a presentation graphics program
that you can use to organize, illustrate, and deliver your ideas.
Use this tool to professionally and effectively present your
message at informal meetings, audience presentations, or even
over the Internet.

You can add *OfficeArt* text and drawing effects, charts, and
animations to illustrate your *slideshows*. You can also create
dynamic *presentations* that include multimedia features such as
sounds, movies, and pictures from the Clip Gallery.

Backgrounds: Adding Patterns

Patterns add interest to a drawing on a slide. You can add
a pattern to rectangles and ellipses that you've drawn. The
pattern is made up of a single color and white, or two colors.
Patterns can either be lines or dots, or artistic patterns like
spheres and shingles.

Steps
1. Select the drawing that you want to add a pattern to.
2. Click the drop-down menu arrow to the right of the Fill
   Color icon on the Drawing toolbar.
3. Choose Fill Effects from the list.
4. Choose the Patterns tab from the Fill Effects dialog box.
5. Choose a pattern by clicking it, then click OK for it to fill
   your drawing.

 TIP   You can change the colors of the fill pattern by using the
drop-down Foreground and Background lists in the Fill Effects

continues

continued

dialog box. If you click the Preview button, you can see the effect on your drawing (you may have to move the dialog box to see the drawing).

Backgrounds: Adding Shading

PowerPoint enables you to add a shaded background to the rectangles and ellipses you've drawn. The shading creates a gradient effect between the foreground and background colors, and you can change the direction and style of the shading.

There are also preset gradients, and some of these have effects that you can't get by shading two colors.

Steps

1. Select the drawing that you want to add shading to.
2. Click the drop-down menu arrow to the right of the Fill Color icon on the Drawing toolbar.
3. Choose Fill Effects from the list.
4. Choose the Patterns tab from the Fill Effects dialog box.
5. Choose your gradient design, and click OK. The gradient appears in your drawing.

 TIP Make sure your gradient colors contrast with the color of any text you put in the box.

Backgrounds: Adding Textures

Another way to add interest to rectangles and ellipses that you've drawn is to add a texture—an image that's suitable for a background because it varies only slightly. PowerPoint offers you various types of paper and marble textures. These often add a more sophisticated touch than a gradient background.

Steps

1. Select the drawing that you want to add a texture to.
2. Click the drop-down menu arrow to the right of the Fill Color icon on the Drawing toolbar.

3. Choose Fill Effects from the list.

4. Choose the Textures tab from the Fill Effects dialog box.

5. Choose your texture, and click OK. The texture appears in your drawing.

Bulleted Lists: Creating

Bulleted lists are a major part of presentations. They make it easy for people to see and understand your important points. Often a slide with a bulleted list leads to a series of slides, each dealing with one point on the list.

Steps

1. Choose one of the bulleted list layouts from the Slide Layout dialog box, and click OK. If you're changing what is already on a slide layout, you select the new layout and click Reapply.

2. Choose Apply and enter a bulleted point. Then press the Enter key.

3. The bullet appears automatically, ready for you to enter another point. The new bullet appears when you press Enter after inputting the text for the preceding bullet.

4. When you've entered all your points, click the slide background or choose New Slide from the Common Tasks window.

If you create your presentation in Outline View, you can indent points in the outline, and PowerPoint will convert these to a bulleted list when you go to Slide View.

Don't make your bulleted list too long; aim for no more than six bullets with no more than six words in each. If you can't do this easily, you should consider putting your information on two or more slides.

Whenever a slide layout refers to text, it actually means a bulleted list.

POWERPOINT

TIP If you accidentally press the Enter key and have no more points to list, press the Backspace key to remove the bullet.

Bulleted Lists: Placeholders

Among the placeholder types in the AutoLayouts for new slides is a bulleted list. Many of the layouts include text with bullets because bullets are a popular method for listing speaking points.

Steps

1. Create or display a slide that contains a bulleted list placeholder.

2. The placeholder contains a bullet followed by `Click to add text`. Click this text. The insertion point appears, ready for typing.

3. Type the text for your first bullet point, and then press Enter. A bullet appears on the next line, followed by the insertion point.

4. Type your next bullet point and press Enter.

5. Repeat Step 4 until you have added all the points for the slide. Click outside the text block to view the text on the slide.

See also "Text: Adding to Placeholders" and "Bulleted Lists: Creating."

Charts: Adding Titles

You can add a title to organization charts or to charts that display amounts, such as column charts.

Steps

1. If you have already created an organization chart, double-click it to edit it.

2. At the top of the chart the words `Chart Title` appear.

3. Select these words, and then type your own title.

4. Close the Microsoft Organization Chart dialog box, and select Yes to save your changes. This will bring the slide you were working on back into view.

5. Click the slide to return to it.

Charts: Formatting Fonts

You can change any of the fonts used in a chart. Whether it's the legend, the labels along the bottom or up the sides, or the chart title, they can all be changed. If you've edited charts in Excel you'll understand how to change them in PowerPoint; double-click any text.

Steps

1. Double-click your chart to edit it.

2. Double-click any text in the chart.

3. In the tabbed dialog box, choose Fonts.

4. Choose the Font, Style, and Point Size, and click OK.

5. Click the slide background to see your changed chart.

Charts: Moving

Chart objects are as easy to move as other objects. Just drag and drop. You can move the chart on a page or slide to overlap other objects if desired.

Steps

1. Click the chart to select it.

2. Drag the chart to its new position on the page and release the mouse button.

3. Click outside the chart's selection handles to deselect it, or repeat Step 2 to further position the chart.

You can click the Undo button on the Standard toolbar to move the chart back to its previous position.

POWERPOINT

Charts: Resizing

PowerPoint creates a chart for you in a default size, but you can change the size of the chart to suit the slide where it is placed. A chart is an object, and you resize it the same way you resize other objects—by dragging handles.

Steps

1. Select the chart so that handles appear surrounding the chart.

2. Drag one of these handles and release the mouse button when the chart is the size you want.

   If you drag a corner handle, the height and width of the chart change proportionately. Dragging a middle handle on the left or right changes only the width; dragging a middle handle on the top or bottom of the chart adjusts only the height.

Charts: Resizing Objects

You can resize individual objects within a chart by using the sizing handles of the selected object.

Steps

1. Double-click the chart.

2. Select the object you want to resize, such as the *plot area*, legend, or drawn object.

3. Drag an object handle to resize the object.

4. Click outside the chart to deselect it.

Charts: Rotating

Charts are not *rotated* the same way as other objects. When you select a chart, the rotate tools are dimmed and therefore unavailable. You can, however, rotate the plot area of a 3-D chart to change the angle from which you view the plotted series.

Steps

1. Double-click the chart you want to rotate.

2. Choose Chart, 3-D View.

3. Enter a rotation degree (number from 0 to 360) in the Rotation box.

   Alternatively, click the left or right rotation buttons to rotate the plot area 10 degrees at a time. You can observe the results in the preview box.

   If the Right Angle Axes check box is cleared, the Perspective setting becomes available. You can experiment with these settings along with the Elevation setting until you have rotated the plot area where you want it.

5. Click Apply to see the results on the actual chart without closing the dialog box. (You may have to move the dialog box out of the way to see the chart.) You can choose Default to return the chart to the default rotation settings. When you are finished with the changes, choose OK.

Charts: Selecting Custom Types

Current PowerPoint 95 users know this feature as Chart AutoFormat. The options are now available as custom charts in the Chart Type dialog box.

Custom charts serve as templates or built-in styles that allow additional formatting and chart options. Some of the options available for custom charts are colors, fills, patterns, a legend, gridlines, data labels, a secondary axis, and placements for chart elements. You can use a custom chart type or create your own.

Steps

1. Double-click a chart or chart placeholder to select it. The Chart menu and toolbars appear.

2. From the Chart menu, choose Chart Type to display the Chart Type dialog box.

3. Choose the Custom Types tab.

4. In the Select From area, select Built-in (it's probably already selected), and then select a type in the Chart Type list box. Observe the look of the custom type in the Sample box, and note the description below it.

5. Try other chart types to view their effects. Choose OK to apply the effects of the built-in custom chart.

NOTE To save the styles of a chart you have created as a custom type, first double-click the chart to select it in Microsoft Graph. Follow the previous Steps 2 and 3. Select the User-defined option button, and then click Add. Give the chart a name and description, and choose OK. The chart name is added as a user-defined chart type. You can choose this chart again later to use as a custom chart type. ■

Clip Art: Adding Objects

Images make a presentation more memorable. PowerPoint installs a clip art library and a browser so that you can select the appropriate images for your presentation.

Images can be dragged around the slide to position them, and you can change the size of an image by dragging on one of the eight handles (small black boxes) that appear around the image when you select it. Hold down the Shift key as you do this to keep the image's original proportions.

You can also put clip art in a slide by selecting one of the layouts that incorporate clip art. Double-click the Double-click here to add clip art prompt on the slide.

If you want to add clip art but can't find a suitable image, try using AutoClipArt from the Tools menu. This analyzes the text in your presentation and suggests suitable clip art from the library.

Steps

1. Choose Insert, Picture, and choose Clip Art from the submenu.

2. Choose a category from the Clip Gallery.

3. Double-click the image that you want. It appears on your slide.

TIP Don't let the clip art overpower your message. Choose clip art that will enhance your presentation but not distract from it by being the wrong size, color, or inappropriate for your presentation topic.

Data: Copying

You can create charts in PowerPoint by entering the figures into a datasheet. However, if you have the figures in a spreadsheet such as Microsoft Excel, you can copy the figures directly into the PowerPoint datasheet. This saves you time and avoids the possibility of errors.

While you can cut and paste complete charts made in Excel or other spreadsheets, copying the figures means that you can edit the values even if you transfer your presentation to another computer.

Steps

1. Open your spreadsheet program, select the cells, and choose Edit, Copy.

2. Close the spreadsheet program and open PowerPoint.

3. Open Microsoft Chart by choosing Insert, Chart.

4. Choose Edit, Paste.

Datasheets: Adding Data

PowerPoint enables you to add your data to charts in the same way as a spreadsheet. When you create a chart you'll see a grid of numbers. This is called a datasheet, and each part of the grid is a cell. The column chart visible behind the datasheet contains columns that vary in height according to the values on the datasheet—higher values give longer columns.

POWERPOINT

To put your own values onto the chart, replace the labels (like 1st Qtr, 2nd Qtr, East, and West) with labels of your own. Then replace the numbers with your own values, and press the Backspace key to remove any figures in cells that you don't need. If you need to show more series, add more values in the first empty column of cells; if you need to show more areas, add values to the next empty row.

Charts like the default column chart are useful when you need to show the relationship between several sets of numbers as they change over time. If you want to show other relationships, like the proportion of parts of a whole thing (for example, the areas of spending that make up a budget), you should use a pie chart.

Steps

1. Click the cells in the datasheet that you want to change. You can use the Tab and arrow keys to move around in the datasheet. The chart will reflect your changes as soon as you select another cell.

2. When you've made all your changes, click the slide background. The slide will update to reflect your changes.

Drawings: Adding Shadows

If you draw rectangles or ellipses, you can add a shadow to them to make them stand out from the page. The shadow gives a 3-D effect, but if you want a true 3-D effect, see the section "Objects: Adding 3-D Effects."

Steps

1. Select the object that you want to add a shadow to.

2. On the Drawing toolbar, click the Shadow icon. A box will appear for selection of effect choices and a Shadow Settings button will also appear.

3. Choose the shadow you want.

4. If the shadow effect is not enough for your taste, click the Shadow Settings button.

5. Click the Shadow Settings button as many times as you want to make the shadow more obvious.

 TIP Shadows look most natural when they fall toward the bottom right. To achieve this, click the Nudge Shadow Down button several times, followed by the same number of clicks on the Nudge Shadow Right button; both of these buttons are in the Shadow Settings toolbar.

Fills: Adding Colors

When you use the drawing tools to draw a rectangle or ellipse, they are filled with the current fill color. If you want to change this, you can change the fill to another color or an option from the Fill Effects dialog boxes. If the fill color you want is not displayed, you can add more colors by selecting them from the Colors dialog box.

Steps

1. Select the rectangle or ellipse you want to change.
2. On the Drawing toolbar, click the arrow next to the Fill Color icon.
3. Either choose a color from those displayed, or choose More Fill Colors (if all choices are grayed out, you haven't selected anything).
4. In the Colors dialog box, click the Standard tab if necessary, and choose a color by clicking it.
5. If you can't see a shade you like, click the Custom tab and choose a color by clicking it or entering values in the boxes.

Fonts: Changing

PowerPoint templates come with fonts that will definitely be installed on every computer. This means that you may have fonts that are more suited to your presentation. If you want to change the font throughout your presentation, see "Presentation Templates: Changing Typeface and Text Alignment."

POWERPOINT

Just as you can change fonts in a word processing document, you may want to change the font on just one slide.

Steps

1. Select the text you want to change by highlighting it.
2. Choose a font from the drop-down list on the Formatting toolbar.

Handouts: Creating

It's a good idea to give people something to take away after your presentation. PowerPoint lets you print *handouts*—all or part of your presentation on plain paper, with two, three, or six miniatures of your slides on each sheet. If you have a color printer, you can reproduce the slides in color; otherwise PowerPoint shows your colors as shades of gray.

Steps

1. When your presentation is complete, choose File, Print.
2. At the bottom of the Print dialog box, select Handouts in the Print What list box.
3. If you only want to print certain slides, click the Slides option button in the Print Range section of the Print dialog box, then enter the numbers of the slides you want to print.
4. Click OK to start your slides printing.

You might want to restrict your handouts to those slides that only show the most important points. Alternatively, you could prepare a handout in your word processor and cut and paste charts from PowerPoint.

Lines: Changing

When you draw lines you can vary the thickness and also show them as solid, dashed, or dotted.

Steps

1. On the drawing toolbar, click the Line Style button to adjust the width or thickness of the line or make a doubled line.

2. Click the Dash Style button to change to a dashed or dotted line.

3. Click the Arrow Style button to add an arrow head to your line.

TIP If you click the Line Style button, and then choose More Lines, you'll go to a dialog box that enables you to change everything about your line.

Masters: Handout

The Handout Master is used to format the handouts you want to pass out to your audience. It displays several slide image placeholders. You can add page numbers, date and time, headers and footers, and graphic objects to your Handout Master; however, whatever you add will appear on every page of your handouts.

Steps

1. Open the presentation you want to edit.

2. Choose View, Master, Handout Master. The Handout Master appears along with the Handout Master toolbar and the Master toolbar.

3. Click buttons on the Handout Master to set various layouts of slide placeholders on the page—2, 3, or 6 slides per handout page.

4. If you want to change any header and footer information choose View, Header and Footer. See also "Printing: Handouts" for more information on changing headers and footers.

5. Choose Close on the Master toolbar to close the Handout Master.

TIP To view the Handout Master, you can pull down the View menu and press Shift while clicking Outline; or press Shift and click the Outline View button at the lower left of the screen.

NOTE   If you have deleted or changed any of the headers or footers and want to restore them to the default, follow these steps. While the Handout Master is open on the screen, click Handout Master Layout on the Common Tasks toolbar. In the Handout Master Layout dialog box, choose the item you want to restore and choose OK. ■

Masters: Notes

Notes Master offers a way for you to organize an upcoming presentation. At the top of the page is a graphic of one slide. At the bottom of the page is a Notes placeholder containing a copy of the text from the slide. This section is useful to the speaker for organizing the talk.

Steps

1. Open the presentation you want to edit, or create a new presentation.

2. Choose View, Master, Notes Master. The Notes Master appears along with the Master toolbar.

3. To change text styles, click within the text on any line of the Notes part of the page, and then use the Formatting toolbar to format the text.

4. If you want to change any header and footer information, choose View, Header and Footer. See "Printing: Handouts" for more information on changing headers and footers.

5. Choose Close on the Master toolbar to close the Notes Master.

Masters: Slide

Slide Masters control the background in a slideshow and define the styles of the text and titles that appear in the presentation. Slide Masters also can contain any objects you want to appear in every slide of a presentation.

TIP To view the Slide Master, you can hold the Shift key and click the Slide View button at the bottom left of the screen.

Steps

1. Open the presentation.

2. Choose View, Master, Slide Master. The Slide Master appears along with the Master toolbar.

3. To change text styles, click within any line of text, and then use the Formatting toolbar to format the text. Apply designs by choosing Apply Design on the Common Tasks taskbar.

4. If you want to change the footer information, choose View, Header and Footer. On the Slide tab, make any changes, and then choose Apply to All.

5. Choose Close on the Master toolbar to close the Slide Master.

Masters: Title

The Title Master defines the formatting and arrangement of the title slide of the presentation. It allows you to define a unique appearance for the title slide, separate from the design of the other slides.

Steps

1. Open the presentation you want to edit.

2. Choose View, Master, Title Master.

3. Change text styles and apply designs the same as for slides.

4. Choose Close on the Master toolbar to close the Title Master.

Navigating: Slide Navigator

During the delivery of a presentation you can use the *Slide Navigator* to monitor your location in a slideshow and jump to a slide out of the presentation sequence.

POWERPOINT

Steps

1. Begin a slideshow by clicking the Slide Show button at the lower left or by choosing View, Slide Show.

2. Moving your mouse to the lower-left corner of the screen, click the icon at the bottom left of the screen. From the Slide Show pop-up menu, choose Go and then choose Slide Navigator. The Slide Navigator dialog box appears.

3. In the Slide Titles list box, double-click the slide title you want to show. Alternatively, select the slide title and choose Go To.

NOTE The slideshow continues forward in its sequence from the slide you jumped to. If you skipped over slides, they will not be shown unless you return to the Slide Navigator and select the slides. ■

Navigating: Through Animations

After you create the slides for your presentation, you can add or change *animations* and set custom timing of animations for a slide.

NOTE Animate quickly by choosing from several preset animations. Select an object to animate. From the Slide Show menu, choose Preset Animation and select an animation. ■

Steps

1. Display the slide you want to animate.

2. From the Slide Show menu, choose Custom Animation. If an object has not had animation applied, its name appears in the Slide Objects Without Animation list box on the Timing tab.

3. Click Animate to move object names to the Animation Order list, which makes them available for further customization.

4. In the Animation Order list box, change the order in which animations are played for the selected slide by selecting an object name and clicking the up-and down-arrow buttons.

5. Select an object in the Animation Order list box and then apply the following options from the tabs in the bulleted list following these steps.

6. Click the Preview button to run the animation in the preview window. Choose OK when you are satisfied with the animation settings.

- On the Timing tab, choose whether to animate the selected object and set to initiate by mouse click or set timing.

- On the Effects tab, choose animation, sound, and other effects.

- On the Chart Effects tab, choose options available only for chart objects.

- On the Play Settings tab, choose options available only for movie or sound objects.

NOTE Instead of using the Custom Animation dialog box to set timings, you can set them automatically while you rehearse the slideshow. From the Slide Show menu, choose Rehearse Timings. The slideshow starts with the Rehearsal dialog box displayed. Advance through each animation on the slide at the speed you want the timing to be automatically recorded. ■

Navigating: Through Presentations

As your presentation grows in size, it is essential to know how to navigate from slide to slide. You might need to move from one slide to another to add, delete, or rearrange content.

Steps

1. Press the PageUp key to display the previous slide, and press the PageDown key to display the next slide in the presentation.

POWERPOINT

2. Use the Slide Changer buttons, which are located just below the Slide Changer's scroll bar. Clicking the double-up arrow or double-down arrow buttons move you up or down through the slide sequence in the same way as using the PageUp or PageDown keys.

3. Drag the scroll box in the Slide Changer to move through the slide sequence. PowerPoint displays a slide number indicator, such as "Slide: 3 of 8," as you drag the scroll box.

Objects: Adding 3-D Effects

If you draw rectangles or ellipses, you can add a 3-D effect to them to make them stand out from the page.

Steps

1. Select the object that you want to add the 3-D effect to.

2. On the Drawing toolbar, click the 3-D icon to display the choices box.

3. Click the effect you want.

4. You can modify the 3-D effect by clicking the 3-D Settings button.

5. Click the buttons as many times as you want to modify the 3-D effect.

Objects: Adding AutoShapes

PowerPoint comes equipped with a number of predefined shapes called *AutoShapes*. These shapes are fully adjustable in size, and many include an additional adjusting handle to reshape the object in some way. You access AutoShapes on the Drawing toolbar.

PowerPoint 97 has added new AutoShape categories such as action buttons, block arrows, callouts, flowchart symbols, and stars and banners.

Steps

1. Display the slide or object to which you want to add the AutoShape.

2. On the Drawing toolbar, click AutoShapes. On the pop-up menu, point to a category, and then click the shape you want.

3. With the cross-hair shaped pointer, click where you want to place the AutoShape and drag to the size you want. You can reposition and resize the shape later.

    Depending on which shape you draw, you probably see a fill color inside the shape. Use the Fill Color tool on the Drawing toolbar to change or remove the fill color.

See also "Objects: Moving Around" and "Objects: Resizing and Cropping."

NOTE   Four common AutoShapes appear on the Drawing toolbar, so you don't have to use the AutoShapes menu to select them: Line, Arrow, Rectangle, and Oval. ■

TIP   The rectangle shape draws a square and the oval shape draws a circle if you hold down the Shift key as you drag the shape. Holding down the Shift key maintains the shape's width-to-height ratio.

Objects: Changing AutoShapes

After you have drawn an AutoShape, you can change it to another AutoShape. You might do this if you have already added color and styles to the shape and want to change the shape without starting over.

Steps

1. Select the object whose shape you want to change.

2. On the Drawing toolbar, choose Draw, and then point to Change AutoShape.

3. Choose a category and a new shape. The shape changes, but the color and other styles are applied to the new shape.

 TIP You can change a shape to a 3-D object by selecting it and then clicking the 3-D button on the Drawing toolbar.

Objects: Changing the Order of Layers

You may want to layer objects on a slide, both to fit more on the slide and to improve the design. Layering objects allows you to overlap them. You might want a text object to fit within a drawn object or provide callouts for a chart. Or, you might want to overlap a drawn object onto a clip art object.

Every object you place on a slide occupies its own layer. No matter how many objects you have on a slide, each object can be sent backward or brought forward relative to any other object in the stack of layers.

 TIP You can bring a group of objects forward or backward by grouping them first before sending them forward or backward. See also "Objects: Ungrouping."

Steps

1. Drag the objects to the position you want; don't be concerned about the wrong ones overlapping or hiding one another.

2. Select one of the objects that you want to change.

3. On the Drawing toolbar, click the D_raw button to pop up the menu.

4. Choose O_rder to display the options on the Order submenu shown in the following table.

   If you are working with only two overlapping objects or groups, then Bring to Front and Bring _Forward may appear to do the same thing. This is also true of Send to Bac_k and Send _Backward.

5. Select one of the options on the Order submenu. The layers change accordingly.

Choose This	To Place the Selected Object
Bring to Front	All the way to the front
Send to Back	All the way to the back
Bring Forward	One step closer to the front
Send Backward	One step closer to the back

Objects: Deleting

You can't delete anything on a PowerPoint slide unless it is part of the Master Slide. You have to select what you want to delete; be careful that you have chosen the right item to delete. If you want to delete text, you can do this by clicking the text to make an insertion point, and then deleting using the Backspace or Delete keys.

If you want to delete a graphic, a chart, or an entire block of text (like a complete bulleted list) you must select the object before deleting it.

Steps

1. Click the object to select it.

2. Press the Delete or Backspace key.

   If the object does not disappear, you may have selected only part of it. Move the point of the arrow cursor over the edge of the object and click; press the Delete or Backspace key.

Objects: Moving Around

You move different kinds of objects according to the type of object they are. Text objects must be selected and dragged by the selection box bordering them. Other kinds of objects can be dragged from anywhere within the object.

POWERPOINT

Steps

1. Click anywhere within the object.

2. Drag the object to a new location and release the mouse button.

TIP To get an object out of your way temporarily, drag it off the slide into the "gray area."

Objects: Placing and Rotating

Any object created in PowerPoint can be rotated with the Free Rotate tool on the Drawing toolbar. The Draw menu contains additional options for rotating and flipping objects. These tools give you the flexibility to be creative with objects, even displaying text objects at any angle.

Steps

1. Select the object you want to rotate.

2. Click the Free Rotate tool button on the Drawing toolbar.

3. Do as the status bar advises: `Position the pointer over a round handle and drag to rotate.`

4. Continue to drag until the object is positioned the way you want, and then release the mouse button.

5. Click a blank part of the slide—or click the Select Objects button on the Drawing toolbar—to discontinue using the Free Rotate tool.

   If you want to rotate additional objects individually, you can click them and use the round handles to rotate them. In other words, the rotate function stays on until it is turned off, either by clicking a blank part of the slide or clicking in the Draw toolbar.

TIP Rotate more than one object at a time by holding down Shift while selecting them. Use any of the free rotate handles to rotate all of the objects at once.

To use the other rotation and flipping tools, select the object and click the D**r**aw button to pop up the Draw menu. Choose Rotate Or Fli**p**, and then select one of the submenu options:

Choose This	To Rotate the Selected Object
Free Rotate	To any angle
Rotate Left	90 degrees to the left
Rotate Right	90 degrees to the right
Flip Horizontal	Flipped side to side (mirrored)
Flip Vertical	Flipped top to bottom (upside down)

 TIP Imported pictures cannot be rotated or flipped, however if you ungroup the picture and regroup its components, you may then be able to rotate or *flip* it.

Objects: Resizing and Cropping

You can *crop* or *resize* objects on the slide to make them larger or smaller. Usually you resize an object by dragging a handle. PowerPoint also allows you to crop certain picture objects—photos, bitmaps, or clip art.

To resize an object, you select it and then drag a sizing handle until the object is the shape and size you want. To resize the object proportionally, hold down the Shift key while dragging a corner handle.

Steps

1. Select the object you want to resize.
2. Choose F**o**rmat, **O**bject, and then click the Size tab.
3. In the Size area, enter the percentages you want in the **H**eight and **W**idth spin boxes.
4. Click the Lock **A**spect Ratio check box to maintain the object's ratio between height and width.
5. Choose OK.

TIP To restore the proportions of a resized picture object, right-click it and choose Format Picture on the shortcut menu. On the Size tab, click Reset, and then choose OK.

Objects: Ungrouping

You can group objects together in order to manipulate them as a group instead of individually. After you have grouped multiple objects, they act as a single object. Then, you can move, resize, rotate, copy, cut, paste, or perform other operations on the objects. Afterwards, you may want to ungroup them to their individual separate objects. For example, you may want to remove one of the objects in the group. Also, to rotate some graphics it is necessary to ungroup components and group them again.

Steps

1. Select the grouped object.

2. Click the Draw button on the Drawing toolbar.

3. Choose Ungroup. Handles appear on the individual objects.

NOTE To regroup objects you just ungrouped, leave them selected. On the Drawing toolbar click Draw, and then choose Regroup. ■

Org Charts: Adding Staff Positions

You may need to add new positions to an organization chart. You can edit an *org chart* by double-clicking it to start the Microsoft Organization Chart application. This allows you to add or remove positions and change the text in the boxes.

If your new org chart takes up more space than before, it will be resized to fit your slide.

Steps

1. Double-click the org chart.

2. Click the position you want to add from the symbols in the Microsoft Organization Chart toolbar.

3. Move the cursor over the position you want to add to and click. Enter name and position details.

4. Choose Exit and Return to [your presentation name] from the Microsoft Organization Chart's File menu.

5. Choose OK when asked if you want to update the object.

Org Charts: Changing Connecting Lines

You can change the thickness and color of a line connecting positions in an organization chart, and you can also make lines dashed. Dashed lines can indicate non-supervisory connections within a company, like someone who passes information to another employee but is not responsible to that employee. Colored connections can be useful to show departments or proposed changes.

Steps

1. Double-click the organization chart to select it, if necessary.

2. Click the line to select it.

3. From the Line menu in Microsoft Organization Chart, choose Thickness, Style, and Color.

4. From the File menu in Microsoft Organization Chart, choose Exit and Return to [your presentation name].

Org Charts: Changing Styles

You can present an organization chart in one of several different styles. You can add styles to charts without affecting the relationships. You can use styles to improve the readability of a chart, change relationships, and identify specific groups or levels.

Steps

1. Double-click the organization chart to edit it.

2. Open the Styles menu in Microsoft Organization Chart.

POWERPOINT

3. Choose a style from the icons on this menu.

4. On the Microsoft Organization Chart File menu, choose Exit and Return to [your presentation name].

Org Charts: Cutting and Pasting Members

You can move members on an organization chart using cut and paste. You can't use drag and drop with org chart boxes, branches, or charts to other applications, but you can move them by selecting the boxes or branches to be moved and using the Edit menu's Cut and Paste commands.

Steps

1. Select the member boxes you want to move. Hold down the Shift key to select multiple boxes.

2. Choose Edit, Cut.

3. Select the box that will be the new manager.

4. Choose Edit, Paste Boxes. The boxes become *subordinates* of the *manager*.

 TIP   Right-click to use the shortcut menu to cut and paste boxes.

CAUTION   Microsoft Organization Chart permits only a single Undo action. If you cut and paste, Undo removes the paste, but you cannot also undo the cut to return the chart to its previous state. Save the chart before cut-and-paste operations so that you can exit without resaving if you don't like the results.

Org Charts: Entering Names, Titles, and Notes

Organization charts show current or projected staffing and reporting responsibilities. They make it clear who works where and who supervises whom.

PowerPoint uses the Microsoft Organization Chart application. When you start this, it opens in its own window and has its own menus. Use the Organization Chart application menus during the time the window is open.

You can enter a name, a position, and lines of comments by typing to replace the placeholders. PowerPoint requires that you type a name and position for each box. If you don't have all the details, highlight the placeholder and delete it. It's usually better to type something like **To be hired** so that your audience will understand the significance of this box. If you don't enter any comments, the placeholder for comments will not print.

If you do not want to use one of the boxes that appear when you start up the Organization Chart application, you must delete it, otherwise it will appear in the chart on your slide.

Steps

1. Choose the Organization Chart slide layout when you create a new slide.

2. Enter the title, then double-click to create an organization chart.

3. Type the name for the first box, and press the Enter key. There's no need to delete the placeholder.

4. Type the position. If necessary, press Enter and add comments.

5. Click each box in turn, and add names and positions in the same way.

6. Go to the Microsoft Organization Chart menu and choose File, Exit and Return to [your presentation name]. Choose OK when asked if you want to update the object.

Org Charts: Formatting Text

You can often make an organization chart more interesting by putting names in a contrasting font to the positions.

Steps

1. Double-click the organization chart if necessary, to edit it.

2. Highlight the text you want to alter.

3. In the Microsoft Organization Chart window, click Text, Font.

4. Change the Font, Style, and Point Size, and click OK.

5. In the Microsoft Organization Chart window, choose Exit and Return to [your presentation name]. Click Yes to accept changes.

Org Charts: Moving Members Around

Don't count on that beautifully arranged organization chart to stay accurate for long. If your chart shows people in an organization, surely someone will get promoted—or demoted! Others will come and go or be assigned different positions than the organization chart shows. You can keep your org chart current by dragging members to move them to their new locations on the org chart.

Steps

1. Double-click the organization chart if necessary, to edit it.

2. Drag the member's box over its new manager box or co-worker box.

3. Release the mouse button.

Outlines: Dragging and Dropping Text

PowerPoint allows you to move and copy text by using its drag-and-drop feature. This feature can be used in Slide View, Notes View, and Outline View to move or copy text to a new location within the selected placeholder.

Steps

1. Select the text to be moved.

2. Drag the text to another part of the outline, releasing the mouse button when the shadow insertion point is positioned where you want to place the text.

NOTE When you move text within the presentation outline, you are changing the text content of the slides. Be sure to review the appearance of each slide after moving text in the outline. ■

Outlines: Editing Text

It's possible to create a presentation in Outline View, or import an outline from a word processor. Even if you create your presentation in Slide View, you also create an outline. As Outline View lets you see the words of all your slides at once, it's a great place for checking the message of your presentation without distracting backgrounds or multimedia effects.

You can change the text as you would in a word processor, but you can also change the order of slides, promote subtopics to topics or demote topics to subtopics, and even change the order of items in bulleted lists.

Steps

1. Change to Outline View, if necessary.

2. Make any changes to the text by clicking an insertion point and editing.

3. If necessary, select a slide and use the buttons on the left side of the screen to change the slide's position or to change the position of its content.

TIP If you collapse a presentation to see just the slide titles, you can often see where another slide would be useful.

Outlines: Expanding and Collapsing Levels

When you display your presentation in Outline View, you see all the text that appears on your slides. If you want to restrict this view to just displaying the slide titles, you can click the

Collapse button on the left side of the Outline View screen. This will show only the titles of any slides that you have selected. To see all the contents once more, click the Expand button.

Steps

1. Switch to Outline View, if necessary.
2. Click the slide you want to collapse.
3. Click the minus button (Collapse) to see only the titles.
4. Click the plus button (Expand) to see the entire contents of the slide.

TIP If you want to collapse or expand all your slides, choose Edit, Select All.

Outlines: Moving Text

In PowerPoint's Outline View of a presentation you can rearrange the outline text by several methods. The Outlining toolbar makes the job easy, but if you prefer to drag text or cut and paste, these methods will work too.

Steps

1. Select the entire slide or specific lines to move. You can include slides or content of the slides such as bulleted text or both.
2. Click the Move Up or Move Down button on the Outlining toolbar until the text is placed as needed for the presentation.
3. Click the Promote or Demote button on the Outlining toolbar if the text should change levels.

Outlines: Moving Text with Cut and Paste

You can modify the content of your outline by moving outline text using cut and paste.

Steps

1. Select the text to be moved.

2. Choose Edit, Cut. Alternatively, right-click the text and choose Cut from the shortcut menu.

3. Click to place the insertion point where the text should be placed.

4. Choose Edit, Paste. Alternatively, right-click the text and choose Paste from the shortcut menu.

Overhead Transparencies: Creating

Transparencies are one way you can show your presentation. They are the cheapest way of getting the message across, but can't show animations and other multimedia effects.

You create transparencies on letter-sized sheets of transparent material. This comes in versions for laser or inkjet printers. Inkjet printers usually let you print in color, to get the most benefit from your slides.

You'll need an overhead projector; there are special models with extra power for showing presentations.

Steps

1. Choose File, Print to display the Print Dialog box. Select Transparencies in the Print What drop-down list. You may want to have a trial run on paper before printing transparencies.

2. If necessary, load the printer with transparency material.

3. Click OK, and your transparencies start to print.

TIP   You can store transparencies in clear, plastic wallets that fit in a three-ring binder. When you give the presentation you can lay the binder flat, open the rings, and lay the transparency in the wallet on the overhead projector before returning it to the binder.

POWERPOINT

Page Layout: Changing

You may discover as you're working on a slide that the information is best presented in another layout.

PowerPoint lets you exchange one layout for another. If you created a subtitle, for example, and then change to a layout that has no subtitle, your text remains on-screen but will probably be moved. However, you won't lose it.

Steps

1. In the Common Tasks window, click Slide Layout.
2. Select a layout to replace the layout you're already using.
3. Click Apply.

 TIP If all you want to do is add some extra item (such as a chart, picture, or table) to a slide that doesn't have this built-in, just go to the Insert menu and choose the item from it.

Presentation Templates: Changing Backgrounds

You can change the background of your presentation templates.

Steps

1. Choose Format, Background.
2. Drop down the list in the Background Fill section of the Background dialog box.
3. You can choose single colors from the palette, select Fill Effects to use gradients or textures, or use a picture as a background.
4. You can select Preview to see how your slide looks without permanently changing it.
5. When you're done, click Apply to change only this slide or Apply to All to change all slides in your presentation.

 TIP To save an altered template to use again, choose File, Save As and choose Presentation Template (*.pot) on the Save as Type drop-down menu at the bottom of the Save As dialog box.

Presentation Templates: Changing Typeface and Text Alignment

If you like a template but want it to be different, you can customize it any way that you want. You can save your altered template under a new name, and every layout variation will reflect the changes that you make.

The templates in PowerPoint are designed to use fonts that will definitely be on any computer that has PowerPoint installed. Your computer may have other fonts that could be more suitable than those in the PowerPoint templates. It's also possible to make a completely new template from scratch. You can change the typeface and the text alignment.

Steps

1. Choose View, Master, Slide Master.

2. Select any text and choose a new typeface, or change the alignment of the text.

3. When you've made all your changes, click the Close button in the Master window.

Previewing: Presentations

You have prepared the slides with the information you need to convey and enhanced them with special effects and animation. Now it is time to preview the slideshow on-screen as it will be delivered to a live audience.

You can choose to run the entire slideshow, or a selected group of slides, and advance the slides manually or let the presentation run with preset *timing* for each slide. You make these choices by setting the options for running the slideshow.

Steps

1. Open the presentation in PowerPoint to the first slide.

2. Choose Slide Show, Set Up Show.

3. Choose options from the Set Up Show dialog box.

4. Choose OK after setting the options.

POWERPOINT

After the options are set, you are ready to run the show. To run the show, click the Slide Show button.

If you are running the show manually or have not set timing, you advance to the next slide by clicking the left mouse button or by pressing the spacebar, the N key, the right arrow key, the down arrow key, or the PageDown key.

When you get to the end of the slideshow, the next click or press as if to go to the next slide brings you back to the Slide View.

TIP   You can click the right mouse button during a presentation to choose options for controlling the slideshow, such as blacking the screen or going to a slide out of order.

Printing: Handouts

It is common, but not absolutely necessary, to print handouts of the slides in a presentation for the viewers. PowerPoint makes it easy to group a number of slides on each page. First, you'll want to print header and footer information on the handouts.

Steps

1. Choose View, Header and Footer to display the Header and Footer dialog box.

2. Choose the Notes and Handouts tab.

3. Choose the appropriate check boxes: Date And Time, Header, Page Number, Footer.

   For the date and time, you can also choose to Update Automatically or fill in a Fixed time. Fill in text if you chose a header and footer.

4. Choose Apply to All.

In the Print dialog box, you can print handouts by choosing one of the three Handouts choices in the Print What drop-down list:

■ Handouts (2 slides per page)

■ Handouts (3 slides per page)

■ Handouts (6 slides per page)

(If you want one page-size slide per page, you can print the slides.) Choose other options the same as for slides and choose OK.

NOTE The Fra<u>me</u> Slides check box is automatically selected when you choose to print handouts. Frames around the slides make the handouts easier to read; however, the check box can be deselected if desired. ■

Printing: Notes

Notes Pages contain a reduced slide at the top of the page and speaker's notes at the bottom of the page—a very convenient speaking tool to keep slides and notes synchronized.

Choose header and footer information—which can contain page numbers and the date and time—the same as for handouts (see also "Printing: Handouts").

Steps

1. Choose <u>F</u>ile, <u>P</u>rint to display the Print Dialog box.

2. Choose Notes Pages in the Print What drop-down list.

3. Choose other options the same as for slides, and then choose OK to print the Notes Pages.

Printing: Outlines

Because an *outline* serves as an overview of your presentation, you may want to print the outline to include with the audience handouts. Or, use the outline as a table of contents for a report. An outline prints as it appears in the Outline View at the time you choose to print, therefore you must change outline options first.

POWERPOINT

Steps

1. Choose from the following options in Outline View:

   * On the Outlining toolbar, click Collapse All to print only the slide titles; or click Expand All to print all levels of text.

   * On the Outlining toolbar, click Show Formatting to show or hide formatting that will print.

   * On the Standard toolbar, click the Zoom box and change the zoom scale.

   * On the View menu, choose Header and Footer, and click the Notes and Handouts tab. Select header and footer options that will print on the outline. (If you already selected these options for the Notes Pages or handouts, they will print on the outline also.)

2. Choose File, Print to display the Print dialog box.

3. In the Print What drop-down list, choose Outline View.

4. Select other options, the same as for printing slides, and then choose OK.

Printing: Presentation Materials

PowerPoint lets you print any component of a presentation: slides, handouts, Notes Pages, and an outline. Each of the components can be selected in the Print dialog box—the component does not need to be visible on-screen, as long as the presentation you are printing is the active one.

Steps

1. Open the presentation. Choose File, Print to display the Print dialog box.

2. In the Print What drop-down list, choose Slides (without animation) or Slides (with animation).

3. Choose a Print Range: All, Current Slide, or Slides (by list of numbers).

4. In the Copies area, set Number of Copies and check whether to Collate.

5. Choose any appropriate check boxes at the bottom of the dialog box, and then choose OK. The slides print, one per page.

TIP Click the Print button to print the presentation using the default settings in the Print dialog box. A box appears on the lower-right part of the screen showing which page is currently being printed.

Slides: Creating Output

Slide output puts your presentation onto 35-millimeter *slides*. These take up very little space and can be used in slide projectors that can easily be found or rented.

It's possible to put your presentation onto slides using a machine, but because these machines are so expensive many people use a commercial service.

You can use a local service by saving your presentation on a disk and taking it to a local company. You'll find local companies in the Yellow Pages under Desktop Publishing.

Alternatively, you can use the built-in service in PowerPoint. This requires that your computer can connect to the Internet. You send your files via modem to a company called Genigraphics; they convert your file into 35-millimeter slides and send them to you next day by an overnight delivery service.

Steps

1. Choose File, Send To, and choose Genigraphics from the list.

2. Follow the instructions in the Genigraphics Wizard.

TIP Many slide projectors used in professional presentations use the Kodak Carousel system; experienced presenters buy a carousel magazine of their own to hold their slides.

Slides: Deleting

If you want to delete a slide, you need to be in *Slide Sorter View*.

Note that if you delete a slide, you delete all its contents. You can select the contents and copy and paste them to other slides if you need to.

Steps

1. Change to Slide Sorter View, if necessary.
2. Select the slide you want to delete by clicking it.
3. Press the Delete or Backspace key.

Slides: Moving Around

After you have created a slide presentation, you can easily rearrange the order of the slides. You can drag the slides around in Outline View (see also "Outlines: Moving Text"). However, a simpler and more pictorial method is to use the Slide Sorter View. You can move slides within a presentation or between presentations.

Steps

1. Open the presentation and go to Slide Sorter View by clicking the Slide Sorter View button. Or, choose View, Slide Sorter.
2. Drag a slide to the position where you want to move it. As you move the mouse pointer, a vertical line appears between slides indicating the location where the slide will be placed.
3. Release the mouse button when the vertical line is at the position where you want to place the slide. Repeat Steps 2 and 3 until you have rearranged the slides in the right order.

Slides: Moving Between Presentations

You can move slides from one presentation to another by opening the source and destination presentations and using the commands on the Window menu.

Steps

1. Open both presentations and display them in Slide Sorter View.

2. From the Window menu, choose Arrange All to display both presentations side-by-side.

3. Drag the slide you want to move from one presentation to the other presentation.

TIP You can move more than one slide at a time by selecting them using Shift+click before dragging.

Tables: Adding Backgrounds

You may find that if you add a table to a slide, the table may need to have more emphasis. When Office is installed, PowerPoint uses Microsoft Word to create tables. Therefore, you have to use the Word formatting features to add a background to your table.

If you create a table, you'll notice that the menus and toolbars change to those of Word, even though the title bar still reads PowerPoint. The relevant feature in Word is the Format, Borders and Shading command.

Steps

1. Double-click the table to edit it.

2. Drag across the cells that you want to add a background to.

3. Choose Format, Borders and Shading.

4. Choose the Shading tab and either Cells or Tables in the Apply To list box under the Preview box.

5. Choose the shading you want, click OK, then click the slide background.

POWERPOINT

Tables: Adding Columns

Because a table in PowerPoint is created in Word (without most users being aware of the change) you use the Word commands to add columns to your table. If you double-click your table to edit it, the Word menus and toolbars appear. The Table menu lists all the commands that Word offers.

Steps

1. Double-click the table to edit it.

2. Move the cursor so that it is above the top outer edge of the column to the right of where you want the new column to appear. The cursor is actually outside the table and pointing down at the column you are selecting.

3. When the cursor changes to a black downward-pointing arrow, click to select the column.

4. Choose Table, Insert Column.

Tables: Adding Rows

You can insert additional rows in a table using Word's Table commands.

Steps

1. Double-click the table to edit it.

2. Click an insertion point anywhere in the row below where you want the new row to appear.

3. Choose Table, Insert Row.

Tables: Changing Column and Row Width

You can adjust columns or rows to fit the widest or longest data.

Steps

1. Select the columns or rows you want to adjust.

2. In the selected area, double-click a column gridline to adjust columns, or double-click a row gridline to adjust rows. The selected columns or rows will be adjusted to fit the widest or longest data.

3. To control the precise measurements of the columns or rows, choose Table, Cell Height and Width.

4. Select options on the Row or Column tabs to set the exact measurements.

NOTE To make selected columns the same width, choose Table, Distribute Columns Evenly. To make selected rows the same width, choose Table, Distribute Rows Evenly. ■

Tables: Changing Row Height

You can change row height in a table by using the mouse to drag to make the row taller or shorter. Make sure you have selected a column or row before you do this, or you'll throw everything out of alignment.

Steps

1. Position the mouse pointer on the row gridline below the row you want to change, making sure that the mouse pointer becomes a two-headed arrow.

2. Drag the gridline up or down and release the mouse button when the row is the height you want.

TIP Hold down the Shift key while you drag the gridlines to also change the width or height of the table (instead of affecting the width or height of the adjacent column or row).

Although Powerpoint's Undo function is limited to one step, Word's is not, so when you're editing a table you have a greater ability to recover from your mistakes.

Tables: Creating

Tables are a useful way of showing pieces of related information. PowerPoint uses Microsoft Word to create tables, so you may already know how to create a table in this way.

POWERPOINT

You can choose the Table Layout when you create a new slide, or you can add a table to any slide by clicking the Insert Microsoft Word Table button on the Standard toolbar.

Steps

1. Double-click the Table Layout slide to create a table.

2. Enter the number of rows and columns you need.

3. Type your information into the first cell of the table, and then press the Tab key.

4. Move through the table entering data in this way, and enter data in the last cell. Don't press Tab at this point.

5. Click the background of the slide to make your slide appear with the table on it.

TIP   If you don't want to put any information in a table cell, press Tab and the cursor will move to the next cell.

Tables: Moving Columns

Whether you spend a lot or a little time setting up a table, you will often want to move a column or row from its current position, perhaps for legibility or to improve its design for a presentation.

Steps

1. Double-click the table to activate it in Word.

2. Select the column by clicking just above the column while the pointer shape is a black down arrow.

   Alternatively, select a cell in the column, and then choose Table, Select Column.

3. With the mouse pointer positioned on the column, drag left or right to position the shadow insertion point on the new location for the column, and then release the mouse button. The column is moved to the new position.

TIP   To move more than one adjacent column or row, drag to select multiple columns and rows, and then follow the same steps to move them.

Tables: Moving Rows

You can reorganize your table information by moving the rows in a table.

Steps

1. Double-click the table to activate it in Word.

2. Drag to select all of the cells in the row you want to move. Alternatively, position the insertion point in a cell in the row you want to move; choose Table, Select Row.

3. With the mouse pointer positioned on the row, drag up or down to position the shadow insertion point on the new location for the row, and then release the mouse button. The row is moved to the new position.

Tables: Table AutoFormat

Inserting a table in PowerPoint or double-clicking the table placeholder created by the Table *AutoLayout* gives you a Microsoft Word table. When you edit the table, you automatically activate Word, making the Word commands and features available. One of these features is Table AutoFormat, which is used to enhance the appearance of the table with pre-defined formats.

Steps

1. Select the table by double-clicking it. The Word menu and toolbars appear and the table gridlines, selection border, and rulers are displayed on the table.

2. Choose Table, Table AutoFormat. Alternatively, right-click the selected table and choose Table AutoFormat from the shortcut menu.

3. In the Formats list box of the Table AutoFormat dialog box, choose one of the 39 formats and observe the sample in the Preview box.

4. Select or deselect the check boxes to add or subtract specific formats of the AutoFormat design—Borders,

Shading, Font, Color, and Autofit. Experiment with each one to see the effect in the Preview box.

5. In the Apply Special Formats To section, select check boxes to use a different format for these parts of the table: Heading Rows, First Column, Last Row, Last Column.

6. Choose OK. The formats are applied to the table. Click outside the table to deselect it.

CAUTION   Don't apply any formatting to the table before you use Table AutoFormat because you will lose that formatting to the formatting AutoFormat chooses. You can, however, make further formatting changes *after* using AutoFormat.

Text: Adding Shadows

Just as text can be made bold or italic, it can also have a shadow applied to it. The effect is subtle and cannot be increased or decreased. You can't see the effects of the changes you've made until you close the Shadow Settings dialog box and click something else in the slide.

Steps

1. Select the text you want to have a shadow.

2. Click the shadow button on the Formatting toolbar.

Text: Adding to Existing

Text can be altered or added to once it has been put on the page.

Steps

1. Move the cursor over the text that you want to add to. The cursor changes from an arrow to an I-beam.

2. Click the insertion point where you want to add text.

3. Type your new text.

4. To see the result, click a blank area of the slide.

Text: Adding to Placeholders

Whenever you add a new slide, you'll see an area of the slide with words like "Click to add title." This is called a *placeholder*, it's text that tells you what to do. When you click the words the placeholder changes to show a flashing insertion point; you can now add the text you want.

For example, you could start a new slide that has an area marked "Click to add title." You can click this area, and type **1998 Marketing Plan**; this text will now appear on your slide.

When you move on to click another placeholder or go on to another slide, the border around your text disappears.

Steps

1. Click a placeholder.

2. Type your text and click another placeholder to go to another slide.

TIP   If you don't enter any text in a placeholder, the placeholder itself will not appear on your slide.

Text: Copying

If you have text on your slide that you want to appear elsewhere, you can copy this text. You can use the same methods as you would in Microsoft Word. The simplest method is probably to hold down the Control button while you drag the text.

Steps

1. Highlight the text you want to copy by dragging across it.

2. Press the Control key (Ctrl) and hold it.

3. Drag the text you want to copy to its new location.

4. Release the mouse button, then release the Control key.

POWERPOINT

The text loses its original formatting and assumes that of the text into which it is inserted, or if you drop it outside another text area, it goes to the default text format.

Text: Deleting

You delete text in PowerPoint the way you delete in a word processor; either select the text and press the Backspace key, or click an insertion point and use the Backspace or Delete keys.

Steps
1. Select the slide in Slide View.
2. Click the text; an insertion point appears.
3. Use the Backspace or Delete keys to remove characters.

 TIP When you have an insertion point in text, the Backspace key removes characters to the left and the Delete key removes characters to the right.

Text: Moving

To move an entire box of text in PowerPoint, you move it as an object. But, you also can move text around within the text object—to rearrange paragraphs, for example.

Steps
1. Click the edge of the text object. The selection box appears around the text.
2. Drag the selection box to its new location and release the mouse button.

Text: Moving Within a Text Object

You can move text within a text object.

Steps
1. Select the text to be moved.

2. Drag the selected text and release the mouse button when the shadow insertion point is positioned where you want to place the moved text.

If you prefer, you can use the Edit menu or shortcut menu to cut and paste text within the text box.

Text: Spell Checking

Always check the spelling in a presentation before the audience sees it. To check the spelling, use PowerPoint's spelling checker, which checks both spelling and letter case.

Steps

1. Open the presentation you want to check.

2. Click the Spelling button on the Standard toolbar or press F7. Alternatively, choose Tools, Spelling. The spelling check begins.

   If PowerPoint finds a potential error, the Spelling dialog box appears. (Otherwise there is a box telling you The spelling check is complete.)

3. A suggested spelling or case appears in the Change To text box (unless you disabled the Always Suggest feature). Beneath this suggestion, there may be a list of additional suggestions. You can then take one of the actions shown in the bulleted list at the end of these steps.

4. After you make your selection, the spelling checker continues checking the presentation. When it has finished checking the entire presentation, it displays a message to that effect. Choose OK to close the message box.

   • To continue without correcting the word, choose Ignore.

   • To ignore this and all further instances of this word, choose Ignore All.

- To correct only this instance of the word, choose one of the suggested alternatives, or type the correction in the Change To text box, and choose Change.

- To correct this and all further instances of the word, choose one of the suggested alternatives, or type the correction in the Change To text box, and then choose Change All. PowerPoint doesn't prompt you to confirm the subsequent changes.

- To add the word in the Change To text box to the dictionary listed in the Add Words To text box, choose Add. If the word differs from the word highlighted in the slide, PowerPoint also replaces the highlighted word with the correct word. To select a different dictionary, select the Add Words To text box to list available dictionaries and then choose a dictionary.

- If you have disabled the Always Suggest feature, choose Suggest to have PowerPoint suggest a correct spelling.

After using the spelling checker, carefully proof the presentation for errors that a spelling checker can't detect.

TIP   The Spelling dialog box now has an AutoCorrect button. If you want to add the word and its correct spelling to the AutoCorrect list, click AutoCorrect before clicking Change.

NOTE   PowerPoint 97 has an automatic spelling feature, just like Word 97. As you type, potentially misspelled words are marked with a red *wavy line*. Correct the word or right-click the word to choose a suggested correction. ■

Tools: Meeting Minder

The purpose of the *Meeting Minder* is to give the presenter a way to take meeting minutes and notes electronically. Those notes and minutes can then be imported into Microsoft Word and other word processors and edited, or included in another presentation outline. Use the Meeting Minder during a presentation to keep track of questions, discussions, and any notes regarding the presentation.

Steps

1. Begin a slideshow by clicking the Slide Show button at the lower left, or choose View, Slide Show.

2. During the slideshow, click the Slide Show pop-up menu icon in the lower-left corner, or click the right mouse button.

3. From the pop-up menu, choose Meeting Minder to display the Meeting Minder dialog box.

4. Use the Meeting Minutes tab to display an editable area for typing text, such as the minutes for a meeting.

5. Use the Action Items tab to record items (such as a job) that have been assigned, to whom they have been assigned, and the due date.

6. After using the tabs as needed, choose OK or press Enter to remove the Meeting Minder. Note that you cannot proceed through the slideshow while the dialog box is displayed.

Transition Sounds: Adding

You can add sounds whenever a new slide appears; if necessary, the sound can play continuously until the next slide appears.

Steps

1. Change to Slide Sorter View, if necessary.

2. Select the slide you want to add sound to by clicking it.

3. Click the Slide Transition button on the Slide Sorter toolbar.

4. Choose a sound from the drop-down list.

POWERPOINT

Transition Timing: Changing

If you set up special effects that occur when you change from slide to slide, these changes may take place too swiftly to be easily noticed.

You can change the timings from fast (the default) to medium or slow. Factors that affect the timing include:

- The nature of the *transition* (some effects like Fade through Black are obvious and usually work best at fast speed).

- The difference between consecutive slides (an effect is more obvious if a slide is very different from the slide that precedes it).

- Your own taste.

Steps

1. If necessary, change to Slide Sorter View.

2. Click the slide to select it, then click the Transition button on the Slide Sorter toolbar.

3. In the Slide Transition dialog box, click the option button for Slow, Medium, or Fast. The preview images change to show you the effect.

4. Click Apply to change only this slide, or Apply to All to change all slides in this presentation.

TIP The preview images in the dialog box (the dog and the key) are very different, so they tend to overstate the effect of transitions.

Views: Outline

PowerPoint contains various *views* to facilitate preparing each part of a presentation. You can move among these views to check the overall look of the presentation or to fine-tune individual parts. You can use the View menu or the View buttons in the lower-left corner (above the status bar) to change views.

In Outline View you view the text of the entire presentation, add slides, delete slides; and edit, format, and alter slide text. You can rearrange slides, along with body text elements, by dragging, and indenting text (called *promoting* and *demoting*).

Steps

1. Choose View, Outline View.
2. Once in Outline View, click anywhere in the text of a slide to make it active.
3. Update slide content or add new slides and content until your updates are finished.

Outline View is a good place to plan your presentation and to look at the logical progression of your arguments.

Views: Slide

The outline interacts with other views in PowerPoint, most notably the Slide View. Most of the time creating a presentation is spent in the Slide View. This is where you perform many of PowerPoint's creative functions, such as building charts and tables, editing text, and drawing. In Slide View, you work with only one slide at a time.

Steps

1. Choose View, Slide View.
2. Make the desired modifications to the slide.
3. Move to other slides and make necessary modifications. You can move from slide to slide by using the *Slide Changer.*

TIP   When you drag the scroll box up or down on the Slide Changer, a small ScreenTip pops up next to the Slide Changer showing the number and title of the slide. As you scroll up or down, the ScreenTip changes accordingly. You also can navigate through the slides by clicking the blank area of the Slide Changer.

See also "Navigating: Through Presentations."

Wizards: AutoContent

Wizards are used throughout Office 97 applications to walk you step-by-step through creative tasks. Office Assistant, formerly the Answer Wizard, presents help on tasks as you work. In PowerPoint, *AutoContent Wizard* guides you through setting up a presentation. Another Wizard, *Pack and Go*, packs up the components of the presentation for you to take with you.

When you launch PowerPoint, the PowerPoint dialog box is displayed, allowing you to open a presentation using a template, blank presentation, existing presentation, or the AutoContent Wizard. The AutoContent Wizard guides you in selecting content templates that cover a variety of topics for popular presentation uses, such as flyers, calendars of events, status meetings, information *kiosks*, and Web pages.

Steps

1. In the opening PowerPoint dialog box, choose AutoContent Wizard. The Wizard starts.

    In general, you click Next to progress through the dialog boxes. The chart on the left side highlights a block in green to show the step you're currently in. You can click the Back button to return to a previous task, or click the block representing the topic you're interested in on the left side of the dialog box.

2. Click Next. Choose a button for the general category of the subject of your presentation, and then choose a more specific type from the list box.

3. Click Next and continue selecting options and choosing Next until you reach the Finish step.

4. Click Finish. PowerPoint creates a nicely formatted presentation.

NOTE   If PowerPoint is already past the opening screen, you can still start AutoContent Wizard. Choose File, New. In the New Presentation dialog box, click the Presentations tab, and then double-click the AutoContent Wizard icon. (Clicking the New icon on the Standard toolbar opens the New Slide dialog box, not the New Presentation dialog box.) ■

After AutoContent Wizard creates a presentation, you should run the slideshow or browse the slides. Then, you can customize any parts you want to change. You are likely to have a number of text placeholders to fill in that are specific to the type of presentation you created.

Wizards: Pack and Go

The Pack And Go Wizard assembles your presentation for carrying to other sites. Pack And Go gathers together your presentation file and all your linked files (such as sound and movie clips), compresses them, and bundles them into a convenient package on a disk. (Pack And Go will use as many disks as it needs.) Pack And Go will prevent you from accidentally leaving behind a file that your presentation needs.

Steps

1. (Optional) Open the presentation in PowerPoint. (The Wizard will let you name the presentation even if it isn't open, but you do need to have PowerPoint running.)

2. Choose File, Pack And Go.

   Similar to the other Wizards, you click Next to progress to each step in the Wizard while a green box highlights the step you are on in the chart at the left side of the dialog box.

3. Click Next and proceed through each step selecting options for the presentation, destination, links, and viewer until you reach the Finish step.

4. Have a disk in the drive you specified and click Finish. PowerPoint compresses the presentation and copies it to disk.

TIP Remember to run Pack And Go again if you make any changes to your presentation.

Glossary

ActiveX controls   Reusable and programmable elements, such as controls, that can be used in Microsoft products to enhance their capabilities, including creating Web pages.

Address Book   Documents, forms, letters, and other types of documents created in Word 97 can have information contained in the Outlook Address Book inserted with a click of the mouse.

aggregate function   A function like SUM or AVG that calculates a value based on a group of records. These functions require that a table be sorted by the group in order to be determined.

alignment   How a cell entry is positioned in a cell, both horizontally and vertically.

animation   In PowerPoint, special moving effects and sounds that can be added to objects and transitions in a slideshow.

append   Adding records to the end of a table.

applet   A small application unable to run by itself. When you purchase an application, it may come with additional applets. For example, Office comes with applets for manipulating fonts (WordArt) and drawing charts (MS Graph).

archive   The removal of selected items to another location for storage and occasional future access. A file that is not stored in a mail folder cannot be archived.

aspect ratio   The relationship between height and width. Drawing settings often let you lock the aspect ratio to avoid distorting an object or picture during resizing.

auditing   The process of checking for errors or relationships in a worksheet.

AutoCalculate   An Excel feature that supplies a quick total in a worksheet.

AutoComplete   An Excel feature that makes it easy to enter repeated text items in a column.

AutoContent Wizard   In PowerPoint, a feature that creates an entire presentation based on a few choices by the user.

AutoCorrect   In Office applications, a spelling dictionary for correcting misspelled words automatically.

AutoFormat   An Excel feature that applies a set of pre-defined formatting choices to reports, tables, and lists. Also, a feature used in PowerPoint (for a Word table) that applies formatting to enhance the appearance of a table.

AutoLayouts   The slide layout templates for creating new slides. AutoLayouts contain placeholders for various combinations of objects.

AutoNumber   A sequential number field that is automatically entered as a default value by Access when the record is created. You can edit the value in an AutoNumber field without affecting the next value.

AutoShapes   Drawing tools for creating objects and pictures.

AutoSum   An Excel feature that enables you to sum adjacent columns or rows automatically.

AutoSummarize   A feature in Word 97 that creates a summary or abstract of the document.

Binder file   A collection of programs saved together in one file. Similar to a three-ring notebook, it has sections that can contain different programs such as Word documents, Excel workbooks and worksheets, PowerPoint presentation files, and so on.

Binder template   A binder used as a pattern for creating other binders. Speeds up the creation of new binders.

bound control   A control or object on a form or a report that displays the data from a table, query, or SQL Select statement.

Briefcase   A Windows 95 option that allows multiple users on a network to work with the same Binder files and incorporate all changes.

calculated control   A control or object on a form or report that displays the value of an expression. Normally calculated controls are evaluated at runtime and are not stored in your database.

Calendar   An Outlook feature that contains events, a date navigator for quick viewing of specific dates, a list of appointments, a taskpad that lets you outline your To-Do list, and a meeting planner.

chart   A graphic representation of data, also called a graph.

chart type   The type of chart or graph, such as column, bar, area, pie, line, and so on.

Chart Wizard   An Excel feature that automates the creation of a chart.

check box   An HTML control placed in a Word document for Internet or intranet use. Placing a check in the check box toggles the action on; removing the check toggles the action off.

child table   A table in a relationship between two tables where the values displayed are controlled by the value in the other table. A child table may display zero, one, or more related records. Depending upon how the relationship is set up, Access may display one record or more than one record should there be more than one matching set of records.

clip art   Graphic pictures, often offered as collections, for inserting into documents.

Clip Gallery   In Office programs, a collection of clip art, pictures, sounds, and videos, some of which are stored on a CD. Choose clips from the Clip Gallery to add to documents, spreadsheets, slides, and objects. Additional clips can be added to the Clip Gallery.

conditional formatting   Excel 97 provides a tool to automatically format the results in cells according to a pre-defined set of conditions.

contact   A contact is a person or organization that you correspond with. You can store information about contacts such as job titles, phone numbers, addresses, e-mail addresses, Internet e-mail addresses, and notes.

control   An object on an Access form or report. Controls can be text labels, graphics like lines or boxes; text boxes that are bound to data, or unbound to data. You can have controls that display pictures, hyperlinks, OLE objects, or point to other files on disk. Also a data-entry object commonly used in Excel forms, such as scrolling lists or check boxes.

ControlSource   The table, query, or SQL Select statement that serves as the source of the data displayed in a control. Not all controls can display data; only ones with this particular property.

criteria   The basis for selection in a query, established by entering it on a line in the Query Design grid.

crop In graphics programs, reduce the size of a picture object by using this tool that trims the edges instead of shrinking the image.

data mapping An Excel feature that enables you to see the relationships between numbers and geographic features.

data type The type of information that is allowed to be entered into an Access field. A data type determines the size of the values entered, and the operations that can be performed on that field.

database An Access file that contains all of the tables, relationships, forms, queries, reports, and other objects that make up an information system.

Database window The central tabbed dialog box in Access that displays a list of your tables, queries, forms, reports, and macros.

Database Wizard An Access tool for automating the creation of database tables.

datasheet A compact display of the data in your table that is similar in appearance and operation to a spreadsheet.

Date/Time A particular data type that stores information about a date and time in serial date format. Access displays a date or time, but stores a numerical equivalent internally. That allows this field to be used in date and time calculations.

default value The value automatically entered into a field when a record is created. You can change that value.

demoting In an outline, moving an item down a level in the outline hierarchy.

dependents In Excel, cells that contain formulas that refer to other cells.

detail section   The part of a form or report that displays data from an individual record. Depending upon the way a form is set up, you may see none, one, or many detail sections.

event   An activity that lasts 24 hours or longer. An annual event such as an anniversary occurs yearly on a specific date, while an event occurs once and can last for one day or several days. An event or annual event shows time as free when viewed by others.

exclusive   Opening a database, table, record, or other object so that no one else can access it at the same time. Many operations on tables and databases in Access require that they be opened exclusively.

Export Text Wizard   Used to export data in an Access table to a text file when creating links between text files and the current database, or in links to an HTML file.

Expression Builder   A design tool that helps you create expressions that you can use in calculations and properties.

field   The information in one column of a database, form, or table. Also, a named container of a particular data type that can store values.

filter   A particular way of selecting and organizing data in your table.

filter by form   Access 97 provides the means to speed the access of data through a view of the form. Enter the desired data in the appropriate field of the filter form.

filter by selection   Select the desired data directly in the table and click the Filter by Selection button to start the filter process.

filter for input   Enter desired data in the Filter For box after selecting the field to be filtered.

flip In PowerPoint, the act of turning an object upside down or mirroring from left to right.

folder Used in Outlook to contain all Outlook elements and other documents stored on your computer. Folders allow organization of appointments, faxes, e-mail messages, and documents into easily accessible items.

footer In a Word document, the optional text at the bottom of each page. In PowerPoint, the optional text at the bottom of presentation handouts, notes, and slides.

form A designed display used to enter, view, or print data. Also, an organized and formatted worksheet that facilitates data entry.

formula Calculations you enter in a worksheet.

function A predefined formula that performs a specific operation in Excel.

group (of objects) More than one object combined to use as a single object. The user selects all of the objects and chooses a program command to perform the grouping. Also, a set of records with the same value in a field.

handouts In a PowerPoint presentation, printed copies of the slides in a slideshow that are handed out to the audience.

header In PowerPoint, optional text at the top of presentation handouts, notes, and slides. In a Word or Excel document, the optional text at the top of each page.

HTML (Hypertext Markup Language) A set of programming commands and controls used in creating Internet and intranet applications.

Hyperlink Text that is linked to other text in Internet or intranet applications which moves the viewer to the linked text. Also in Access, a field type that contains a description and a pointer to an address on the Internet or an intranet in URL or UNC form.

index An organized listing of values in a field or in a set of fields.

input mask A way of controlling the characters that can be entered into a field.

insert An operation in which a field or record is added to any part of a table.

join The method used for returning values based on the relationship between two tables.

Journal An Outlook feature that you can use to record interactions with important contacts, to record items or documents that are significant to you, and to record activities of all types.

key The index that is used to specify unique values in a table.

kiosk A booth at a trade show or convention. A PowerPoint slideshow can be set up to run unattended at a kiosk.

Layout Preview A preview that Access creates based on the first set of records in your file. This may or may not be representative of your final output.

Left Pane The part of the Binder window that displays the icons, and the binder's sections or documents.

Letter Wizard A tool in Word 97 that speeds the creation of common documents, automatically checking common information such as salutations and greetings, capitalization, and providing access to standard documents with pre-defined formatting.

linked data A data source outside your database that is referenced from within an Access table.

list In Excel, information that contains similar sets of data; also referred to as a database.

list box An HTML control placed in a Word document for Internet or intranet use. Click one of the items in the list.

Lookup A table that serves as the data source for a field based on a matching set of values in the two tables.

manager A box in an org chart that has other boxes (subordinates) reporting to it.

Meeting Minder In PowerPoint, the feature that lets the presenter take notes on-screen during a slideshow.

Memo A field that points to a data file on disk. Memo fields are small, but point to fields (generally text) of any size.

Microsoft Exchange An optional program that can be installed with Windows 95 to send documents via fax or e-mail. Includes a wizard that guides you through initial configuration.

Notes Pages In a PowerPoint presentation, the view (or printed copies) of the notes used by the speaker during a slideshow.

null A value that indicates that the value was not specified or is unavailable.

object Any type of data item, such as a picture you draw, clip art from a collection of pictures, a text container such as the title object or bullet point object in PowerPoint, a chart you create in Excel or PowerPoint, or a sound or video clip. Also, anything in Access that can be named and described with a set of properties.

Office Assistant An intelligent tool developed for use with all Office products to simplify user help.

OfficeArt A set of graphics provided with Office 97 to be used in any of the Office products.

org chart   Short for Microsoft Organization Chart, an add-in application available in PowerPoint for creating graphic organization charts.

outline   In a PowerPoint presentation, the view or printout that contains all of the text from slides in a slideshow. The outline is used to organize and rearrange slides in the show.

Outline View   In Microsoft Word, Outline View shows you a hierarchical arrangement of your documents.

outlining   An Excel feature that enables you to expand or contract worksheets or reports so that you see more or less detail.

Pack and Go   In PowerPoint, the feature that packages (compresses and copies) the components of a presentation for carrying on disk to where it will be shown.

parameterized query   A type of query in which the values returned are based upon the parameter provided at runtime.

parent table   The table in a relationship that controls the display of records in the other table. A parent table requires unique values (a primary key), and can match up to another table with no, one, or many related records.

paste function   An Excel feature that automates the process of entering a function.

Performance Analyzer   Access 97 can recommend changes to how your tables are organized to improve performance using the Performance Analyzer.

placeholder   A dotted line box that appears when you create a new PowerPoint slide. The placeholder contains instructions to click or double-click to add text or an object.

plot area   The graphic part of a chart where the series of data is plotted.

precedents   Cells that are referred to by a formula.

presentation   A collection of slides, speaker notes, handouts, and an outline for demonstration at a meeting.

primary key   An index that is unique, and uniquely identifies the records in a table. You can have any number of unique indexes, but only one primary key.

profiles   A group of settings that define how Outlook is set up for a particular user. A profile can contain any number of information services. Generally, you only need one user profile. If you sometimes need to work with a different set of information services, you may create an additional profile to use those services. If more than one person uses the same computer, each person should have a separate profile to keep personal items secure.

promoting   In an outline, moving an item up a level in the outline hierarchy.

properties   The settings associated with an object, as displayed in a Property sheet when that object is selected.

query   A method for selecting and organizing the records in your table, or in a set of related tables. Queries are used as the basis for displaying values in forms and reports. Access can translate queries into SQL syntax.

record   The information in one row of a database, form, or table.

referential integrity   A set of inter-table database rules that controls how data is updated, deleted, or inserted.

relationships   The manner in which the data in two or more tables can be linked together. Relationships between tables can be one-to-one or one-to-many; with three tables combined through two one-to-many relationships to give a many-to-many relationship. It is through table relationships that information can be extracted.

Remote mail   An Outlook feature that allows you to retrieve your mail from another location outside your current network.

replica   A copy of a database.

report   A read-only printable display or data based on a query or table. Reports can be designed, and contain some special features for data organization and display that aren't allowed in forms.

resizing   Changing the size of an object, often done by selecting and dragging resizing handles that appear in the outline of the object when clicked.

Right Pane   The part of the Binder window that displays the contents of a section or document.

rotate   Turning an object around a point to view it at another angle or perspective.

routing slip   An electronic form to be completed that enables routing of binders to one or more recipients.

rules   Expressions that automatically enter or validate data in a table or between tables in a database.

Rushmore   A technology for query optimization that improves record selection dramatically.

section   A new or existing document added to a binder.

Simple Query Wizard   A tool for creating quick queries of the data in tables, using Access 97's intelligence to automatically open required tables.

slide   An individual screen in a slideshow.

Slide Changer   On a PowerPoint slide, the scroll bar on the right side of the window used for moving through a slideshow.

Slide Navigator   A dialog box for changing the order in which slides are shown during a slideshow.

Slide Sorter View   In PowerPoint, the view that shows all the slides of a slideshow in miniature. This view is useful for rearranging slides and attaching transition effects to slides.

slideshow   In PowerPoint, a series of slides displayed in sequence, controlled manually or automatically, and with or without animation effects.

sort   An order for viewing the records in your tables based on the value in a field or set of fields. When you specify an index order, your table is ordered at runtime by the values in that index.

Spelling and Grammar tool   When set, Word 97 will automatically check your text for spelling and grammar errors as you type, indicating questionable sections with a wavy underline.

Structured Query Language (SQL)   A means for accessing data through simple phrasing of the desired information.

subforms   Forms that can be displayed within other forms.

subordinate   A box in an org chart that reports to a manager.

tab order   The order in which you can tab through the fields in a form.

table   A designed container for sets of values.

Table Analyzer Wizard   An Access 97 tool to identify un-structured data and its relationships, recommending how to best use the data in a relational database.

task   A task is a personal or work-related duty or errand you want to track through completion. A task can occur once or repeat (a recurring task). A recurring task can repeat at regu-lar intervals or repeat based on the date you mark the task complete. For example, you may need to send a report on the last Monday of every month.

Template Wizard   An Excel feature that enables you to quickly create professional-looking data entry forms.

text box   An HTML control for entering text placed in a Word document for Internet or intranet use.

timing   The setting you can change to determine how long each slide or slide animation appears during a slideshow.

tracer lines   Lines showing the flow of data through the worksheet by connecting the active cell with related cells; used with the Excel auditing feature.

transition   In PowerPoint, a special effect used to introduce a slide during a slideshow. For example, you can checkerboard across or down.

unbound control   A control or object that does not display data from a data source.

validation   Rules used to determine if the values entered into a field or set of fields are allowed.

wavy line   Word 97 indicates words that it does not find in its dictionary with a wavy line underlining the words.

Index

Symbols

3-D effects
  adding
    objects
      (Powerpoint 97),
      336
    shapes (Word 97),
      119-120

A

Access 97
  action queries
    creating, 156-157
    deleting, 157-158
    features, 156
    make table, 158
    update, 159
  append queries
    AutoNumber
      values, 156
    features, 155
    procedures, 155
  Briefcase
    features, 159
    procedures,
      159-160
  calculated fields
    creating, 161-162
    features, 160
    group by
      expressions, 162
    procedures,
      160-161
  controls
    appearance, 166
    bound, 162-163

    calculated, 163-164
    changing, 162
    editing, 165
    properties, 163
    types, 162
    unbound, 164-165
    wizards, 162-163
  data
    changing, 170
    copying, 166
    cutting, 167
    pasting, 169-170
  databases
    backing up,
      170-171
    blank, 172
    compacting,
      171-172
    encrypting,
      174-175
    new, 172-174
  forms, calculated
    fields, 160
  hyperlinks,
    finding, 160
  properties,
    DisplayControl, 163
  reports, calculated
    fields, 160

**accessing backups
(Word 97), 44-45**

**action queries
(Access 97)**
  creating, 156-157
  deleting, 157-158
  features, 156
  make table, 158
  update, 159

adding
  3-D effects
    objects
      (PowerPoint 97),
      336
    shapes (Word 97),
      119-120
  Address Book entries
    (Outlook), 21
  appointments
    calendar (Outlook),
      21-22
  AutoShapes objects
    (PowerPoint 97),
      336-337
  backgrounds, tables
    (PowerPoint 97),
      357
  borders (Word 97),
    47-48
  captions
    (Word 97), 50
  cells, tables
    (Word 97), 130-131
  check boxes, forms
    (Excel 97), 278
  colors
    drawing objects
      (Word 97), 57
    fills (PowerPoint
      97), 329
    text (Word 97), 57
    worksheets
      (Excel 97),
      253-254
  columns, tables
    (PowerPoint 97),
      358

Check out Que® Books on the World Wide Web
http://www.mcp.com/que

As the biggest software release in computer history, Windows 95 continues to redefine the computer industry. Click here for the latest info on our Windows 95 books

Make computing quick and easy with these products designed exclusively for new and casual users

examine the latest releases in word processing, spreadsheets, operating systems, and suites

The Internet, The World Wide Web, CompuServe®, America Online®, Prodigy® —it's a world of ever-changing information. Don't get left behind!

find out about new additions to our site, new bestsellers and hot topics

In-depth information on high-end topics: find the best reference books for databases, programming, networking, and client/server technologies

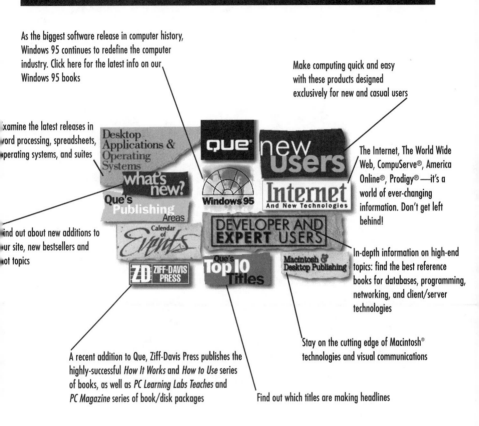

Stay on the cutting edge of Macintosh® technologies and visual communications

A recent addition to Que, Ziff-Davis Press publishes the highly-successful *How It Works* and *How to Use* series of books, as well as *PC Learning Labs Teaches* and *PC Magazine* series of book/disk packages

Find out which titles are making headlines

With 6 separate publishing groups, Que develops products for many specific market segments and areas of computer technology. Explore our Web Site and you'll find information on best-selling titles, newly published titles, upcoming products, authors, and much more.

- Stay informed on the latest industry trends and products available

- Visit our online bookstore for the latest information and editions

- Download software from Que's library of the best shareware and freeware